COLONEL
PADDY

COLONEL PADDY

THE MAN WHO DARED

PATRICK MARRINAN

Lieutenant Colonel Robert Blair Mayne ('Colonel Paddy'). *Royal Ulster Rifles Museum*

For those who dared

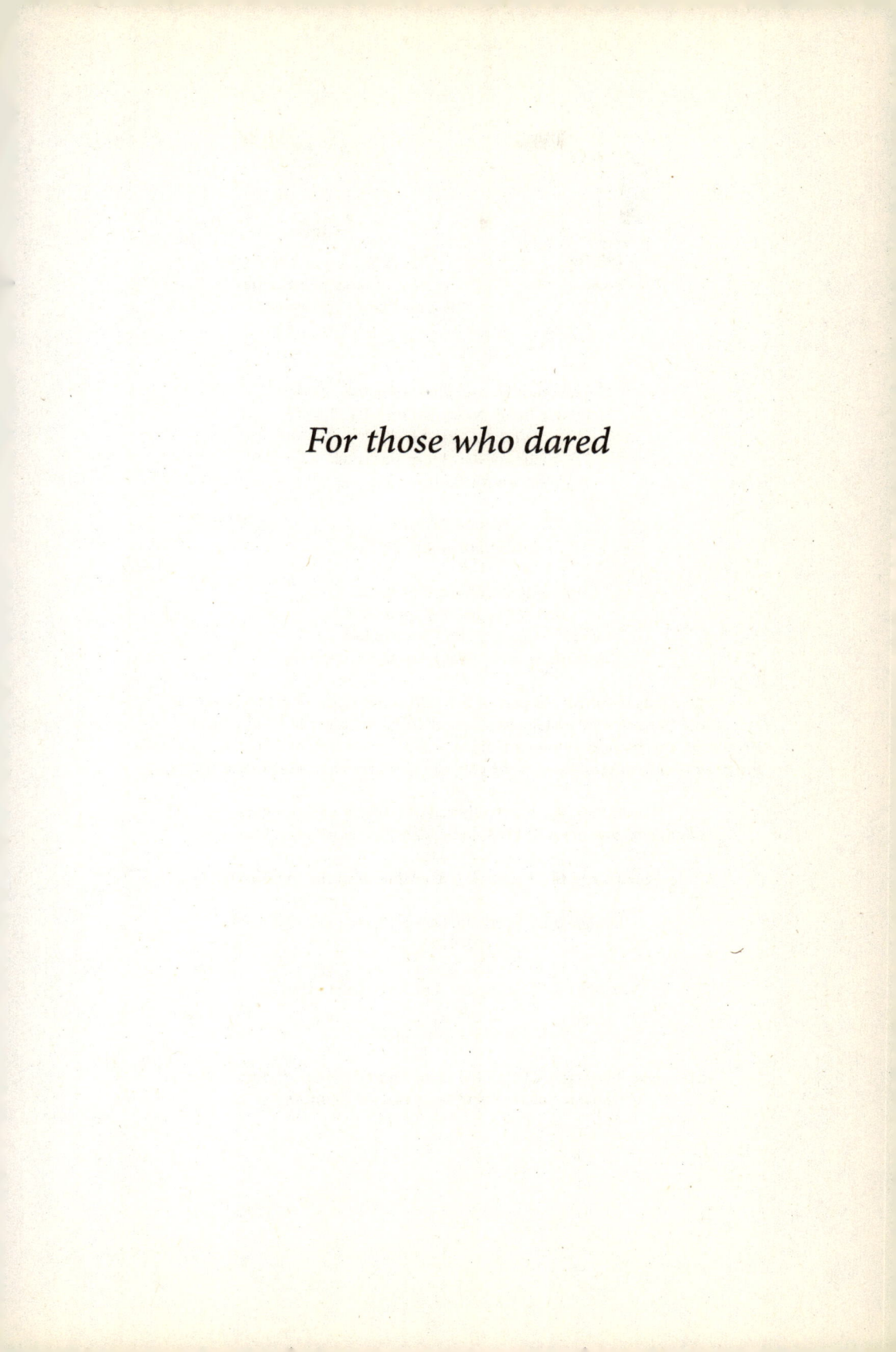

Published 1983 by
Pretani Press

This edition published 2013 by
Colourpoint Books
an imprint of Colourpoint Creative Ltd

Colourpoint House, Jubilee Business Park
21 Jubilee Road, Newtownards, BT23 4YH
Tel: 028 9182 6339
E-mail: sales@colourpoint.co.uk
Web: www.colourpoint.co.uk

Second Edition
Fifth Impression, 2023

Copyright © Colourpoint Books, 2013
Text © Patrick Marrinan, 2013
Maps © Colourpoint Creative Ltd, 2013
Illustrations © As acknowledged in captions

All rights reserved. No part of this publication may be reproduced, stored in a retrieval system or transmitted in any form or by any means, electronic, mechanical, photocopying, scanning, recording or otherwise, without the prior written permission of the copyright owners and publisher of this book.

The author has asserted his right under the Copyright, Designs and Patents Act, 1988, to be identified as author of this work.

A catalogue record for this book is available from the British Library.

Designed by April Sky Design, Newtownards
Tel: 028 9182 7195

Printed by CPI Group UK Ltd, Croydon CR0 4YY

ISBN 978-1-78073-041-7

Rear cover: The statue of Colonel Blair 'Paddy' Mayne that stands in Conway Square, Newtownards. *(M Johnston)*

Contents

Foreword to the First Edition 9
Foreword to the Second Edition 11
Key to Abbreviations... 15
1 In the beginning was the end 17
2 Syrian Interlude 25
3 Desert Saga 31
4 Reprieve.. 40
5 A-Hunting we must go....................................... 49
6 Rift in the lute 53
7 The Black Camel 57
8 Stocktaking 70
9 Death or glory.. 79
10 Singing in the wilderness................................... 93
11 Intermission 109
12 Spearhead.. 116
13 Augusta 125
14 Bon Viaggio!... 138
15 Termoli.. 144
16 Tempered steel 149
17 Nemesis 156
18 Vive la France!.. 164
19 Blood and guts 174
20 Operation Irish Terrier 184
21 Ringing out the bells 198
22 A borderline case 203
Epilogue 215
Index 219

Foreword to First Edition

WHAT A PRIVILEGE it is to write this Foreword. It comes to me not because, like many others, I served with Colonel Mayne from the pioneer days in the desert but because during the European Campaign I was his Padre.

I have so much for which to thank him. When the Regiment was training in Scotland for its part in the invasion of France, the services of a Chaplain were required. I was instructed to report to the Colonel to be looked over. As he was good enough to accept me I was then given the opportunity of ministering to the most remarkable group of men I have ever known. I have to thank Paddy for that.

Much more was to follow for which I shall never cease to be grateful. Unlike the veterans of Africa and Sicily and Italy I was a new boy, untried in the fires of war. Yet from the moment we met Paddy offered me his friendship and his trust. More than that he gave me his full support in all that I undertook. No Commanding Officer ever backed his Chaplain more whole-heartedly.

In part this was due to the respect Paddy had for what the Christian Church, in its properly inclusive manner, stands for. But there was more to it than that. Paddy cared deeply and passionately for the welfare of his men. In a real sense I was seen as a fellow-worker. Our spheres of responsibility were different but we were both concerned for the care of the Regiment and all that pertained to its good.

Paddy was the embodiment, on a large scale, of initiative, courage, daring, determination but at the same time he was sensitive and shy.

Personal relationships could provide problems. Partly because I was a minister and also because so quickly we found ourselves on the same 'air length' we enjoyed a quality of comradeship which, as passing years confirmed, was precious to us both.

The accident which brought his legendary life to an end revealed the regard of his fellow-countrymen. I had never conducted such a funeral and cannot think I shall ever see one like it. No salute could have been more impressive. A giant among men, in physical stature as in his own multi-coloured personality, was with us no more – except in grateful remembrance, dear to very many and specially so to me.

J Fraser McLuskey

26 March 1983

The Right Reverend Dr J Fraser McLuskey, MC, MA, BD,
former Moderator of the General Assembly
of the Church of Scotland

Foreword to Second Edition

He was an Air-Commando, a leader of the most daredevil and most dangerous regiment in the British Army, the SAS. He was the scourge of the Nazis; Hitler ordered that he was to be shot on sight. He was the personification of Irish courage, but he was also the most loveable character ever to come out of Ulster. My father and mother John and Jane Adamson knew him well, for he used to call at our house on Main Street, Conlig, Newtownards, for sandwiches and a cup of tea. He never appeared to them the natural soldier that he was, but rather one of nature's gentlemen.

My family has a long tradition of serving in the British Army. My great grandfather John Adamson was stationed in Clandeboye, County Down around 1870 and married my great grandmother Roseanne Gamble in 1873. When John left the Army they went to live in Bolton, Lancashire, where the family ran a cotton mill and John took over its direction. My grandfather Samuel and his brother William both joined the Army following in the family tradition. They served in the Boer War (1899-1901). Following Winston Churchill's policy decision during the Second World War to prepare an enterprise with specially trained troops of the hunter class, the name 'Commando' for these troops was chosen from the guerrilla fighters of the Boer War.

My maternal grandfather Robert Kerr served in the Royal Field Artillery during the First World War. The cousin of both my maternal granny Isabella Sloan and paternal granny Martha Sloan, who were sisters, was William Sloan of Roseneath Cottage, Conlig. William died on 1 July 1916, as a volunteer soldier of the 36th (Ulster) Division, on the first day of the Battle of the Somme. He has no known grave. Granny's sister Hannah's husband Herbie McPeake fought throughout the First World War and survived. Several of my uncles and aunts served throughout the Second World War and also survived, although my Polish uncle died soon after the War ended. For those who fought and died in both World Wars I formed the Somme Association in 1990, with its headquarters now in the Somme Heritage Centre, Conlig.

Because of my family history and my parents' friendship with Blair Mayne, I was always interested in guerrilla warfare. During the First World War General Paul von Lettow-Vorbeck, German Commander of the East African theatre, conducted a brilliant guerrilla war against the Royal African Rifles. At the same time in the Middle East, TE Lawrence was enjoying great success using hit and run tactics against the Turks. Hauptmann (Captain) Theodor von Hippel served under Lettow-Vorbeck in Africa and after the war became a strong advocate of those tactics pioneered by his former commander and of Lawrence of Arabia.

Hippel's vision was reminiscent of that of David Stirling, founder of the British SAS. When Hippel approached the Reichswehr, however, his idea was rebuffed because of the antagonism of the traditionalist Prussian officers. Nevertheless he then found an ally in Admiral Wilhem Canaris, commander of the German Intelligence Service, the Abwehr. Canaris gave the go-ahead for a Unit that became known as the Lehr und Bau Kompanie z.b.V. 800 (or Training and Construction Company number 800) on 25 October 1939. This was the Brandenburg German Special Forces Unit, one of whom was Herr Jopp Hoven, who had operated as a spy in Belfast prior to the outbreak of war. Until 1944 it was an OKH (Oberkommando des Heeres) High Command Unit rather than a unit of the regular army (Heer).

Colonel Paddy was first published by the Ulster Press. Patrick Marrinan acknowledged with gratitude his debt to the following for their help and co-operation; the Mayne family; Sgt-Major Robert Bennett, MM; Lt-Commander John St John Coates; James W Vitty, former Chief Librarian of the Linen Hall Library, Belfast; Rt Reverend Dr J Frazer McLuskey, MC, MA, DD; Corporal William Hull; the editor of the TV Post; Miss Muriel Moore; Marshall Mark Esq, MA and Rory T O'Kelly Esq, Solicitor.

FOREWORD TO SECOND EDITION

With the help of my friends David and Rosaleen Adamson, I edited and published a revised text of Patrick's book in 1983 under my imprint of *Pretani Press*. This could not have been possible without the help of my oldest friends Andy and Agnes Tyrie, Brian and Jennifer Craig and Edmund and Kathleen Irvine, to whose son Eddie I gave the proceeds of this and my own book *The Identity of Ulster* to sponsor him into motor racing. *Pretani Press* itself would not have succeeded without the help of Jackie Hewitt, the management and the staff and students of the Farset Youth Project, of Louis West, Tommy and Billy Aiken and the staff and friends of the Ainsworth Community Centre. I was also grateful to Joe English and Stephen Lowe for their historical research. The cartography of the original edition was by my friend Anne Johnston, whose maps adorn all of my books. I also appreciated the help of Ken and Anne Sterritt, David Stirling, President of the Special Air Service Regimental Association, Colonel Robin Charley and the staff of the Royal Ulster Rifles Regimental Museum, Waring Street, Belfast, and the committee and management of the Shankill Social Sports and Recreational Club, Belfast.

But most of all I have to thank the Reverend Dr J McCluskey MC, MA, DD, who agreed to write the foreword for me. The Reverend McCluskey was a very special person who had spent several months on a travel scholarship in Germany before the War and he became interested in the Confessional Church. This was made up of those opposed to Adolf Hitler and to the attempts by the Nazis to control the National Protestant Church. It was here that he met his future wife Irene Calaminus, the daughter of a Pastor in the Confessional Church. In 1942 he took leave of absence from his chaplaincy in the University of Glasgow and, after parachute training, was posted to the Special Air Service, serving in France, Germany and Norway. He was awarded the Military Cross and became famous as the Parachute Padre, writing a book of his exploits in that name. He died in Edinburgh on 24 July 2005.

I was so glad to have known him and it is indeed a great privilege and pleasure for me to welcome this new edition, with his original foreword, of my friend Patrick's classic and incomparable story of *Colonel Paddy, The man who dared*. There have been many books and articles on Blair Mayne, but Patrick's book is quite simply the best.

On this occasion I would like to thank the publishers Malcolm and Wesley Johnston of Colourpoint Creative Ltd and Jacky Hawkes. I would also like to acknowledge the cooperation Patrick's children – Paulyn, Yvonne, Patrick and Carmel – and I wish to thank Paulyn for her contribution in bringing this project to fruition. Also my colleague Helen Brooker of Pretani Associates, chair of the Ullans Academy promoting Common Identity, and her husband David; Nikki Tumelty, who has typed my scripts and my wife Kerry, all of whom have done so much to bring this venture to a successful conclusion.

Dr Ian Adamson OBE
October 2013

Publishers Note

The publishers gratefully acknowledge the assistance of:
Paulyn Marrinan Quinn, SC
Dr Ian Adamson
The staff of the Royal Ulster Rifles Regimental Museum

Key to Abbreviations

AA – Anti-Aircraft *(gun)*
CO – Commanding Officer
DSO – Distinguished Service Order *(medal)*
GHQ – General Headquarters
HQ – Headquarters
LCA – Landing Craft, Assault
LCI – Landing Craft, Infantry
LRDG – Long Range Desert Group
POW – Prisoner of War
RAF – Royal Air Force
SAS – Special Air Service
SIG – Special Interrogation Group
SOE – Special Operations Executive
SRS – Special Raiding Squadron
SS – Schutz-Staffe *(German unit – 'Protection Squadron')*
VC – Victoria Cross *(medal)*

CHAPTER 1

In the beginning was the end

Through the dimly lit streets of the sleepy town of Newtownards, near Belfast, the red Riley sports car roared on its way, and then with a screeching of brakes swung into Mill Street.

Suddenly, ahead there loomed up an unlighted lorry – and too late the car driver saw it. With a deafening thud metal crashed against metal, and the sports car bounced across the roadway into a telegraph pole and stopped. Over the steering wheel a giant figure slumped, and all was silent except for the hiss-hiss of an overhead cable short-circuiting on the bent pole.

It was 3.00 am on that dark December night in 1955, and the man who had been top-most among the bravest soldiers in the British Army – or in any army – was dead, and tomorrow all Ireland would mourn his passing.

Down from the nearby shores of Strangford Lough the looming wail of a distant water bird rent the air, and then all was silent again. Strangely, nobody seemed to have heard the crash, but busman James Alexander, who lived in the street, looked out of his door and saw lights flashing from overhead electric wires and a motorcar on the footpath with headlamps shining and its engine running. He thought that the Electricity Board employees were repairing the cables, and went off to bed.

A few hundred yards away, on Scrabo Hill overlooking Newtownards, the Mayne family were asleep in their secluded mansion home, Mount Pleasant, with its forty acre woodland estate, unaware that the favourite son of Ulster, their own boy Blair, now lay broken and dead in the valley below. Next morning they were to be shocked out of reason and for Mrs Mayne, his adored and dedicated mother, it was to be a sentence of death.

At first it seemed impossible that such a mighty and apparently indestructible warrior could have been vanquished, and that his splendid figure would never be seen again on his native soil. For days and weeks to come a pall of gloom seemed to hang over the land where he was born.

Lieutenant Colonel Robert Blair Mayne, DSO, DSO, DSO, DSO; Légion d'Honneur, ('Colonel Paddy' to his contemporaries, and now to history), was not just another hero in an area where heroes abound; he was a symbol of Ulster's warrior tradition and a legend in his own lifetime. Lawrence of Arabia was a light-weight in comparison with this man of action, whose exploits had already been recorded by a dozen writers since the war, and whose deeds of daring would be recalled whenever brave men gathered to talk of battles near and long ago.

Before the call to action began the world-wide build-up of Colonel Paddy, he was already a national figure in sport, capped six times for Ireland at rugby football and also a distinguished amateur heavyweight boxer.

He was born at Mount Pleasant on 11 January 1915, the second youngest of a lively family of six children which included two other boys and three girls. Brother Tom was killed in a shooting accident in 1932, and the following year William led the remaining brotherhood into the amateur boxing inner ring by winning the RUC Light Heavyweight Championship.

Blair set off on his own athletic career without undue delay. Even as an under-teenager, he astonished everyone around him with his strength and agility. At eleven years old, he could drive a golf ball as far as an experienced grown-up; at 18 he could rip a telephone directory in half, and lift 400lb bar bells above his head; at 21, he won the Irish Universities Heavyweight Boxing Championship; and at 23, he collected the first of his half-dozen International Rugby Football caps for Ireland.

Rugby was always his prime interest in sport, and it was through this that he became involved in boxing. He began his scholastic education at Regent House School, Newtownards, and then went to Queen's

University, Belfast, where he started to study law. There was a very well equipped gymnasium at the university and an excellent training staff, headed by a tough former professional heavyweight boxing champion of Ireland. It was in order to get fit, and keep fit, for the rugby field that the university players used to go into the fighting ring.

Chief of the training team was burly, beetle-browed 'Big Davy' Magill, who had fought Joe Bloomfield and Tommy Gibbons in sensational ring battles. He was, indeed, sometimes too tough for some of his youthful university trainees, bashing them so hard that they chucked in boxing and switched their athletic exercises to swimming, rowing, tennis or squash.

When Big Davy took over Paddy as a pugilistic pupil at first he felt no regard for one whom, though he was six foot three inches tall, broad-shouldered and weighing fifteen stone, he reckoned was "a bit of a softie." (In those days Paddy was still quietly-spoken and generally very gentlemanly – to strangers, anyway!) Big Davy, rather a roughneck himself, concluded that any time spent on training this overgrown fop to learn boxing would be just wasted time. He resolved to re-kindle the young man's interest in rugby, and have done with him.

So with a sly smile, he invited Paddy into the gymnasium ring for a friendly spar! Ten minutes later Big Davy opened his eyes to find that a group of university medical students were applying cold water treatment to him in order to wake him up. The fop had K-O'ed him.

Now that youthful Master Mayne was standing over him, looking very worried and nervously apologising for what had happened. But this time it was Big Davy who changed his views, and realising that this awkward-looking pupil of his was a natural hitter, decided that he could develop his talents by further detailed instruction on the noble art of fisticuffs. So, round to it (and round-by-round to it!) they got.

Very soon afterwards, Paddy Mayne fought Cecil Beamish, one of his First XV rugby team-mates, for the right to represent Queen's University in the Irish Universities Championship to be held at Trinity College, Dublin.

Cecil Beamish, a member of the famous Royal Air Force and Rugby Football family, was a powerfully-built and quick-moving six-footer, with the hardest right-hand punch in Ireland. Like Paddy Mayne, he was rather shy in character. But because of the aura of fame which had been won in the rugby field for his family by his brother George (the late Air Marshal Sir George Beamish) and brother Victor (the flying ace who died in action a month after spotting the German pocket battleships, *Scharnhorst* and *Gneisenau*, when they were making their memorable dash up the English Channel in February 1942) Cecil Beamish had a massive following when he squared up to Paddy Mayne.

In Round Two he suffered the same fate as Big Davy. The slogging match could just as easily have gone the other way, but it didn't. So, for a time, this splendid sportsman stayed a fallen idol. Later, he was to make fresh fame as a golfer, and represent Ireland many a time.

And Mayne? He had to meet one more challenger before he could stand up as the champion of the Irish Universities. This was Houston, a rugged, heavy-built man of only five foot ten inches. In the first round, it really looked as if he was going to outgun the redoubtable Paddy. But in Round Two, a smashing right-swinger sent him sprawling through the ropes, and though he staggered to his feet and bravely clambered back again into the ring one of the judges jumped in, just in time to call a halt before he crashed again.

A month later Mayne fought Karl Luntz of Liverpool University in the British Universities Heavyweight final. Luntz, a giant Boer, had practically taken a lease of the title and was now defending it for the fourth time. This six foot six inch South African outstripped the Northern Irishman in height, but more narrowly in ringcraft; he only just defeated Paddy on points.

So now, back to the rugby field. Paddy poured his boundless fervour into the game – and what personal fame flowed out of it! Top rugby critics said he was one of the finest forwards in the world. Dr Danie-Craven, who managed the famous South African Springboks before the Second World War, rated him among the sixteen greatest forwards of all time, and few rubgy fans in Ulster would challenge his assessment.

In South Africa, where Paddy toured with the British Lions Rugby team in 1938, his fifteen stone of rawboned Irish energy, combined with the speed of a deer, won for him the respect which the sturdy Springboks reserve for few. Off the field, his now growing eccentric habits alarmed some of his acquaintances, but delighted most.

Sometimes he mixed up night with day, and on one occasion he turned up at his hotel at noon with a large buck on his shoulder, his evening dress suit looking as if it had been worn by a poacher for months. His story to his British Lion team-mates was that he had fallen in with some game hunters at a night coffee stall and had gone off with them on a hunting expedition into the veldt. The buck he had shot himself with a borrowed rifle. This was not surprising when one learns that Mayne was a crack shot, well up to Bisley[1] standards!

He revelled in that South African tour, enjoying the folk as much as the rugby. He liked the landscape too, though comparing South Africa scenic qualities with the lush beauty of his native Ireland he was once heard to say (no doubt during some cheerful bar-room argument), "South Africa has an ugly face. That must be to conceal her riches under the surface."

On the playing field the game was everything to Paddy, but if he thought for one moment that his opposite numbers were indulging in too much rough stuff, then he was only too happy to accommodate them with some of his own. It happened once at Ravenhill, in Belfast, when Ireland were playing Wales and three Welsh forwards had forsaken rugby for all-in wrestling and fisticuffs. Suddenly, with dynamic fury, Mayne cut loose and one after the other the offenders were knocked out. The large crowd went hysterical, but Paddy soon forgot and that night he and his Welshmen were drinking together in a friendly pub like blood-brothers.

It was during the same year of 1938 that Mayne was admitted to the Roll of Solicitors. Frankly, he was bored and unhappy. It was probably because of this that one night while celebrating with a friend, Ted Griffiths (who later won the Distinguished Flying Cross (DFC) over Germany with the RAF), he joined him in filling in a couple of Territorial Army enlistment forms. It may have been a joke – for the letters were posted without a stamp.

But if the legal profession did not capture the imagination of Mr Blair Mayne at the start many of the characters aroused his personal interest. And how much did he stir up theirs! The Bar and the Law Society, from the Lord Chief Justice, Lord MacDermott, down to the humblest Solicitor's clerk, deeply admired and liked him and recognised him as one of the liveliest Irish personalities of all time. After the dark clouds of war had gone the Law Society was pleased to appoint him as its Secretary, and this position he held until the time of his tragic death.

Even to the end, though, Paddy's eccentricity remained with him. Despite his high and responsible office he was just as liable, when,

---

1 A village in Surrey, which is noted for its rifle shooting ranges.

out on an occasional frolic, to clear a tavern bar of a bunch of coal-heavers or toughies as he had been to shoot up a troop of Germans in the faraway desert. Women, as lovers, he had no time for, but to them he was always gentlemanly and correct. His mother, of course, was on a pedestal all of her own, and the bond of love between them was almost spiritual in its intensity. Also, for his sisters, Barbara and Frances, he had the warmest affection.

At his funeral it seemed that almost every profession and every walk of life was represented. From Britain old comrades of his regiment, the famous Special Air Service (SAS), answered the call and paraded proudly in the two-mile-long cortege. Along the sidewalks women and children wept. In the Northern Ireland Legal Quarterly the scholarly and gentle Probate Registrar, James Lindsay, wrote this tribute:

"In the midst of great battles the warrior comes into his own. When a nation fights for its existence, its soldiers of ardour and daring receive the salutation of the people. Adulation often fades when years of peace come, but in the midst of the struggle – especially when it is fierce and deadly – those who dominate by their boldness and gallantry receive grateful acclaim. And so when our country was confronted with the horror and might of the Third Reich, when it faced the menace of the U-boats, the threat of invasion and the deadly blitz, gratitude and admiration were evoked by inspiring deeds of valour. Our legal profession was indeed proud of a Solicitor-soldier who had proved himself of the highest temper and quality. In Africa, in Sicily, in Italy, in France, the fame of Blair Mayne became almost legendary. His name will be forever linked with the Special Air Service – a unit born in the desert, formed to harass and attack and destroy the enemy's lines of communication. Many accounts have been written about the exploits of this body. In all these, generous tributes are paid to the leading and formidable part played by Blair Mayne. We read of his daring; his rugged and forceful leadership; his ruthlessness – he asked for no quarter from the enemy and he gave none; his great care for the men under him; his shrewd judgement of character; his hatred of pretence and freedom from vanity; and above all his great personal prowess. And so, when the war ended and Colonel Mayne came back to civilian life with his wealth of fame and the unique distinction of having been awarded the DSO with three Bars, as well as having been admitted to the Legion of Honour by

Decree of the French Republic, his appointment by the Council of the Incorporated Law Society to be Secretary of the Society met with the warm approval of the Solicitors' profession.

The transition from the limitless battlefield to the confines of a world Council Chamber and library was not without its pains. In this new world of filing cabinet, memorandum and minute book he had to learn that results could not be achieved by swift and direct action, and that many goals could be reached only by patient progress through orderly procedure. Those great hands which so skilfully handled the gun, the grenade and other weapons of death, found the pen less easy to wield than the sword. Often in the humdrum of daily routine, the tingle and stab of recollection brought him back to the vast eternity of the desert, the battlefields of Sicily and Italy, the wooded valleys of France, the lairs of the Maquis. Small wonder that on occasions he would fain have shaken off the trammels of this ordered, conventional world.

But the adjustment took place – never ended completely, but helped greatly by the return to the profession of many who had served in the war and who in some measure were faced with similar problems of their own. To these he gave all the assistance in his power, especially to those whose studies had been interrupted by the conflict.

He carried out his duties as Secretary with quiet courtesy; oftimes with an insight that brought him directly to the heart of the problem.

His great gifts of organisation ensured that all the public and social functions of the Law Society were arranged with quiet efficiency. On formal occasions he represented the Society with dignity and poise. Each Armistice Day he led his brethren into the Great Hall of the Royal Courts of Justice, a figure of towering strength adorned with a gleaming array of decoration. During the Two Minutes Silence each heart had its own thoughts; through his mind great tides of memory must have flowed of which his calm, impassive countenance gave no sign. His nature was reserved, revealing itself fully to but few. Though courteous, considerate and tolerant, he often maintained an air of aloofness. Sometimes those who presumed upon his courtesy by showing an undue familiarity were withered to silence by his glance or a dryly spoken word. He had his moments of brooding and strange sensitivity, but to those who knew the depth of his complex character these were understandable and fell into place. Less apparent than his great strength and toughness was a gentleness and wonderful kindness. One manifestation of the gentler side of his nature was his love of trees and shrubs and flowers; much of his great physical energy had of late been devoted to gardening in which he found an increasing joy. One could not fail to be touched by the shy pride with which, in his garden, he pointed out the beauty of a rare bloom. It is a tragedy that his life should have been suddenly cut off in his forty-first year. In military annals he will be encircled with the halo of martial renown; in the legal profession he will be remembered as a beloved friend and brother."

It is a remarkable tribute coming from a man equally shy and modest, equally fond of the beauties of nature and equally solicitous for the welfare of others.

The greatness of Blair Mayne as shown during the war years had left its mark on his life before and after those black years of uncertainty, and never again will those who knew him be able to place him in any light other than this blaze of courage and daring. And yet it is amusing to reflect that when as an anti-aircraft (AA) gunner he applied for a transfer to the fighting Royal Ulster Rifles a stuffy adjutant duly reported that this young lieutenant was unpromising material for a combat regiment, was undisciplined and unruly and generally unreliable. It is indeed well that his criticisms were ignored and that this natural-born leader was not tethered to some nettle-rank AA battery in Belfast for the duration. It might well have been a case of:

"Full many a gem of purest ray serene
The dark unfathom's caves of ocean bear:
Full many a flower is born to blush unseen,
And waste its sweetness on the desert air."[2]

The transfer from the AA Regiment came on the 4 April 1940, and it was only after a short spell with the Royal Ulster Rifles that Blair Mayne, with restless impatience for real action, got himself transferred to the 11th Scots Commando. And so the web of fate was woven and greatness was assured for this fine Ulsterman.

---

2 Thomas Gray, 'Elegy written in a County Churchyard', 1751

CHAPTER 2

Syrian Interlude

IT WAS WHILE serving with the 11th Scottish Commando that Paddy Mayne formed a friendship with a very gallant officer, Major (later Lieutenant Colonel) Geoffrey Keyes. He was the elder son of the famous First World War hero, Admiral Sir Roger Keyes VC, who led the valiant naval attack to block the German U-boat base in the captured Belgian port of Zeebrugge on the night of 22/23 April 1918. Now, as Admiral of the Fleet Lord Keyes, he had launched the imaginative, revolutionary idea of Commando operations.

Geoffrey Keyes doted on his father, and from his boyhood days had been determined to emulate him. He did not, however, share his renowned father's love of the Royal Navy, and after completing his schooling at Eton he entered the Royal Military Academy at Sandhurst, duly passed out and was posted to the Royal Scots Greys in February 1937.

This famous cavalry regiment was then about to be partially dismounted and mechanised. In October 1938, Geoffrey Keyes found himself involved in the Jewish-Arab feuding in Palestine, then a British mandate. In the Spring of 1940 he returned to Britain as a volunteer for the Narvik Expeditionary Force which had just been formed to attack the German invaders then occupying this Norwegian port of such strategic value. (No doubt Geoffrey's sporting interest in skiing added a further incentive to the Scandinavian visit.) The onslaught, late in May, was a success – and so was Geoffrey – but the fall of Belgium and the looming threat of disaster in France forced the Allied Command to withdraw from Norway within the following fortnight.

For Geoffrey Keyes, ever-impatient for action now, it meant frustration and a return to the Royal Scots Greys depot at Edinburgh.

But men of his calibre are not for long thwarted, and by the end of July Geoffrey had contrived to get himself transferred to the 11th Scots Commando. A few days later he was introduced in the bar of the Douglas Hotel, Galashiels, to a powerfully-built young Irishman who had just been posted to the same unit. His name was Lieutenant Blair Mayne, and Geoffrey Keyes decided there and then that if there was to be trouble anywhere, he would like to have this softly spoken, hard-fisted giant by his side.

It was mutual, this friendship which started off at the bar. Both men were fine sports – as well as free spenders. To them both, physical fitness was a joy in itself. They were also outdoor types, fond of fishing and shooting. 'Geoff' Keyes was a splendid horseman and a very skilful skier. 'Paddy' Mayne was a boxing blue and a rugby international. They were, in brief, the *crème de la crème* of English and Irish manhood, and their future as soldiers required no crystal ball to foretell.

Geoffrey was happily married. Paddy had no real interest in the fair sex beyond his adored mother. So, they both gravitated to the bar during the rare leisure breaks they got from the rigorous spartan training which they were forced to undergo by their Commanding Officer, Colonel Pedder.

Together with their brother officers over a merry cup they often sang the newly composed marching song:

"Fra a' the crack regiments cam oor men,
The pick of the Heilands and Lowlands and a'
The stout-hearted Irish fra mountain and bog
And gunners and infantry gallant and braw.
And noo we're away, lads, to meet the foe,
We'll fight in the desert, the hill and the plain,
And though as yet we've no honours to show,
They'll ken the 'Black Hackle', afore we come home."[1]

They had not to wait too long for the real McCoy. In December 1940, 5,000 Commandos were embarked and their destination was to

---

1 Known as 'The 11th (Scottish) Commando March'

be the Italian Island of Pantellaria, between Sicily and Tunisia, where the Italian Air Force was operating from a very large modernised aerodrome and was inflicting crushing damage and destruction upon British shipping. Then, at the last moment this bold Commando venture was abandoned and the three troop-carrying steamers were ordered to set off for the Middle East via the Cape of Good Hope.

They sailed away on the 29 January 1941, and after an unusually pleasant voyage rolled up at the Great Bitter Lake, about twenty miles up the Suez Canal, and landed near Geneifa. There they were warmly welcomed by the Commander-in-Chief of the Middle East, General Sir Archibald Wavell, and that doughty old Irish warrior, General Sir John Dill. Military morale could hardly have been higher, and every man was now ready and eager for his battle. Soon, they were to be amalgamated with other Commando units into a composite group already known as 'Layforce' under the command of Lieutenant Colonel Robert (Lucky) Laycock.

All was booming at this minute on the Western Desert Front. Early in February, the British had driven the Italians back from the frontier of Egypt to almost half-way across Libya, capturing 130,000 prisoners.

Then came a drastic change. The Germans had arrived in the field. They were pouring infantry reinforcements and tanks into North Africa under a dynamic leader, General Erwin Rommel, and were sweeping down through Yugoslavia and Greece to the British-protected island of Crete. A desperate rearguard action there by a Layforce contingent, led personally by Robert Laycock, failed to hold the island.

Geoffrey Keyes and Paddy Mayne missed the Crete operation, and they were lucky, for more than seventy percent of the Commandos engaged there were lost.

Instead, Geoffrey and Paddy were sent on garrison duty to Cyprus. This was a far more peaceful island, over three hundred miles away, and for months they had lolled about in the sun – and wondered what ever they were doing in the Army.[2]

---

[2] During this period Belfast and its environs, ill-prepared for attack, suffered four air raids. The first bombs fell on the night of 7 April 1941, killing 13 people. A huge raid then followed on 15 April, leaving 745 dead, the greatest number of casualties in one night lost in any city during the course of the War: 100,000 people abandoned the burning city for the safety of the countryside. On the night of the 4 May the shipyards of East Belfast were bombed, leaving another 150 dead. Altogether the Belfast Blitz cost the lives of 942 citizens; 56,000 houses and the shipyards were damaged.

On the 3 June 1941, siesta time was over, and they were embarked for Egypt. Promptly on arrival they were transferred to other ships and taken to the coast of Syria (just about one hundred miles back beyond Cyprus) for an attack upon the Vichy French on the mainland.

What strange twists of fate were happening in those days of high drama! When the aged French hero, Marshal Pétain, had signed the Armistice with the all-conquering Germans on the 22 June of the previous year, there was no other course open to him; but the subsequent collaboration of his Vichy Government split the French nation right down the middle and left behind it seams which years later had still not been healed.

In the summer of 1941, perfidy, duplicity and dishonour held the field and national traditions of France which had endured for centuries were jettisoned without a blush of shame.

But for Geoffrey and Paddy the Syrian campaign was to give them their first opportunity of proving their worth in battle, and they seized it with both hands. Their enthusiasm was fully shared by all ranks of the 11th Commando, much to the discomfort of Vichy General Dentz and his renegades.

Lieutenant Blair Mayne earned himself a mention in despatches for his initiative and courage in the Litani River engagement, where his troop had landed behind the French lines. Now let him tell you in his own words what happened, in the account which he sent at the time to his RAF brother, Douglas:

> "We did a good piece of work when we landed behind the French lines at Litani. We were fired on as we landed, but got off the beach with a couple of casualties – then we saw a lot of men and transport about 600 yards up the road. I couldn't understand it as they seemed to be firing the wrong way, but might have been Aussies – there was quite a lot of cover – kind of hayfield. I crawled up to 50 yards or so and heard them talking French, so I started whaling grenades at them and my men opened fire. After about five minutes up went a white flag. There were about 40 of them – two machine guns and a mortar – a nice bag to start with. We had only a couple of men hurt. They had been firing at McGonigal's[3] crowd who had landed further north. We left

---

[3] Eoin McGonigal, a fellow Ulsterman and a great friend of Paddy, was later killed in the desert.

those prisoners and pushed on. McGarren, a Cameronian, was in charge of my forward sections and he got stuck, so we went round him. I had about fifteen men, it got hilly and hard going and Frenchies all over the place – eventually we came to a path which we followed and came on a dozen mules and knew that there must be something somewhere – we came on it just round the corner – about thirty of those fellows sitting twenty yards away. I was round first with my revolver and the sergeant had a T. Gun. Were they surprised! I called on them to 'feltez vers à la planche', but they seemed to be a bit slow on the uptake; one of them lifted a rifle and I am afraid that he had not even time to be sorry. This was a sort of HQ place with typewriters, ammunition, revolvers, bombs, and, more to the point, beer and food. We had been going about six hours and were ready for it. While we were dining the phone rang. We didn't answer it but followed the wire and got another bull – four machine guns, two light machine guns, two mortars and forty more prisoners. We only lost two men (sounds like a German communiqué)."

But while Lieutenant Mayne's troops got off lightly others were not so lucky, and amongst the fallen was their tough, straight-talking Commanding Officer, Colonel Pedder. Paddy, who was deeply attached to him, was grief-stricken with this loss.

It seemed all so tragic and unnecessary that British soldiers should fall to the gunfire of former allies, some of them black Senegalese and Algerians, who had not the remotest idea of what it was all about.

In the event, the Syrian campaign was soon over and a sadly depleted 11th Commando returned to Cyprus. Geoffrey Keyes, then only twenty-four years of age, was promoted to Lieutenant Colonel and appointed acting commander of the unit. He was also awarded the Military Cross for exceptional gallantry, and no comrade in the Commando would quarrel with this. He had well earned it, but there were murmurings of criticism about his appointment as CO and the word 'nepotism' was often bandied about.

Then, alas, with the immaturity of his years, young Geoffrey began to take himself much too seriously. He assumed the role of a strict disciplinarian, which quickly rankled his fellow officers and men.

Nobody more strongly resented this change of personality than Paddy, who believed in complete relaxation after the tough experience of combat, and found drinking parties the best cure for frayed nerves. This did not line up, however, with the new CO's ideas of military discipline and decorum and inevitably friction sprang up between him and several of his more full-blooded officers, who included Lieutenants Paddy Mayne, Eoin McGonigal and Bill Fraser, all close chums.

Now, because of the Navy's growing need for every British ship in the tense Mediterranean struggle, none were any longer available for Commando raids. So it was decided at GHQ in Cairo that Layforce should be disbanded. The choice of future service was offered to the officers and men. They could rejoin their former regiments, or wait at the Middle East Commando Depot in Geneifa for the projected formation of some new desert raider units.

While these alternatives were being considered, Lieutenant Mayne and his erstwhile friend Lieutenant Colonel Keyes had a stormy meeting which resulted in the Irishman's temper flaring up – and a crashing blow being struck that knocked poor Geoffrey unconscious. Immediately afterwards Paddy was put under close arrest.

That a phase of transient vanity and pride should have blighted the friendship of these two outstanding characters was a tragedy, and one that was to be unredeemed because of the heroic death in action on the night of the 17/18 November 1941, of Colonel Keyes. He had been leading a raid 250 miles behind the enemy lines to capture General Rommel in the German Afrika Korps HQ, at Beda Littoria, Libya.

It narrowly failed; this, the far-and-away most daring exploit of the Second World War up to this time, and no wonder it earned for Geoffrey Keyes the posthumous award of the highest decoration in the British Armed Services, the coveted Victoria Cross.

The pity is that it was not pinned on his proud young breast by the Sovereign whom he served so splendidly.

CHAPTER 3

Desert Saga

LIKE A CORNERED beast, powerfully-built young Lieutenant Robert Blair Mayne paced up and down a cramped detention centre in the desert scrub a hundred miles from Cairo. For several weeks he had been under close arrest for knocking out his Commanding Officer and the boredom of captivity filled him with mounting anger. Not only that, his promising career in the Army seemed to be in ruins even before he had fulfilled one burning desire – to go into action against the real enemy.

Suddenly, the bolts were drawn back and he was released to meet face to face a younger, but senior officer, Captain David Stirling, another Commando man and a most ambitious and courageous soldier who was later to win legendary renown in the desert as 'The Phantom Major'.

A few weeks earlier he had severely injured his back during a parachuting practice on the Egyptian coast at Mersa Matruh. Then, while lying almost paralysed in a bed at the Scottish Military Hospital in Alexandria, he had worked out (and mapped out in detail) his plan for a highly trained but minute striking force of about sixty parachute raiders which could be dropped in groups of a dozen on selected targets far behind the enemy lines.

The idea had sprouted in his mind after watching the lightning effect of the German airborne invasion of Crete. Surely, the desert was just the place for such a British force! Hundreds of miles of enemy supply lines stretching along the coast road were obviously highly vulnerable.

So were the lightly protected airfields and repair depots which studded the coastal strip.

Now that the seacraft were no longer available for Commando landings, what could be more simple than to drop the raiding troops by parachute near to any of these vulnerable targets, hide in the desert scrub during daylight, and await the cover of darkness to attack the packed enemy planes with timebombs! Then back to the shelter of the desert and a rendezvous with the Long Range Desert Group (LRDG), a reconnaissance unit now operating over an area stretching into thousands of square miles.

The idea captured the imagination of General Claude Auchinleck, the new Commander-in-Chief of the Middle East who had just taken over from General Archibald Wavell. 'The Auk', as he was always known to his troops, ordered the set-up of a trial unit of six officers and sixty men to be trained by David Stirling for action in November, when he planned to launch a main offensive against General Rommel's Army. The unit was to be called 'L Detachment of the Special Air Service'.

Now Stirling was off on a recruiting mission. His first capture was Lieutenant Jock Lewis, then running Commando night patrols in the besieged port of Tobruk. He was both a daring soldier and a fine scholar, with remarkable organising ability. He fell in with the plan right away.

Next, Stirling repaired to the Commando depot at Geneifa where he collected four more officers, including Eoin McGonigal and Bill Fraser. Not surprisingly they mentioned the name of their old friend Paddy Mayne, and also that unhappy beast of a temper which had resulted in his consignment to the desert jailhouse nearby. Stirling had already heard some lively stories about this colourful character, and thought that he could steer his fire in the direction where it would hurt the enemy instead of his superior officer.

So, the meeting was arranged and the two bombshells faced up to one another. But, on this historic occasion, no explosion! Instead, as the pair stood a few feet apart eyeing each other cautiously Paddy quietly braced himself up for another brasshat wigging, for the set trash of moral lecture considered appropriate for such occasions. He had been given basins of it out here in the smelly sweat-house and now all he wanted was a speedy court martial and whatever punishment the brasshats saw fit to impose.

But very soon Paddy's heart was bounding with joy as he heard David Stirling inviting him to join the SAS (Special Air Service). For most it would have been Hobson's choice, but not for Lieutenant Blair Mayne. This was what he *really* wanted – a chance to fight alongside tough, adventuresome men of courage in a field that offered greater freedom of action and more scope for individual purpose than normal infantry troops.

Little did this happy volunteer think, for all his instantaneous enthusiasm, that he was now about to set out on a long rocky road that was to lead to fame and the leadership of one of the most glittering regiments in the British Army.

The embryo unit, however, was not to be born without due labour pains. The chairborne warriors back in Whitehall did not take too kindly to the news of the formation of a Special Air Service unit. As far as they were concerned, the idea of a small, highly organised group of raiders prowling behind enemy lines in the desert, blowing up planes, petrol dumps, railways and trucks seemed too far-fetched and was likely to be doomed before the show ever got under way. Not only that, but war materials and supplies of every kind were badly needed at home and should not be squandered on some hare-brained outfit with such a remote chance of success.

Thus, when Paddy Mayne and his Commanding Officer, Captain David Stirling, arrived at their provisional new base at Kabrit, a village in the Suez Canal Zone, on the edge of the Great Bitter Lake about one hundred miles from Cairo, a forlorn sight greeted them. You could hardly have called it a camp, rather, a dump! Two small tents for personal use and one large supply tent, containing a few battered old chairs and one table. This was to be the 'home' for the first fifty volunteers of the winged dagger men, who were already trundling along their way in three-ton trucks.

But if the Whitehall brasshats imagined that they had dampened the spirits of this highly irregular team of daredevils, they would have to put their ornate thinking caps on again. Because, with an ingenuity which was to manifest itself more and more in the months to come, they became, overnight, one of the most luxuriously equipped units in the British Army.

How did it happen? A rapid reconnaissance of the surrounding country, a wide plain broken only by protruding rocks, showed that a splendidly equipped camp belonging to the New Zealand Division was unoccupied while they were away on manoeuvres. So, that night, a dozen SAS men in a three-tonner bluffed their way through the camp entrance past an Indian guard, piled up a load of fifteen tents, chairs, tables, hurricane lamps, wash basins, kitchen utensils, cups and crockery – and from the three large tents also a piano and a bar.

"We didn't exactly steal them", one of Paddy's men was heard to explain some time later. "We only borrowed 'em." The raiders were never tracked down. But the New Zealanders were quickly able to replace their own furniture losses.

Meantime, this bunch of teaktough SAS boys, who had all been through strenuous Commando training courses before being posted to the Middle East, embarked on further exercises which would make any average strong man wilt. Apart from the regular activities such as rifle practice, weapon training and rigorous physical drill, the recruits were required to leap from a truck travelling at 30 mph and make a 100 mile forced march across the desert, carrying a heavy pack. Tough bodily endurance and flash-point brain reaction were essential if the Germans and Italians were going to be caught napping.

Young Paddy Mayne entered into the whole training course with so much gusto that it spurred the others on. They watched in silent admiration as he showed them how to navigate a boat, climb rocks, drive any vehicle, transmit morse signals, expertly strip any type of enemy weapon, and use explosives. A little chemistry shop was set up near the rifle range, and experiments were carried out with different combinations of plastic and thermite. Finally, through the inventive genius of Jock Lewis, a light-weight sticky bomb, powerful enough to blow up a plane, was devised.

The next move was to practise infiltrating into enemy aerodromes by night, and there was only one way to do that – try it out on their own airfields. The largest was Heliopolis, the main aerodrome for Cairo, and this was selected as the target. The RAF were confident that their airfields were well guarded and that these saucy SAS men would be repulsed and red-faced with embarrassment as they were marched off to the guardroom. Equally, cheeky Paddy Mayne was sure that they could slip in, put labels instead of bombs on the planes and sneak away undetected.

It was a blazing hot morning in October 1941, when Paddy led a group of ten men – there were three other groups – on the first thirty mile 'leg' of the ninety mile stretch from their base at Kabrit to the Heliopolis aerodrome, where the RAF waited, warned in advance that an attempt would be made any night to get through and attack the bombers they were protecting.

Each of the raiders carried his own supply of bully beef, biscuits and four water bottles containing a pint apiece. They marched across the desert by night, and lay under camouflaged rough cloth sacks on the hard sand by day and tried to sleep. Raging thirst began to torment them before long, but they pressed on steadily for three nights until they reached the outskirts of Heliopolis aerodrome.

And Paddy? Hefty, strong, and fresh as ever after the gruelling ordeal of the march, though also personally parching for water, he suppressed a chuckle as he and his men noiselessly cut their way through a barbed-wire fence surrounding the two mile perimeter. Then, as silently, they stole up to the symmetrical rows of parked Bombay aircraft and pasted on them more than forty labels, just as they had promised to do.

The other three SAS groups also turned up during the night and duly decorated the rest of the air fleet. Red faces were ten-a-penny among the RAF élite next day, when the memos started to drop like confetti: "Steps must be taken at once to remedy the defence system at Heliopolis."

In Kabrit there was now both an RAF camp and a Naval camp known as HM Saunders – and how the capers of the SAS boys amused everyone! The Naval mess was the focal point of the combined camps social activities, and it was truly a jovial centre in that dreary set-up in the flat barren wilderness of the coastal desert. Prices were most reasonable: dinner for two shillings and drink and cigarettes duty free. There was swimming and it was very pleasant to sunbathe and then dip in as the heat grew more intense. Paddy loved to spend his evenings in that matey mess drinking and chatting with his friends for hours on end.

And the friends he made were of outstanding character. David Stirling himself, a tall, handsome Scottish aristocrat with a drawling, well-bred voice and a heart of gold; Captain Lord Jellico, son of the famous Admiral, brave and unassuming, but very sociable; Captain Malcolm Pleydell, the Medical Officer who was to become his close friend; Captain Randolph Churchill, son of the great Winston, a fellow he found intolerably rude on occasions, but still liked; and a host of RAF and Naval officers who were the salt of the earth (and of the sky and sea!)

The other ranks were equally comradely, and Paddy spent many happy hours in the Sergeants' Mess. "A dangerous place to go," he wrote to his brother Douglas. "You can never be quite certain of what is in your glass." As the training was really so very tough these off-duty sprees did ease the tension.

After several weeks drilling at this 'ground work', as Jock Lewis called it, they took to the air and started the real job, parachute jumping. For this they borrowed a Bombay bomber from their next door neighbours in the RAF camp.

Paddy Mayne didn't like it himself, but there was no option if he intended to stay with this happy band of adventurers and, by George! he wanted to be with them. So holding his heaving tummy somewhere between his tonsils he took the plunge – and found it was not as bad as he had imagined. But it was still bad enough, this jumping into space with the earth rushing up to you like an erupting volcano. What a relief, then, to feel the sharp tug on the harness and to look up at the white billowy canopy overhead. But these practice drops, of course, were in daylight and the reality would be done in the inky blackness of night, perhaps with ack-ack fire coming up from below and a lively reception committee awaiting you on the ground if you survived the drop.

Paddy, however, was not given to morbid forebodings. He was decisively a man of action; a man who, once embarked on a set course, had no doubts or fears. It was simply a question of mental discipline and he had mastered it.

Ahead of him now was only one objective and that was the successful execution of the November raid which David Stirling had planned on five German aerodromes behind their front lines on the north-west of Libya. It was an ambitious plan and much depended on its outcome. The only way that the SAS could continue was to prove its real use. The fate of Laycock's Commando had demonstrated this.

The overall strategy in the Middle East was clear to hardly anyone at this time, and a kind of stalemate seemed to have set in. But Lieutenant Mayne knew that his fellow Ulsterman, General Auchinleck, was breeding no idle worms. He and another Irishman, General Alan Cunningham, were hard at it in GHQ planning the big November thrust that was to drive the Afrika Korps back across the desert and relieve beleaguered Tobruk.

This had all been done once before by General Wavell and that most dashing and colourful field commander of his, General Richard O'Connor, but Winston Churchill's tight-rope antics over Greece had stripped them of their laurels (by slimming them of their strength) and opened the door to Rommel and his Afrika Korps. By this insistence on backing the Greeks against the Germans – much against their own wishes, it may be said – Churchill had demonstrated a dangerous pigheadedness which was this time to cost his country dearly, though, at other times, it served it superbly.

Now, in the desert the date for the attack on the aerodromes was fixed for the night of the 17 November and this meant that five separate groups would have to be dropped on the 16 November so that they could reconnoitre the ground beforehand.

First they were transported to Bagush, a forward RAF airfield near the front line, where they were entertained rather like men doomed to destruction. As one man wrote shortly afterwards:

> "An Officer waited on us at the table and he looked at us in such a way that we could imagine him saying, 'I will give them all I can, as these poor chaps may not be coming back again'. It was just like having whatever you wished before going to the gallows."

At 10.30 pm on that black November night they roared away in five Bombay bombers to an unknown fate. Each group had been instructed to retreat to a chosen meeting spot in the desert hinterland after its task had been completed. There, the Long Range Desert Group would be awaiting them in trucks.

General Auchinleck's offensive was timed for dawn on the 18 November and every man of the SAS felt justly proud of the part his unit was being asked to play. There were high hopes that the raid would throw the Germans and Italians off balance and that the main attack would then surge through the front line.

But things went sadly wrong, as one of the men who lived through it, formerly Sergeant-Major Bob Bennett, from Oxford, now recalls:

> "The moment we climbed aboard the planes taking us to the dropping zones the weather turned its back on the Met men's

forecasts and began to deteriorate rapidly. Dust storms blew up, and by the time we reached the area we seemed to be flying blind, and the objectives below were completely obscured. It was cold inside that dank bomber – bitterly, uncomfortably cold.

There could be no turning back, however, for any of us. Paddy had made up his mind that, as this was our first big show, we were going to let everyone see what we were capable of doing. But as we tumbled out, a thirty-mile-an-hour gale scattered us in all directions. Our containers, with supplies of bombs and food, drifted out of sight. Some of our chaps were dragged along on their faces and must have died in agony. I saw two seriously injured. One had a broken leg and the other a back injury, and we had to leave them where they lay. I heard, some weeks later, that they had been captured and had their fingers cut off.

Paddy broke his toe in the fall, but insisted on limping towards the direction of gun flashes due North. We still had a few bombs, enough to do some damage, so we decided to push on. We spent the night in a wadi, sitting back to back to keep warm, with a blanket over our heads. Then came torrential rain. The wadi became a river and we watched helplessly as the rest of our supplies were washed away. Fortunately, we were able to fill our bottles with rainwater and this, I think, saved our lives.

It was a long walk back to the rendezvous – 36 miles. Paddy was tight-lipped and silent. He was so choked up with disappointment that I couldn't get a word out of him. He was always like that when things went wrong. But I could see from the look of determination on his face that he would come back again, alone if necessary, and that there would be no mistake next time."

Mercifully, the Long Range Desert Group Patrol was waiting for them with tea, bully beef and cigarettes. What a relief for all of them after their frightful ordeal!

Soon they were bumping over the desert en route to their base at Kabrit, and nothing much happened except an attack by an Italian Savoya plane which dispersed them temporarily but did no damage. At Siwa Oasis they were transferred to transport planes and ferried back to base.

For Paddy, slumped forward in his seat, everything was gall and his thoughts shifted uneasily from the poor chaps whom he'd had to abandon in the desert to the abortive raid itself. How had the other fellows fared? he asked himself. What of his Belfast friend and fellow officer, Eoin McGonigal, who had taken off with his section in the Bombay Bomber which had preceded his own off the runway, how had he got on? Then, the resourceful David Stirling and Jock Lewis, had they achieved any success?

He now recalled the discussion they had, just before take-off, about cancelling the operation – and how, with a gust of bravado, he had opposed it. "I joined the unit," he had said, "to fight, and if I don't get a crack at the enemy soon, I may have to indulge in a few practice rounds with some of the chaps at Headquarters." How stupid of him, and how stupid of the others, too, to have shrugged off the advice tendered by the RAF officers who knew so much more about these things than they did! And now, if the others had failed as he had, the whole future of the SAS would be in jeopardy. He knew that many conservative-minded officers had been sniping at them for months up at Headquarters and now they would probably break out in the open with howls of derision.

The only ray of hope remaining was that the other raiders, despite the unfriendly elements, might have pulled it off.

But it was not to be. Back as base, the broken and dejected remnants came limping home, each and all with a tale of disaster and none with any good news. The final roll call showed that out of fifty-five men and seven officers engaged in the venture, only eighteen men and four officers returned. Paddy's friend, McGonigal, was missing and it was hoped that at the worst he might be a prisoner. In fact, he died, only a few days after his capture, from injuries received when landing.

What was now urgently needed was a striking success to boost morale for the SAS boys and keep the jaundiced eyes of their detractors away from them.

In the north, the launching of Auchinleck's new offensive had not gone off too well and General Cunningham had been replaced at the height of the fray by General Ritchie. It was not until early December, and after heavy losses in men and armour, that the Eighth Army got the upper hand and forced Rommel to withdraw far beyond Tobruk into Tripolitania.

On the 8 December 1941, Britain declared war on Japan and the war had now become a world one in the truest sense of the word.

CHAPTER 4

Reprieve

NOVEMBER 25 1941, a decisive day for Captain David Stirling and Lieutenant Blair Mayne – and also for Generals Sir Alan Cunningham and Neil Ritchie!

For in the morning General Cunningham, Commander-in-Chief of the Eighth Army, was replaced by General Ritchie, Chief of Staff, Middle East Command. David Stirling was interviewed by both of them in turn, to find out what he and his men had observed on the Gazala–Tobruk coast road in the form of enemy reinforcements, especially tank strength. He was able to report that he saw only supply trucks, no armour whatever. Neither of the generals said anything critical of his recent experiences, and he withdrew from the meeting greatly relieved. The SAS was going to be allowed to live to fight another day, but David had made up his mind that the *modus operandi* must be changed. For the time being, deep penetration on land using 30-cwt trucks, the same type as those of the Long Range Desert Group (LRDG), would replace airborne raids.

David Stirling had to wait at Headquarters for several days before he could button-hole just the right man to help him make his next step. This was Brigadier John Marriott, then commanding the 22nd Guards Brigade, who promptly referred and seconded him and his unit to Brigadier Denys Reid whose force had just fought a brilliant campaign crowned by the capture of Jalo, an oasis in the Sahara Desert 150 miles south of the Mediterranean coastline. It was not an impressive spot, a few scattered villages of mud huts, and the water in this sand sea was

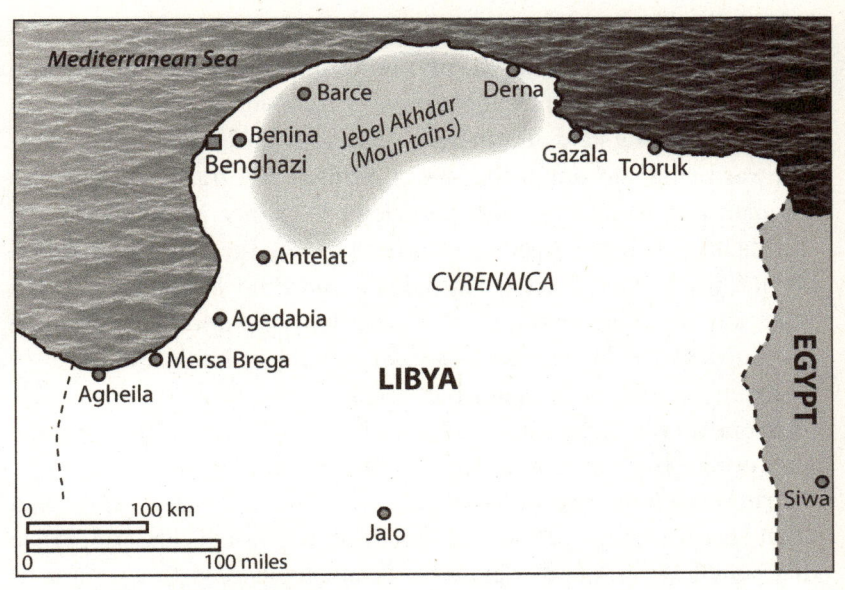

Map of eastern Libya in late 1941.

hardly drinkable. An old fort did give part of it a certain 'Beau Geste' touch, but the attractive thing was that Jalo, although out of the main tide of battle, was within striking range of many juicy targets such as Agheila, Benghazi and Sirte on the sea shore, and with hundreds of miles of coastline thrown in for good measure.

Across the sand sea eastward was Siwa, base of the Long Range Desert Group, and two days after Stirling and his men arrived a squadron of the outfit moved into Jalo to set up a forward base for reconnaissance, aimed at keeping the Afrika Korps very close under the microscope. It was a role which the LRDG had been performing for sixteen months and they had done it well. To these highly skilled navigators the desert was like an ocean which they roamed for months on end with their petrol dumps and food depots hidden away in the most unlikely places, enabling them to operate continuously in forward areas without the necessity of returning to base.

Stirling enlisted their aid and it was arranged that they would ferry the SAS to within a few miles of Agedabia aerodrome and take them back after they had carried out their appointed task of blowing up aircraft parked around the perimeter of the field. The date for the operation was fixed for the 21 December.

Blair Mayne had by this time grown a red beard and looked more like a Viking pirate than a British Army officer, but the sun and the training had made him a man of iron. Now more than ever he was determined to rally to Stirling's aid and make a success of the SAS. The Agedabia raid was being laid out at the special request of Brigadier Reid, who was planning to link up with his friend Brigadier Marriott and his Guards Brigade in the Agedabia–Antelat area on the 22 December and felt that the hornets' nest at Agedabia aerodrome should be well out of the way when he arrived there. Enemy bombers and fighters can be very uncomfortable neighbours as past experience had proved.

Stirling agreed to the plan but decided to squeeze in two earlier raids, one on the night of the 14 December at Sirte aerodrome, and the other on the 16 December at Agheila aerodrome.

Sirte was a long way off, nearly four hundred miles, but report had it that here was the largest air base on the entire North Coast of Africa. That suited Stirling and Mayne fine and they agreed to attend to it together. A pretty formidable combination indeed.

Agheila was a 'mere' 180-odd miles off and this target was assigned to Jock Lewis. The attack on Agedabia would be led by Bill Fraser.

So, on the 8 December, in the half light of dawn and with a cold biting wind cutting across their faces, Stirling and Mayne and thirty-seven of the LRDG and the SAS set off in seven trucks fully stocked with the baggage of desert travel in wartime, guns, ammo, petrol, blankets, camouflage nets, food, water, cooking utensils, and last, but not least in value, spades for digging out the lorries when they got stuck in the mud ('unsticking', as the boys called it in their more polite moments.)

In three days they had covered 280 miles undiscovered, but on the fourth they were spotted and attacked by an Italian reconnaissance plane. No damage was suffered except now the enemy would know they were there. And, true enough, within half an hour three bombers roared up, and strafed and bombed the scrub where the raiders had taken refuge. But again their luck was in, and no damage was suffered.

It was, however, a nerve-wracking ordeal, lying flat down and blindly hoping that bombs and bullets would miss somehow and that death would be held at bay a little longer. In the lonely primeval vastness of the desert this game of hide-and-seek seemed oddly out of place, strangely unreal and wrong.

The why's and wherefore's of international politics and intrigues did not seem to belong and yet, to Blair Mayne, rolling over on the hard earth and watching the bombers disappearing in the distant haze, it was all too real. Ten or twelve German or Italian young men had with grim determination set about them hell bent on one thing only – to blast them all into eternity. Blair did not complain; this was war, total war, and he was in it up to the hilt. Today, by the nature of things they were the hunted; tomorrow they would be the hunters and the destruction of the enemy was their primary objective at all times.

Soon they were on their way again, and by nightfall they hoped they would be at the selected rendezvous three miles from their target. But again an enemy plane flew high overhead, on reconnaissance this time, and now they feared that all aerodromes and supply depots ahead of them would be ringed with iron and their plans frustrated. Even worse could be expected, but turning back was gall to them which they couldn't take, with the future of their unit so precariously in the balance.

Now darkness laid her mantle over them protectively and a sense of security returned. Suddenly, they were nearly astride the coastal road and almost there! Sergeant Mike Sadler, the LRDG navigator, had done his job well and now there they were within sight of enemy patrols restlessly and anxiously scouting up and down the roads.

Stirling thought hard and fast on the best plan to outwit them. The element of surprise had been partly lost and now something new would have to be devised. Quick as a flash it came to him. Blair Mayne and some of the men would attack Tamit aerodrome thirty miles west of Sirte, and he and Sergeant Brough and the rest would proceed to Sirte and try their luck there. This way they had two chances of success, and success was something they had to have this trip, or else… It didn't bear thinking about. Zero hour was fixed for 2300 hours on the following night and he waved goodbye to Mayne and his men and wished them all the best in the world.

They needed it, too. After leaving Stirling, Paddy and his men headed south until they came to a large canyon which one of the boys had since described as being as high and as steep as Beachy Head. There was no track, yet by some incredible sixth sense they got their vehicles down through ravines and boulders. By dawn they were within four miles of Tamit and holed up in a wadi which gave them excellent cover. All day they stayed in their hide-away, sleeping, eating, servicing vehicles and getting ready for the business that had brought them there.

Reconnaissance parties were sent out to report on enemy movements and they brought back word that the enemy had shifted all his aircraft from the Sirte aerodrome to the landing ground near Tamit, barely two miles away from their uninvited visitors. This must have happened after the bombing by David, Paddy and the others the previous evening. Middle East Headquarters had, in fact, picked up a message from the Mayor of Sirte reporting that his town was being attacked in strength by British Army patrols, and the local German commander, flapping with justifiable panic at such an imminent threat, must have decided that Tamit, a good thirty miles further away, offered greater security for his squadrons.

The reports which Paddy Mayne's scouts brought in of planes landing like crows in a cornfield must have been very satisfying for him as he quietly handed out his time-bombs to his men. The desert night had now descended on them and he decided that it was time to go, so the nine operatives whom he was going to use were quietly ordered into the trucks. Captain Gus Holliman, of the LRDG, was then asked to make a five-mile detour of Tamit airfield and take three of his trucks down the coastal road for the rendezvous with David Stirling. The other three would travel round to approach the field from the north, then leave Paddy Mayne and his men three miles to cover on foot.

Before he died in the car crash at Newtownards in 1955, Paddy began to write his own so-casual account of this remarkable exploit, his initial success in a fabulous war career. It reads:

"It was just after ten o'clock as we left the truck. An ideal night for the job. No moon, and pleasantly cool for walking. There were four of us, keyed-up, tense, a little nervous. We moved quietly, heading slightly to the right of the North Star.

The desert finished, and we crossed a tarmacadam road – the one Mussolini built to carry his men to the Delta. We were neither expected, nor invited, and we had the initiative. I began to feel happy, we could hear the sea, and after about a hundred yards we came across two wooden huts in a dip. The sound of sleeping came from inside. From the look of them they were not Arabs, so we put some time-bombs on the roof and left. Back up the path we heard voices and hid till they came abreast. I guessed they would lead us to the airfield and they did. They disappeared into a building rather like a Nissen hut with a door at each end. The sound of singing and talking came from inside. I kicked open the door and stood there with my Colt 45, the others at my side with a tommy gun and another automatic. The Germans stared at us. We were a peculiar and frightening sight, bearded and with long, unkept hair. For what seemed an age we just stood there looking at each other in complete silence. I said: 'Good Evening'. At that a young German arose and moved slowly backwards. I shot him, and as he fell, he knocked glasses to the ground from his table. I turned and fired at another some six feet away. He was standing beside the wall as he sagged.

Hawkins, a Londoner, opened up with his tommy-gun. He was a good chap, but he was to leave us soon because of his continual use of a certain epithet.[1] But on this occasion I didn't mind.

The room was by now in pandemonium. So we left, throwing hand grenades to add to the confusion. The dozen or so enemy that we had killed or wounded did not matter much numerically. But we hoped to create a feeling of insecurity and anxiety among the Axis, and to make them waste men on sentry duty. For the same reason we mined the road, forcing their drivers to move cautiously.

The night was livening up. Quite a bit of firing, but none in our direction. We found two dumps of forty gallon petrol drums covered with camouflage netting, and placed sufficient bombs in to destroy the lot.

Then came the greatest thrill. They looked beautiful. Low, sleek, deadly in the air, but strangely impotent now. Thousands of pounds worth of craftsmanship waiting to be destroyed by a little plastic high explosive. As grateful as children on Christmas morning we moved from plane to plane, placing our bombs in the cockpits or petrol tanks.

The bombs were composed of high explosive mixed with thermite, a detonator and a time pencil. These pencils were ingenious devices consisting of a spring, a striker, a capsule of acid, and a retaining wire. When the capsule was broken the acid burned through the wire, released the spring and striker, and so detonated the bomb. The time lag between setting and detonation depended on the thickness of the wire. That night, we had decided on thirty minutes. The thermite was mixed with the explosive to ensure burning.

The planes silhouetted against the night sky were a mixed bag of

---

1 Blair Mayne never tolerated the use of dirty language among his men.

Stuka bombers, Messerschmidt fighters and transports dispersed in a rough circle at intervals of about twenty yards. As I approached one I saw a glow of light in the cockpit. I thought someone was sitting there smoking. So I quietly moved round the rear of the plane and up to the cockpit. I clambered on to the wing and peered inside. Someone had neglected to switch off the panel lights, and the dashboard was softly illuminated. A sharp tug, then a heave, and I had ripped out the dashboard for a souvenir…

We were now running short of bombs. We had wasted too many on telegraph poles, and had been too generous at the petrol hut and around the dumps. But we each had a hand grenade left, so before leaving we tossed them into the cockpits of the last two planes.

Happy and contented, and with empty haversacks, we set off, back to our trucks and the Long Range Desert Group. We hadn't gone far, possibly a quarter of a mile, when there was an explosion. A terrific sheet of flame shot upwards, lighting the area. Feeling slightly naked in the light, we turned and got down in the sand to watch our handiwork. It was magnificent and terribly satisfying to watch the petrol dump blaze.

One by one the German planes joined in the flames. There would be an explosion, a flash of light, then a steady fire. I produced cigarettes and a flask of rum, and we relaxed.

Since our attack on the hut, there had been spasmodic firing, but now everything opened up in a great crescendo. Towards the sea we heard heavy guns, the sky was criss-crossed with anti-aircraft tracer, and there were bursts of ground defence fire as some imaginative gunner started to see shadows moving. We learned later from Army headquarters that they had intercepted a message from the Italian commander of the local garrison to his headquarters in Tripoli to the effect that unless urgent reinforcements were sent they would not be able to hold on. I don't think our little force would have held the area against anything more formidable than a donkey and cart!

The glare from the petrol fire was lessening. So, stubbing our cigarettes in the sand, we continued to walk to the rendezvous point. I had not been too certain of my ability to pinpoint the trucks on our return march, and as I was scared of overshooting, I asked the LRDG to flash a torch every three minutes from two o'clock.

Just when we began to get worried we saw the welcoming light directly in front. There was a great reception awaiting us. The

LRDG were just as pleased at our success as we were. We climbed aboard the trucks, settled ourselves among the petrol, rations and ammunition, and left it to them to get as many miles as possible to a safe hiding place before the enemy fighters came looking for us at dawn."

Paddy's casual reference to his tearing out a dashboard panel is unduly modest. He was one of the most forceful rugby football forwards in the world and a man of freakish muscular power. In his Varsity days he had, without any previous instruction or training, lifted above his head four hundred pounds on a bar-bell with effortless ease. His prodigious feats of strength were well known in his native Ulster.

Now, this night, he had been on the move for about three hours and had caused over a million pounds' worth of damage to the enemy.

Eighty miles of dark, dangerous desert lay ahead before he and his comrades reached their rendezvous with David Stirling and it was eleven o'clock the following morning before they made it.

There they arrived for a heroes' welcome, for although Stirling and Sergeant Brough had been foiled at Sirte by the mass clear-out of the enemy's planes, they had a grandstand view of Paddy's success at Tamit and they were overjoyed. Naturally, David was annoyed that the enemy had suspected from air reconnaissance that a major attack was imminent on the Sirte aerodrome and so had shifted the threatened planes to Tamit but, anyway, the exodus had not saved them in the end.

But typical of the man was his reaction to that empty airfield. Instead of returning to his meeting point with the LRDG with all his ammunition unused, he now set about mining the coastal road with a pile of explosives which he and Brough possessed. But, lest the enemy got alerted, he waited until Paddy's firework display among the parked aircraft had started off.

How David Stirling's heart swelled with joy as he listened to Paddy's account of that Tamit raid! At last the SAS had come into its own – and for the time being, at least, its detractors would have to hold their silly tongues.

For the enemy it would be a cruel blow at a moment when cruel blows could well be done without. And, worst of all, a rash of jitters spread like wildfire from one aerodrome to another, all along the coastal plains.

Those two audacious adventurers, Stirling and Mayne, now became bonded together in a closer comradeship founded on mutual respect and the future took on a more rosy hue. The wild Irishman from Ulster had sloughed off his roughneck reputation and was now accepted as a cunning and daring man of action – a fellow to be reckoned with by friend and foe alike. And now, while his outstanding achievement was being lauded by all he produced another quality that was to enlarge him even more in the eyes of his comrades – modesty; a modesty bordering almost on self-consciousness. It was to stay with him throughout his entire military career.

In Jalo now, Stirling and Mayne awaited anxiously for Jock Lewis's return from the Agheila venture. How had that one come off? Three days after their own arrival in came Jock, with news both good and bad.

The airfield at Agheila had also been deserted, so he and his party had to fall back on a second plan which Jock had stored in that donnish mind of his – an attack on a roadhouse near Mersa Berga which our Intelligence reported was sometimes used as a rendezvous for generals and staff officers who wished to take stock of current events and compare notes. For this raid Jock took a captured Lancia car with him, and masquerading as an Italian staff officer he and the LRDG trucks attached themselves to an enemy convoy on the coastal road.

But when they reached the roadhouse the plan miscarried. The British trucks were suddenly recognised, and the alarm sounded. Jock had to abandon the idea of capturing the generals and staff officers, who, he had reason to believe, were inside the building. Consequently, he had to content himself with shooting up the roadhouse and blowing up thirty or more trucks and cars parked outside. Then he made off without loss, and the desert engulfed him.

A few days later Lieutenant Bill Fraser and his unit returned from their Agebadia raid and reported thirty-seven aircraft destroyed by time-bombs.

This brought the bag total up to sixty-one planes and a large number of trucks destroyed in one week, and the SAS men had good reason for feeling ten feet tall. But, like gambler's luck, their success had to be exploited to the full while Dame Fortune was still smiling. So Stirling, Mayne, Lewis and Fraser put their thinking caps on and got down to some more hard planning.

CHAPTER 5

A-Hunting we must go

ON THE EVE of Christmas, 1941, the 'Roving Four', Stirling, Mayne, Fraser and Lewis, were off once more. Stirling was heading back to Sirte, Mayne to Tamit again, Fraser to Marble Arch this time and Lewis to Nofilia, all on a Santa Claus errand with a load of time-bombs as presents for the Germans and Italians.

Coming so soon after the other raids this was a piece of almost incredible audacity that not even an apprehensive enemy could have envisaged. And this was exactly what these desperadoes were banking on. It was nine o'clock on a perishingly cold night when Paddy Mayne was dropped off in the Wadi Tamit and left with six miles to cover to his target. Zero hour for all was 1.00 am next morning, and the fact that their passage to the area of action was unobserved highly raised their chances of success.

Paddy and five men moved up the wadi cautiously, and reached the airfield two hours later without incident. Twenty-seven planes were parked within their range of vision and they crouched in the cover of a ditch to watch the patrols. Then, stealthily they crept forward and quickly cut the perimeter wire and tiptoed on towards the waiting planes. In each they placed a bomb with a half-hour fuse. But, unluckily, one detonated ten minutes too soon just as Paddy was walking away from the last of the twenty-seven bombers. The deafening explosion which rent the silence of this icy cold, dark night was followed by a pillar of all-illuminating flame.

Paddy called to his men to make a run for it, but as they started Italian

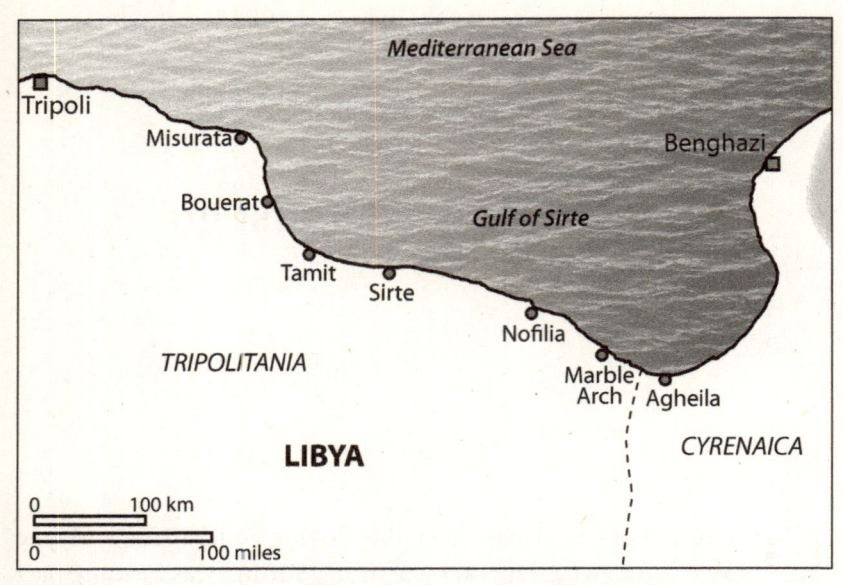

Map of the area of the second daring raid on enemy airfields in Libya.

guards began racing around shouting, "Avanti! Avanti!" Any second now they would open fire. Pulling the pin out of a hand grenade Paddy bawled, "Freund!" in a very un-German-like brogue and tossed it into a group of Italians. Corporal Bob Bennett, who was running alongside him, did likewise and immediately the firing broke out. Behind them all was chaos as bombs exploded and the inferno raged and spread. Trotting and walking, Paddy and his men reached the rendezvous in the wadi twenty-five minutes later and headed back by truck to Jalo.

And next, David Stirling. Alas! Again he was out of luck. First, he had to wait four hours whilst a huge German armoured division rumbled slowly past. Stirling's trucks were heading in the same direction, and had no alternative but to use the same highway. It was not a pleasant prospect, but David was never the man to shirk his duty and presently he was passing armoured cars and tanks and transports, some on the move and others pulled up for the night.

Two miles from the airfield Stirling's trucks hauled in to the side of the road, and he and four of his men went ahead on foot. But when they reached their target it was within an hour of dawn and in front of them stretched a wall of closely webbed barbed wire all round the aerodrome. Inside it armed patrols were pacing up and down, and with the limited time now left to them and the precarious position of the LRDG men in the trucks back on the roadside, David had to call off the attempt and withdrew.

Now there was nothing left but to end with a shooting-up rampage, but first he would have to get the consent of Gus Holliman who was in command to the LRDG men, who were primarily a reconnaissance unit and not supposed to engage in open combat with the enemy if it could be avoided. Here David Stirling encountered no difficulty and soon they were blazing a trail of terror and destruction along the crowded highway, picking on what he called 'soft-skinned' vehicles and tented encampments.

For the enemy, the next half-hour was hell let loose, and then with dawn almost upon them the marauders turned to the desert and headed south.

Back at Jalo, Paddy Mayne was already waiting when Stirling got back, but it was several days before any news of Jock Lewis and Fraser came through – and when it did, how grim! Jock Lewis's raid on Nofilia had gone badly and only two planes had been destroyed when heavy enemy patrols appeared on the scene and drove his party off. At the rendezvous six trucks were waiting and they all set off for Marble Arch to pick up Bill Fraser and his men. En route they were savagely attacked from the air, and Lewis was killed. All the trucks were knocked out but, when the planes flew off, one was salvaged by fitting it up with spares taken from the others. At Marble Arch there was no trace of Bill Fraser, so the remnant of the Lewis patrol headed on for Jalo.

What had happened was that Fraser had also drawn a blank at Marble Arch. Then he had retired to the wrong rendezvous, where he and his four men laid up for almost a week. Next, in despair and fearfully short of water they set forth on a march of two hundred miles to Hasselet, a British outpost. The sufferings endured by these five heroes in the following eight days and the courage shown by all of them should be recorded in the great epics of military history. In the course of this odyssey they shot up a German truck and grabbed two cans of water – a more precious prize to them than anything else in the world at the time. Later, they attacked an Italian lorry which was parked, with many others, in a wadi, and got away with a quantity of food. Finally, they jumped on to a slow moving Mercedes car, overcame the German occupants and drove off along the coastal highway and a traffic tide of enemy transport and armour. After a while they cut into the desert – and found themselves bogged down in a salt marsh. Abandoning the car and their furious prisoners, they marched off once more in the direction of the British lines and two days later were rescued by an armoured patrol. For sheer guts, their achievement could not be bettered.

CHAPTER 6

Rift in the lute

After the Christmas raids of 1941 the Special Air Service returned to their depot at Kabrit to recruit, re-stock and re-equip. Stirling and Mayne now believed that Lieutenant Bill Fraser had suffered the same fate as Jock Lewis and agreed that fresh officers would have to be brought in. To accomplish this and to plan further operations, Stirling hurried off to Cairo and saw General Auchinleck. 'The Auk' proved truly appreciative of what had been achieved, and sanguine of further success.

Now that the Axis forces had been driven from eastern Libya and Benghazi was about to be evacuated, Stirling proposed that the SAS should attack the port of Bouerat, just beyond Tamit and 350 miles to the west.

General Auchinleck, always a soldier of enterprise and trust, gave his consent and authorised the recruitment of six officers and forty men. At the same time he promoted David Stirling to the rank of major and Paddy Mayne to a captaincy. During these busy days David was using the Cairo flat of his diplomat brother Peter as a headquarters and relying on Paddy to keep things going at Kabrit.

And Paddy, though essentially a combat soldier, maintained a stern discipline of his own. In the Sergeants' Mess he would sing and drink all night through, but the moment Reveille sounded he flung off the harlequin's mask and became very much the regimental officer again.

Heaven help anyone who dared to presume upon the familiarity of the night before! Sergeant Bob Bennett, who never missed a party and knew Captain Mayne better than most, had good reason to remember his dual personality.

One cold, wintry night he and two of his pals were on sentry duty and as it seemed to be the height of stupidity to be guarding a camp a hundred miles south east of Cairo, they decided to turn in for a rest. It was 2.30 am, and so far as they knew, all the officers were in slumberland.

Suddenly, they were torn from their own sleep by a voice of thunder. "Guard! Turn out!" Jumping from their bunks, startled and alarmed, they grabbed for their clothes and their rifles but they were not there.

Again the bellowing din shattered the stillness of the night. "Hurry up, you lazy louts! Get a move on!" Shamefacedly, they came out of their tents and stood before Captain Mayne in their underpants and vests.

The night air was spine-chilling. The moon hung low and bright, and behind their officer they saw their uniforms and rifles lying in a heap.

For half an hour the slackers were made to stand there and do arms drill as punishment, and yet when it was all over they were happy, for with this strange unorthodox officer they knew it would go no further.

They knew that on another occasion he had caught a man drunk on guard duty. And after dousing him with a bucketful of water he cracked him on the jaw with his mighty fist and left him unconscious on the sand to be picked up by his comrades.

With Paddy, there were no charge sheets and no detentions, just a rough and ready pay-off justice.

Lieutenant Fitzroy Maclean (later Brigadier Sir Fitzroy Maclean, CBE, MP), a former Foreign Office Secretary and expert linguist who had retired from the diplomatic service at the outbreak of the war, joined the army as a private and was now commissioned in the Cameron Highlanders, was at this moment kicking up his heels in idleness and frustration in Cairo. He was introduced by Peter Stirling to his brother David. In no time at all he had joined the SAS and became immediately involved in the planning of the Bouerat raid which David had decided should take place on the night of the 23/24 January 1942.

On the 10 January, David Stirling returned to Kabrit and blandly informed Paddy Mayne that he would now take over the training of the new recruits and would be out of battle operations until someone else sufficiently experienced in training could be found to replace him and take over duties at the depot.

Paddy almost exploded with indignation. Was this the reward for destroying more than fifty enemy planes in only two operations? Were there not Sergeants and Corporals well fitted to take over this training routine?

Stirling, however, remained adamant and Paddy gruffly remarked at he strode off, "So you're going to leave me sitting on my backside while you hop off to Jalo and have some fun! Don't be surprised if I'm not here when you get back."

"You had better be!" snapped Stirling, and turned away.

The following day Stirling left by air for Jalo with a dozen men. Then, having joined up with a patrol of the LRDG, he set off on the 17 January for Bouerat. It was a mission which Paddy personally felt had by now been enlarged out of all proportion and, in the result, he was proved right. Some machinery, food supplies and some petrol takers were blown up and a small wireless station on the coast was blasted with high explosive. During this operation the unit had run into an ambush outside an Italian fort and had counter-attacked their attackers with such gusto and ferocity that they escaped unscathed, leaving many of the enemy dead and wounded in their wake. But the mass damage planned had not been accomplished.

On the 31 January, they returned to Jalo to learn with dismay that Rommel had counter-attacked in force on the same day on the main front and had retaken the greater part of Cyrenaica (eastern Libya). The Jalo base itself had been evacuated days earlier by the LRDG and now only a rearguard engaged in demolition were there to receive Stirling and his rangers.

The enemy was expected hourly and there was nothing for it but to head for Siwa across the Sand Sea, three hundred miles away as the crows fly – and they weren't going that way.

Back in faraway Kabrit, Captain Paddy Mayne was thoroughly *au fait* with all developments except the fate of Major Stirling's unit which had lost its wireless truck during an air attack in the Wadi Tamit on the 23 January, and had been out of touch ever since. The news of Rommel's thrusting counter-offensive disheartened him greatly; it meant that their own accomplishments at Agedabia and Tamit were now in vain and had only been fleabites to this wily desert fox, Rommel, who seemed to be a jinx to all of the British generals. What now? Would the wearisome see-saw of the desert go on like this forever?

And here he was acting as a glorified RSM to squads of wide-eyed rookies! It really was too much – and after four days of it he took to his bed and buried himself in books. Any fantasy was better than the reality.

The only ray of sunshine was the return of Bill Fraser – to Paddy it was like the recall of Lazarus from the dead, but now he was beset with doubts about David Stirling and his raiding party. What the devil had happened to them? Were they still in the land of the living? It certainly did not look like it.

Then, one day David and his men returned – and for the second time in less than three weeks he and Paddy exchanged angry words. On this occasion it was much more acrimonious, but in the end it finished in a renewal of friendship which never again became strained. The air had been cleared and two strong, dominating personalities had come into harmony and a deeper understanding of each other.

A sergeant-major now took over the recruit training and Paddy gladly bestirred himself from his bed to come to grips with the enemy again. But the opportunity for immediate action was not right at hand because the guerrilla raiding had to go step by step with the High Command's new general plan of operations and Auchinleck was now digging in at Gazala and consolidating for a massive counter-thrust against Rommel which might not materialize for months.

Obviously, the web of airfields in the Benghazi area must be the SAS's next objective, and planning went ahead on those lines. Benghazi Harbour itself was a tempting target, as it was now being used as the principal base for the supply of the Afrika Korps, and Stirling resolved to reserve it for himself.

In the marked area four airfields were listed for raids, and the four Raid Chiefs were named. They were Barce, by Lieutenant Bill Fraser; Slonta by Lieutenant Dodd; Berka by Lieutenant Alston; and a satellite of Berka, by Captain Paddy Mayne. Barce and Slonta, about fifty miles northwest of Benghazi, lay in the Jebel Mountain district, and the Berka aerodromes were on the coastal plain just south of the port.

Now action!

CHAPTER 7

The Black Camel

Paddy and his group moved up from Kabrit to Siwa, on the northern edge of the Sand Sea and to his surprise he found himself in an idyllic oasis which he afterwards described as "a paradise on earth". This fertile area, about three hundred miles from Alexandria, lies in a depression in the desert and measures thirty-six by fifteen miles. It is, in fact, a group of oases and for many years before the war it had modern roads with attractively laid out tree borders of tamarisk and false pepper. There were clumps of palm trees all around and murmuring streams and gardens of great beauty, rich with a thousand different tropical blooms and colours.

The old city of Siwa, now derelict and crumbling with decay, was once a large fortified stronghold. It is like a honeycomb with one house built upon another, and the reason for this was that by custom when a son went off to war his father built him a house – and this was on the parental roof.

In this quaint historic citadel there are nine gates and numerous narrow cavernous streets and alleyways. The natives are Berbers and they have a reputation for evil living. The men are thinly built but the women are well developed and fairly handsome. They do all the work.

In ancient days Siwa had another name. It was known as Jupiter Ammon and it was well-known, even as far back as the reign of Rameses III, in the year 117 BC. The oracle in the temple was of legendary fame and was consulted by Alexander the Great, the Pharaohs, Hannibal, Julius Caesar and Cleopatra, among thousands more.

Christianity came in the fourth century, but the inhabitants were converted by Arab invaders to Islam and, finally, Ben Ali Es Senoussi, founder of the sect bearing his name, imposed his own brand of Islamic Puritanism on them. But even with his draconic rule, the Siwans managed to pursue their own uninhibited ways.

Paddy loved the place and the lore that went with it, and he was lucky to have with him the Arab-speaking Captain Bob Melot to act as interpreter and guide. Together, they walked through the date gardens – the largest in the world, and bought baskets of luscious golden dates for their men, which were as much a delight to the eye as to the tongue. Sometimes, they sampled the local brew, a strong alcoholic liquid called *Lagmi* made from the sap of the date tree.

Cleopatra often spent long holidays in this Garden of Eden and, apart from consulting the oracle about her affairs of the heart, she bathed there regularly in these lovely hot springs. Her special favourite was one known as Ain El Hammam which, besides having sparkling clear water, was encircled by Roman terraces and patios bedecked with trellised flowers and shrubs.

In the scorching heat of the noon-day sun, Paddy and his men followed her example, much to the annoyance on occasion of the local maidens who, by tradition, were obliged to perform their ablutions here on the eve of their wedding day. Still as there were nearly three hundred wells and even a large lake in the oasis, there was never any shortage of bathing space.

In the bazaars almost every kind of fruit was exhibited for sale, oranges, lemons, bananas, apricots, figs, dates, olives and pomegranates. As Sergeant Reg Seekings once remarked to Sergeant Bennett, "You name it, Bob, and they've got it! Every goddam thing but a good pint of beer!"

But even this was not strictly true, for the super-luxury Prince Farouk Hotel had everything. A well-stocked wine cellar, first-class cocktail lounge and food up to the finest Parisian standards. It wasn't cheap but it was more reasonable than Shepheards in Cairo, and Paddy and his fellow officers occasionally paid it a visit.

The place was, understandably, riddled with spies and Army Intelligence advised against social intercourse but it was only natural that this counsel was sometimes disregarded.

In their own encampment at Siwa the SAS boys managed to run a bar and canteen of sorts and amused themselves by having singsongs and card games every now and then. But the serious business of war had to go on, and their sojourns in Siwa were all too short for anything else. So David and Paddy, after a day or two of relaxation, got down to planning the forthcoming raids with their usual thoroughness. There is an old Siwan saying which runs: "Death is a black camel which knocks at every man's door", and while neither of them could deny its truth, both of them were anxious to give that black beast as wide a berth as possible. There was only one way to do this: retain the element of surprise and work out every detail of their operations with utter thoroughness – and make due allowances for all foreseeable emergencies.

The distance from the Siwa base to their trouble rendezvous in Jebel region was roughly four hundred miles, and on the 15 March 1942 the raiders set off in vehicles done up to resemble Afrika Korps staff cars. Three days later they reached their destination, with only one setback – the blowing up of one of the German cars which they had acquired, by a Thermos mine.

The Jebel was a reasonably safe area chiefly because of the natural cover which existed on the slopes leading down from the hills to the escarpment which overlooked the coastal plain, and also because of the friendly natives, the Senussi Bedouins, who proved both helpful and trustworthy. Furthermore, the Jebel was a pleasant place to live in, plenty of water and even fresh food to be purchased from farmers and shepherds.

Paddy Mayne and two men pushed off on their appointed mission and once again the luck of the Irish held and the raid was a success. Fifteen bombers fell to his bombs and he withdrew without loss. He was not entirely free of misfortune, however, and lost his way on the return journey. In a letter to his brother Douglas he describes vividly what happened:

> "At the moment I am about fifteen miles from Benghazi, so I won't be able to post this for some time. We did a raid on the local aerodrome three nights ago and one of the party hasn't returned yet, so we are waiting for him. It's a very pleasant country here, great change from the desert. Some of the people who know the South Downs say that it is very like it – low hills and valleys, lots of wild flowers and long grass. It's like a picnic, only annoying

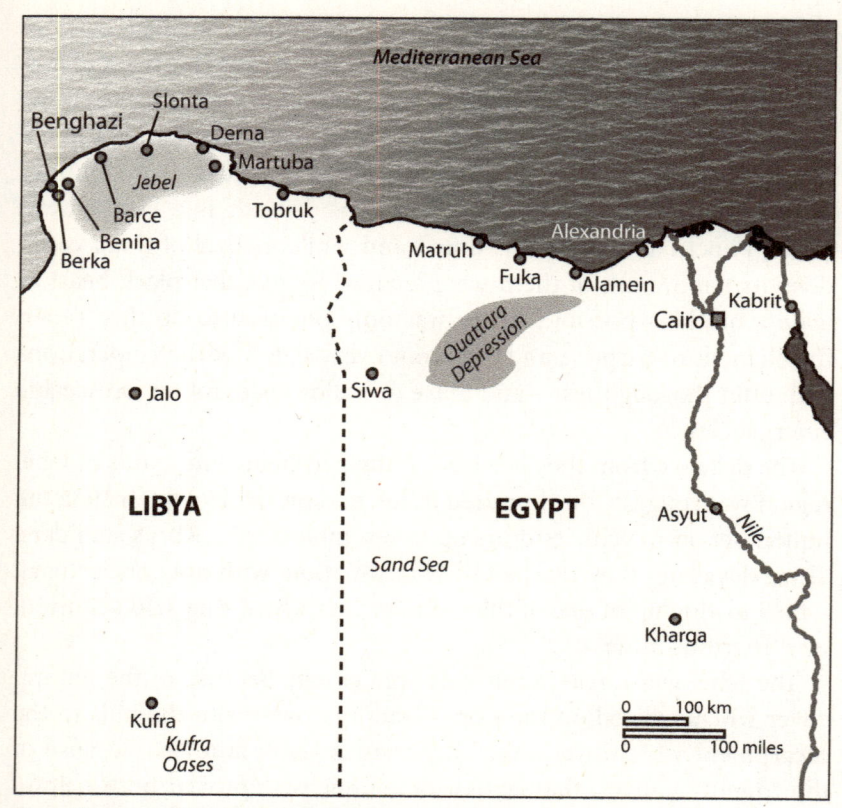

Map of Egypt and eastern Libya in 1942.

thing is the Jerry planes flying about, but we are well camouflaged. Luckily the Italians treat the Senussi very badly and so they will do anything to help us. The day and night after the raid we couldn't find our rendezvous. The maps are awful, we had been walking from 1.30 am to 7 o'clock the next night and couldn't find the damned place anywhere. We must have covered about fifty miles, first of all getting to the aerodrome and then coming away.

It was no good walking round in circles in the dark. I more or less reconciled myself to a two hundred and fifty mile walk to Tobruk and so we (three of us, two corporals and myself) went to the nearest Senussi camp for some water and if possible, a blanket.

The Senussi are very suspicious at first, but once they were sure that we were Inglesi! everything changed and we were ushered into one of the tents, our equipment brought in, blankets put down for a bed.

There was a fire just outside the door and everyone crowded in. First of all they boiled us some eggs which were damned good and then platters of dates and bowls of water and a huge gourd of goat's milk was brought in. I think that the form with this is that they never wash the gourd and the sourer it gets the better they like it and I think they must have liked this stuff very well!

And now listen to this and never disbelieve in luck again or coincidence, or whatever you like to call it. The men who were waiting for us at the rendezvous – and they would have left next morning – had got a chicken which they had bartered for some sugar. They wanted it cooked and they had an English-speaking Arab with them, so they sent him to get it cooked. In that area there must have been thirty or forty different encampments spread over the three odd miles we were from each other and he picked the one that we were lying in to come to – and so we won't have to footslog it across the desert!

We have been here now for two days and the trucks for three and I imagine that every Arab for miles around knows where we are and not one of them would go down and tell the Jerries or the 'Eyeties' where we are."

His companions were Corporals Rose and Bennett and they were to be on many a dangerous adventure together. Paddy regarded both of them as splendid soldiers and the singing Bennett as something more – a lucky companion. Paddy's fellow raiders were not so fortunate and all drew a blank except Bill Fraser, who found and destroyed the only plane that was parked on the Barce aerodrome.

Paddy's triumphs were now becoming legendary and his fame was spreading far beyond the bases and outposts used by the SAS and LRDG.

It was shortly before this last sortie that he had met in Siwa Captain Melot, a former Belgian Air Force man who had fought in the First World War and then married and settled down in Alexandria between the wars. An expert linguist, he had become a firm friend of the Bedouins and had acquired an intimate knowledge of their habits and customs. This made him a very accomplished Intelligence Officer in the desert war, but apart from that he was a fine, courageous soldier who loved to be in the thick of every battle. For a time, he disguised himself as an Arab and lived with the Senussi in the Jebel, gathering vital information about the enemy and his dispositions and then radioing back to British Headquarters.

Paddy at once recognised his worth and was glad when he joined the SAS. Apart from becoming close personal friends they were going to be comrades-in-arms for many moons. Just now Bob Melot was in the Stirling party bound for Benghazi, and had brought along with him two Senussi soldiers for unobtrusive reconnoitring work. Dressed in their native attire, they could move around freely anywhere and this made them extremely useful.

The raid, unfortunately, was another wash-out for David Stirling. Everything went well until he and his group got into Benghazi – which they did, incidentally, with the greatest of ease. Then they found that the canoe which they had brought to enable them to reach shipping in the harbour was damaged and unserviceable. Even so, the water was too rough for such a light craft, and there was nothing that could have been done that night, anyway. A quiet withdrawal was the only course to take just then and the knowledge gathered could be used another time.

Back at the Kabrit depot Stirling talked with his friend Fitzroy Maclean, who had now completed his training there. He entrusted to him the task of experimenting with collapsible small rubber boats, in preparation for the next raid on Benghazi, which he scheduled for the 21 May 1942.

When all was ready, Stirling started off in a Ford shooting brake which had been dolled-up to look like a German Army Staff car. Half-a-dozen men were with him, including Fitzroy Maclean and Randolph Churchill, who had somehow adroitly insinuated himself into the party and was soon to experience the chequered fighting fortunes of the SAS.

They headed straight for Siwa, where they were joined by an LRDG patrol and drove together hundreds of miles across the desert plain and hills. After their long hours of travel they hauled up in a scrubby wadi, from which they had a hillside view of the RAF bombing Benghazi, their own target for the following night.

In the late evening, they emerged from their lair and at 10.00 pm reached the Barce-Benghazi coastal highway and turned along southward to their main objective at Benghazi harbour. A few minutes later as he rounded a bend Stirling had to pull up violently to avoid crashing into a massive wooden bar that blocked the road.

As they were recovering from the shock they found themselves being covered by an Italian sentry with a tommy-gun. It looked like the end of the road for all of them, for in the shadows other armed sentries lurked with tommy-guns at the ready. There just didn't seem to be any way out when, quick as a flash, Fitzroy Maclean started talking to the Italian in his own tongue with an air of great authority, "We are staff officers! And in a hurry!" The barricade was cleared, and they were through in a trice.

But again the raid was dogged by bad luck and, despite checks and double-checks in pre-operational trials only yesterday, the two rubber boats had somehow become punctured and were useless. It seemed fantastic, but it was a fact and so they had no choice but to retire and make their own way back to the rendezvous when they could. There were two more encounters with sentries before they got clear of the harbour, and had it not been for Fitzroy Maclean's command of Italian they would surely have met with disaster. As it was, they had to hide out for almost a day in an empty house in the town until nightfall.

Success, so far, seemed to elude David Stirling at every turn – and the reverse was the case with Paddy Mayne. Why? David thought a lot about it and finally fell under the spell of superstition. The only thing to do was to bring the big Irishman with him on his next visit to Benghazi.

Meanwhile on the 6 May, up on the front line at Gazala, Rommel launched another attack and the whole British defence system was cracking again. Malta was near the point of collapse for want of supplies, and convoys could not get through for the lack of air cover. The blockade had to be broken and the SAS was asked to do it by attacking again the enemy airfields in Cyrenaica on the night of the 13/14 June, when a relief convoy to Malta would try to get through. Gladly Stirling and Mayne accepted and immediately started to plan.

A French unit under Lieutenant Augustin Jordan was chosen to attack airfields in the Derna-Martuba area to the west of Gazala. Paddy Mayne was to attack the Berka aerodrome just south of Benghazi, and David Stirling was to head for Benina just north of Benghazi.

The first of the above was by far the most difficult, being in a region heavily infested with German troops and the idea of getting the French SAS to the target area presented a problem. Then Stirling, always a quick thinker, heard of the Special Interrogation Group (SIG), a band of German Jews who wore captured Afrika Korps uniforms and had volunteered to serve as saboteurs behind the enemy lines. At once it struck him that these men, riding in German trucks, could pass round the enemy desert flank and deliver the French SAS troops in the Derna and Martuba airfields.

Two German prisoners of war were then taken along to help the deception. As captives they had been co-operative and had voiced anti-Nazi views. When asked by Intelligence Officers if they would fight against their former comrades they said they would and surprisingly, and indeed unnecessarily, their word was accepted. One of them, Sergeant Brückner, had served with the French Foreign Legion before the war and been put in a concentration camp by the Nazis when he returned to Germany. Later, with other former legionaries he was conscripted into the 361st Africa Regiment which, because of the desert experience of its men and the cruel brutal cunning which they had developed while in the service of the Foreign Legion, became the most feared German unit in North Africa.

Most German officers regarded them frankly as scum, unprincipled blackguards, akin to the Black and Tans in Ireland, who lived for lust, drink and even murder, but none could deny their fighting effectiveness.

Sergeant Brückner was the embodiment of everything this unit stood for, and he was the man British Intelligence foisted upon the SAS. Paddy Mayne took an instant dislike to him and came very near to clobbering him in the mess at Siwa one evening shortly before the raid took place.

Brückner, a powerful, bull-necked man who spoke both English and French after a fashion, revelled in obscene talk and gestures, especially after some drinking. On this occasion Paddy overheard him giving a particularly lurid account (accompanied by gestures) of his experiences with the local harlot who carried on her business in a greasy old tent. The men with him were obviously enjoying it, but Paddy, who hated obscenity and lechery, bade him to hold his tongue. The German muttered something under his breath but before Paddy, now in a white hot rage, could reach him, Tommy Corps, an ex-heavyweight boxer from Newcastle, stepped in and expertly delivered the anaesthetic.

This ended the evening event but Brückner had his revenge when he was chosen to go with the combined squadron of SAS and SIG in the raids on Derna and Martuba.

When the party moved off, cunningly stowed away in two trucks with the French SAS concealed, the Germans and Jews driving and guarding, it looked as if it might work out well. Certainly David Stirling and Paddy both had reservations, but the leader of the SIG, Captain Herbert Buck, was satisfied and they let him have his way. After all, he was going with them.

Night had fallen when they reached the South Derna aerodrome and Brückner, who had wangled them past the sentries and roadblocks en route, suggested that as he knew the district well he should scout around and see what was going on. Immediately he left the truck he headed straight for the Luftwaffe mess and gave the game away.

All but one of the combined squadron perished and the jubilant Germans flew Brückner back to Berlin where he was accorded a hero's welcome and personally invested with the Iron Cross by the Führer.

On the same fatal night, Paddy Mayne and three of his men arrived at the Berka satellite aerodrome, only to find themselves caught in a RAF raid, with bombs blasting, sirens screaming and fires blazing. It seemed incredible, for Middle East Headquarters had been advised well in advance of the SAS attacks for that night.

However, for the enemy more trouble was to come. Each parked plane had an armed guard and when the air raid passed, a pitched battle began between Paddy's raiders and these guards. Then, in the noise and confusion the guards started firing at one another and the SAS quartet crawled away, blowing up a large petrol dump as they went. At Berka main airfield a French SAS unit was also having a close struggle with the garrison yet somehow managed to destroy eleven bombers before withdrawing. And at Benina, despite another RAF raid, David Stirling and two men were creating merry hell, bombing successfully the only two planes that were on the parking bays and destroying hangars and workshops – and, as good luck would have it – thirty to forty aircraft engines in crates and a couple of bombers.

Not content with this devastation, Stirling also kicked in the guardroom door and flung a grenade at the twenty-odd Germans inside. A carbon copy of Paddy's exploit at Tamit airfield earlier on, it was David's greatest success since he formed the SAS and it had been worth waiting for, although just now the team had little time to survey their handiwork.

Eventually, David and his two comrades reached the rendezvous at noon on the following day, without further incident. Paddy and his party were not so fortunate, for first they lost their bearing and shortly afterwards in the darkness, just in time, they spotted four patrol trucks bearing down on them. There was nothing for it but to disperse and fling themselves to the ground. The trucks still came rattling on and then, just when it seemed they would surely be run over, the convoy halted and disgorged about fifty soldiers who fanned out in every direction, quartering the ground like retriever dogs.

The plight of Paddy and his boys was desperate and he considered jumping to his feet and making a last ditch stand, but on further reflection thought better of it. If daylight would stay away only a little longer they might just escape detection, and so it turned out. Suddenly all four trucks filled up again with troops and were gone.

Now the fugitives were on the move again, and soon found themselves on the border of a large military camp. Capture seemed to be inevitable, but they split their luck and hoped for the best, two of them tramping off and the other two hiding under a garden hedge.

But then soldiers came up in another convoy of lorries and started searching again. One SAS man, Corporal Warburton, could not stand the strain of crouching under the leaves any longer and he leapt up and tried to make a run for it, but was shot down on the instant.

Paddy and Corporal Storey kept moving and found themselves in a Senussi camp where they later met up with Corporal Lilley, their other comrade, who in due course had boldly walked from his hedge covert straight through the crowded German camp and beyond to the distant escarpment. Then, an Italian soldier cycled up and tried to arrest him. Lilley promptly strangled him and continued on his journey until he came upon the Senussi camp and stopped for a breather.

Together again the three SAS men trekked off in the direction of the rendezvous. Before reaching the cover of the hills a German Army Staff car drove up and stopped a short distance away. Paddy wasted no time and ordered his men to drop to the ground and cover the car with their rifles. For him the idea of surrendering was simply out of the question and now, if needs be, he would fight it out to the death. These Germans, however, happened to be not of the same mettle and realising the sort of men they were meeting they decided that discretion was the better part of valour and quietly drove off.

Next morning, Paddy and his men reached the rendezvous and one would have expected that they had now had their bellyful of fighting and danger, just for a day or two. But nothing like it! Promptly Stirling and Mayne decided to borrow a LRDG truck and go off with five more men on a shooting spree along the Benghazi Road. Paddy took the wheel and they were on their way about 7.30 pm in the evening. It was a madcap lark of the highest order and quite unworthy of two such outstanding guerrilla experts. Corporal Lilley was afterwards heard to complain that it was nothing but "a bit of barmy and childish bravado" and it would be hard to gainsay his judgment in this. It very nearly cost them all their lives when a mile from Benina airfield they were halted at a German roadblock.

Let Paddy tell in his own words what happened. To his brother Douglas he wrote:

"I had been raiding Berka drome and after I got back to our rendezvous we decided, the CO and myself, to have a look at Benghazi, so we took a truck. I was driving, the CO beside me and four of our lads in the back – also a free Austrian. Well, we drove on to the road and started gaily down. It was dark and we had headlights on and I got about 5-6 miles when we saw a red light being swung. That didn't worry us, as always before it was only Italians and we only had to shout 'Tedesci' (German) and drive past. But they were getting wise to us and this time we saw a bloody big contraption like a five-barred gate that had got mixed up with a mile or so of barbed wire, and so we stopped. The sentry was in the headlights and, right enough, an Italian. Our Austrian started to do his little piece and shouted out that we were Germans in a hurry and to open the blankety gate. The Wop wasn't so sure so he hollered for the guard – about ten Germans headed by a Sergeant Major, with tommy-guns, grenades and rifles. I was scared to look further in case I saw tanks and machine guns. I gathered later the conversation ran like this:

Fritz: 'What's the password?'
Karl (our Austrian): 'How the ... do we know what the ... password is and don't ask for our ... identity cards either; they are lost and we have been fighting for the past seventy hours against those ... tommies. We have got to get to Benghazi. Some fool put us on the wrong road; we have been driving for the past two hours and now you so and so's, sitting here on your asses in a nice safe job, stop us! Hurry up! Open that gate!'

But Fritz wasn't satisfied so he walked to about three feet from the car to my side. I was sitting there with my colt on my lap and suddenly I remembered that it wasn't cocked, so I pulled it back and the Jerry had a look and then orders the gates to be opened, which they did and in a chorus of 'Guten Nachtens' we drove on. We thought later that he came to the conclusion, the same one that I had come to, that if anyone was going to be hurt he was going to be a very sick man early on."

This near shave should have been enough for Paddy, but now, with his boot pressing the accelerator pedal to the board he thundered on towards Benghazi. Ahead, a squad of Italian soldiers jumped into the highway pointing rifles at them, a real menace, but Paddy never slackened speed. It was his theory that the more furious the assault the easier the victory, and he was now giving a practical demonstration. As he rushed onward and Corporal Reg Seekings trained his Vickers on the now panicking Italians and bawled "Tedeschi! Tedeschi" at the top of his voice, they scattered like a flight of frightened pigeons.

In the next twenty minutes the raiders attacked a transport filling station, a petrol storage tank, a roadhouse, lorries and trailers, and an army encampment, and then turning inland headed for their rendezvous. A German truck came roaring across the plain in an effort to stall them off, but Paddy, driving like a hurricane, left it far behind and reached the shelter of the Wadi Rathara. But the rendezvous was still many miles away when the bumping and lurching of the truck set off one of the bomb fuses and the crew had to make a jump for safety. Seconds later, the vehicle, heavily stocked with bombs and grenades, blew up with a deafening roar and now they had to footslog their way across the roughest countryside for miles around. Then, after what seemed to be hours on end – but was really only one – they came across a Bedouin camp, where they got a friendly greeting. The Arabs even sent off a message to the rendezvous to fetch some LRDG transport, and shortly afterwards they all drove off singing 'Lili Marlene' gustily, the recent dangers and troubles flashed away from their minds as if they had never been experienced.

Back at Siwa, bathing in the cool springs and bathing in the sun, they laughingly compared notes with one another, told of their personal experiences and measured up their recent with their past adventures. Many of their old comrades would never again engage in the cheerful chatter now going on. Some were dead and buried in unmarked graves; some had been wounded and taken prisoner with a doubtful future ahead; and a few had been captured while still fighting fit and were now in a state of uncertainty like the wounded. But the spirit of the SAS, always buoyant in the blackest hour, lived on as ever and memories of happy comradeship in better days compensated a bit for the loss of their good friends.

CHAPTER 8

Stocktaking

AT THEIR HEADQUARTERS in the relaxing atmosphere of the oasis, David Stirling and Paddy Mayne made an assessment of results and were fairly satisfied. Their resolute and charmingly witty French officer, Berge, had gone with Captain Lord Jellicoe by submarine to Crete to attack Heraklion aerodrome and had achieved success in the face of tough opposition. Twenty-one planes had been destroyed, including fourteen Stuka dive bombers. But the price was high; of the original party of half-dozen, three (including Berge), were captured, and one was killed. Captain Lord Jellicoe and a Greek guide got back to the submarine and safety.

These events, however, were being dwarfed almost into insignificance by the current major war news. Rommel was now achieving what seemed to be a decisive victory, which, like a vast tidal wave, was threatening to engulf Egypt itself. Tobruk had fallen in a single day's fighting and nothing seemed capable of holding back the Rommel forward surge. Even the remote oasis of Siwa was now endangered and Stirling and Mayne had to make hurried plans for an immediate evacuation and withdrawal to Kufra, more than three hundred miles away at the southern end of the Great Sand Sea. Their friends of the LRDG were going there too, but even this could not dispel the gloom.

True, their efforts had also helped the relief of Malta to some small extent, as word had just come through that two out of a convoy of seventeen ships had reached the harbour. But this was only small consolation and, as they talked things over, Stirling and Mayne were unanimous on one point – that the war was going awry on a big scale.

Moping about other people's mistakes, however, was not their cup of tea and they started to devise ways and means of helping their fellow countrymen who were taking such a rap up north. Finally, they decided that the SAS would have to be substantially reinforced and motorised. When this was done they would penetrate behind the enemy's lines as before, but this time in strength, and then attack major ports like Tobruk and Benghazi.

Since the closest liaison must be maintained with General Headquarters in Cairo, David made his way there at once with this jointly conceived plan while Paddy headed off with his men to Kufra, a long and dreary journey. Shortly after his departure forward patrols of the advancing Italian army moved into Siwa. Captain Mayne had been lucky again.

So, in another way, was Major Stirling. He had got some real backing in Cairo, where changes were going on at top level. General Sir Claude Auchinleck, Commander-in-Chief of the Middle East Forces, had decided to take over the command of the Eighth Army himself and had planned drastic steps to stop Rommel invading the Nile delta. He had devised a defensive system between El Alamein and Matruh, a masterpiece whose fruits General Montgomery inherited when he and General Alexander replaced Ritchie and Auchinleck. For the moment the front was stabilised.

At Kufra, Paddy received a signal to proceed with a detachment of fifty men to Kabrit, and when he arrived he was greeted enthusiastically by David, who had much to tell him. Firstly, he had requisitioned twenty three-ton lorries and fifteen jeeps, the latter vehicles being small and compact but very powerful. American designed and produced, they were to become the most successful all-purpose vehicle in the British and American armies. With his usual brain snap, Stirling had spotted the possibilities of using such a machine in desert conditions. He tried, unsuccessfully, to armour them with army machine guns, then decided to fit them up with Vickers K guns as used by the RAF for fighter plane machine guns. With their manoeuvrability and power the jeeps were soon to win their spurs as the most dangerous armoured vehicles on either side.

Paddy was delighted with them and promptly drove one for hours in the desert around Kabrit, practising mock attacks and getting to know all the motor machinery.

The second piece of information David had to pass on to Paddy was that on the 3 July they were setting off together from Alexandria for a desert rendezvous 150 miles away to the west and fifty miles south of Mersa Matruh. As usual, the LRDG would act as guides – and, in fact, another section of this splendid group, under Lieutenant Timpson had already set up a base of sorts at this rendezvous. Two days later, David's party arrived bang on course and met up with the waiting section of the LRDG.

The following night had been chosen for five raids on aerodromes in the Bagush-Fuka area, between El Alamein and Mersa Matruh, and this time Stirling decided to have Mayne along with him. They had picked for their target the aerodrome at Bagush, and next morning all parties set out together towards a forward rendezvous. They reached it at noon. The scrub cover was enough to hide them and they settled in for the day.

Dr Malcolm Pleydell, the regimental Medical Officer, in his book *Born of the Desert*, describes his impression of Paddy Mayne at this time:

> "Paddy was a bit different from the others – this sort of fighting was in his blood; he thrived on it. There was no give or take about this method of warfare, and he was out to kill when the opportunity presented itself. There was no question of sparing an enemy – this was war, and war meant killing. No quarter was asked and none was given. Nor can I remember having heard him complain about the enemy's method of warfare in the desert, for to him there were no rules. Once or twice I heard him question the value of the Red Cross, remarking that a soldier who was going to be built up to fight again, should, in his opinion, be a perfectly legitimate target. He observed the rules of the Red Cross, mind you, but his theory was that the day of *noblesse oblige* and the Knights of King Arthur stuff had drawn to a close, and that now it was all or nothing (women and children, bombing of towns, etc did not enter into this argument which concerned only the desert war). Neither did you hear him complain when his friends were killed, but I always felt, although he would say nothing other than giving an expression of sorrow, that a friend's death meant so many lives in a form of personal revenge, a wiping off of the debt as it were ... One only sensed that here was a quietly forceful and rugged leader who could be relied upon in any emergency; a man who

was as ruthless as he was quick witted in action. Later on I used to think that you were as safe as could possibly be when you were with Paddy, because he took such great care of the people who were under him."

Doctor Pleydell's assessment was reached after a close association of many months and in circumstances of great stress, but these factors tend to strengthen, not weaken, its reliability. In fact, all those who served with Mayne speak of his cunning, ruthlessness, resourcefulness and superb courage and remark on the sense of security they felt when operating under his wing.

Resting on the sand a little away from the cheerful chatter of the others, this Irish giant was now turning over in his ice-cold brain the details of the engagement ahead and the best way he could exact the heaviest toll of the enemy. That night they slept alongside or underneath their camouflaged trucks. Next morning they were on to the Qara Matruh track northward bound until they eventually reached the coastal escarpment as darkness fell. En route, they had come on mysterious columns of troops and roadside enemy encampments to all of which they gave the widest possible berth. Several times they had to take cover when enemy planes flew over, but so far as they could judge they were unobserved.

At the top of the escarpment Stirling and Mayne branched off and headed for Bagush. In their three vehicles they had nine men, and there were twenty miles to go. They made it, to within half a mile of the aerodrome, when they slowed down and pulled up just off the highway. The plan was now for Stirling to set up a road block and attack any vehicles that came along while Mayne was making his raid on the aerodrome.

So with five men, he dashed off. It was becoming almost a routine exercise for him now but, cautiously, Paddy was playing no tricks. On the field he found forty planes and after adroitly dodging the patrols he and his team flitted around like shadows, placing their time bombs. Their task accomplished, they withdrew to a vantage point some several hundred yards away to watch the fun. The explosions began, but they counted only twenty-two and Paddy was strangely puzzled. Then he examined one of the spare bombs and discovered the reason – the primer had been put in too early and got damp.

Meanwhile, to the accompaniment of loud guttural shoutings the twenty-two planes blazed merrily and Paddy made his way back to David Stirling's road block. Here, when he heard the news, David gave a flash of his own audacity and genius for novelty. "Now let's drive on to the field," he drawled, "and shoot up the rest of the planes from our trucks."

Paddy was delighted and almost overcome with admiration. This was his friend! The thought of leaving eighteen planes undamaged had already been irritating himself and this was just the thing to soothe his ruffled feelings.

Quickly they checked their Vickers guns and drove off to a point two miles beyond the field. This was their base for operations and the three-ton truck with five men was left there as David and Paddy and the other four went in to the attack. They caught the patrols completely off guard and blasted twelve planes before wheeling off the field in the direction of their waiting truck. Behind them, anti-aircraft shelling broke out, but racing for the escarpment at full speed they were soon out of range. They had to make another eighty miles to the rendezvous due south and now they must expect a rough passage from enemy air patrols – but at least the night would save them for the time being.

As dawn broke they found themselves in open shelterless country, still several miles from the escarpment. Before they could reach its cover they were attacked by aircraft. Two of the vehicles were destroyed and now this SAS eleven had only one jeep in which to make the journey back to the rendezvous. Paddy, who had kept firing at the circling aircraft, now came out of his lair with a handy bottle of whiskey and a broad smile on his face. "Och men," he joked cheerfully, "it could have been worse! It might have been us instead."

As ever, no flapping for this nomad of the desert to whom fear was unknown. So, back on the track again, and three hours later they reached the rendezvous, the first to arrive there.

David Stirling was afire with enthusiasm over this new method of attack that had by splendid chance suddenly sprouted in his brain, and he was restless to develop it further. Paddy Mayne shared his enthusiasm and that night, as they squatted under the stars, they canvassed every aspect of the fresh strategy.

The other raiding parties had not been so fortunate, and as they trickled back to the rendezvous one doleful Jeremiad after another was repeated. True, some success, in the shape of eight planes, forty lorries and three prisoners, had been achieved, but it was a poor pay-off for so much risk and effort.

Then an Italian reconnaissance plane spotted their meeting place and they had to make a moonlight flit of thirty miles to a new hideout at the foot of a small escarpment. This gave them much better cover and was to become their nerve centre of operations for many weeks to come.

What a strange band of shaggy-haired brigands they looked and yet so comradely, informal and jolly! Bob Bennett, the leader of the songster brigade, always ready to lay on light entertainment to lift their hearts. Malcolm Pleydell, the kind, soft-hearted doctor, eager to be father confessor, as well as physician, to anyone. Lord Jellicoe, the jolly and witty conversationalist, and all the others with their strongly individual characters and talents diversifying the communal life and keeping monotony and boredom at bay.

Paddy was Irish and British both, but not so the Southern Irish troopers whom he commanded. They, like the Bedouin, owed no loyalty to anybody but themselves. Today, they were fighting for England and as long as they wore British uniforms they would be fantastically faithful and brave, but once the khaki was put aside they could very quickly strike an anti-British attitude and one could easily visualise them in similar circumstances doing what their fathers before them did after the First World War, shouldering arms with the Irish Republican Army and fighting with a tense hate.

As with the Scots on certain occasions, sentimental ballads about long past English aggression and injustices against their motherland inflamed them to the point of explosion, especially in drink, and at such times they were best left alone.

Paddy had intimate knowledge of this but still could not resist the charming evocative melancholy of the old airs and, despite his loyalty to the Crown, they aroused faint stirrings in his breast. After all, had not his own forbears fought the English with pike and musket in the 1798 rebellion?

Now, in the silver moonlight, the Southerners were singing and what they were singing had something to do with the Easter Rising of 1916 in Dublin when Padraic Pearse and his band raised the tricolour and snatched their hour of glory before facing the firing squads with defiant laughter in their eyes. The heartrending lament drifted across the wadi:

"As down the glen, one Easter morn,
To city fair rode I,
There armed lines of marching men
In squadron passed me by.
No pipe did hum nor battle drum
Did sound its dread tattoo
But the Angelus bell o'er the Liffey swell
Rang out on the foggy dew."

There, but for an accident of birth and time, mused Paddy, I might have been leading my compatriots against the British. And what a rebel leader he would have made in the later rebellion, commanding the much famed Flying Columns that brought the Black and Tans to their knees!

The mournful lilting air continued:

"Back to the glen I rode again
And my heart with grief was sore
For I parted then with valiant men
I never would see more.
But to and fro in my dreams I go
And I kneel and pray for you
For slavery fled, O rebel dead
When you fell in the foggy dew."

Now, with the English out of the way, these fighting sons of fighting men had taken up the Nazi challenge in the cause of freedom. More than 80,000 Southern Irishmen fought under the British flag in the Second World War.[1]

---

[1] There was already a long tradition of Ulster and Irish regiments fighting in the British Army. It has been estimated that at least half of the British Army under Wellington at Waterloo in 1815 were Irishmen. Certainly, according to Wellington himself, "the 27th of Foot (Inniskillings from Ulster) saved the centre of my line at Waterloo." Following the outbreak of the First World War the British Army had raised eighty-two battalions in Ireland by the end of 1914 and of these Ulster had contributed forty-two. Altogether, out of 145,000 voluntary recruits from Ireland, Ulster contributed, in round numbers, 75,000. Belfast stood second on the roll of British cities for numbers of recruits in proportion to population, up to the imposition of universal service. Besides the Irish

Paddy was proud of them. They knew how to fight and they knew how to die. And their English and Scots comrades thought finely of them. As Sergeant Bob Bennett once remarked, while still under the influence of one of these rebel songs:

"Gorblimey, we'll all end up in the IRA if we're not careful."

Those who were destined to outlive the war would never have the good fortune to enjoy this kind of happy experience again; the lonely majesty of the massive desert, the starry skies and, above all, the camaraderie of brave men.

Small raiding parties came and went, but in Stirling's mind the memory stuck of that hefty mobile attack at Bagush, and together with Paddy Mayne he began planning a large-scale jeep raid on the Sidi-Enich airfield nearby the previous target. Then he hurried back to Kabrit to get the extra jeeps that he needed.

In the meantime, Paddy attacked and destroyed fifteen planes at El Daba on the coastline. He suffered no casualties of any kind, and frankly, while others were failing, everything that this man did was attended by success. In a nutshell, and perhaps illogically, his stature was being built up into bold relief by the misfortunes of others; but Paddy would have been the first to protest against any glorification of his deeds at the expense of his comrades. Their courage and daring were not found wanting – only their luck. And Paddy, more than anybody, knew it.

As soon as Stirling got back from Kabrit he fixed the date and time for the attack. He had brought with him a brand new squadron of twenty jeeps and a number of three-ton trucks, and that same night he started practising formation drill in the moonlight. The raid itself was to be by jeep on the following night, and in the late afternoon the motorcade drove off. Some hours later they reached the escarpment and descended to the plain beyond. As they approached the airfield they saw flare paths brightly lit up, with planes circling overhead waiting to be called in, and other planes on the ground revving up for take-off.

The raiding party in their box formation of twenty jeeps roared

---

recruits, a very large number of men born in Ulster were to be found in the Dominion troops, especially among the Canadians, with whom two Ulstermen won the VC. On the 1 July 1916, the 36th (Ulster) Division sustained 5,500 casualties at the Battle of the Somme while the 16th (Irish) Division, in which there were five Ulster Battalions, sustained heavy losses at Messines Ridge.

across the track and opened fire with eighty machine guns. The din was awful, and the Germans were taken completely unawares. Most of their defences were silenced, all in fact except a Breda gun which rattled on throughout the entire action and claimed one victim. Then Stirling pulled out in front, and the others formed into a double column as they swung onto the field and raced along the lines of planes blazing away with tracer and incendiary bullets. A plane coming in to land caught a burst of it as it touched down and exploded immediately.

It was like a scene from Dante's inferno – except worse! Here and there, bombs which had already been loaded in Stukas and Heinkels blew up like claps of thunder. Death, din, fire and destruction raged all around, and, as the mobile crocodile of spitting lead and flame in which Paddy was travelling slowed to make a turn, he leapt from his jeep, rushed forward and thrust a time bomb into a Heinkels bomber which had so far escaped damage. Within seconds it was shattered, and Stirling and his gang were gone as swiftly (though not quite as silently!) as they had come. Dispersing into groups they headed for the rendezvous.

While this terrific – and to the Germans, terrifying – attack had been going on, another group of the SAS had stormed into Bagush and destroyed fifteen planes. This time, however, the Jerries decided to send ground forces as well as aeroplanes to hunt and destroy these British phantoms of the night. But they were unlucky once again as their quarry switched round and destroyed four trucks loaded with heavily armed troops.

The SAS was a serpent with a tongue of fire and best left alone if possible.

CHAPTER 9

Death or glory

PADDY AND DAVID, now on the very crest of the wave, were all for pressing their luck and had already set about making plans when suddenly out of the blue came a startling order from Headquarters. It was to the effect that they and their men were to return at once to Cairo. Transport planes would be flown out with petrol and supplies so that the jeeps and trucks could travel overland to Kabrit, via the dreaded Qattara Depression, but the main body of men was to be taken back by air.

It was a puzzling order at a time like this when the Germans were in a real flap over the desert raids and were calling back troops and armour from the Alamein front to guard their airfields and supply lines. But orders are orders and must be obeyed. So, back to Cairo it was now for Stirling and Mayne, with curiosity in their minds as to what some bright young brains at GHQ might be setting up for them.

The main desert campaign had, of course, been going badly in recent times and that splendid specimen of Irish warrior manhood, General Sir Claude Auchinleck, had paid the price for his defeat at Mersa Matruh by losing his Middle East Command to another Ulsterman, General Alexander, whom he knew and respected greatly. He had, in fact, suggested him as his successor in a private letter to General Sir Alan Brooke, the Chief of General Staff, as early as the 23 June 1942. On the 6 August his transfer to another command had been decided and on the 15 August Alexander took over, with General Montgomery as the new Commanding Officer of the Eighth Army.

Both Stirling and Mayne had liked and respected the Auk, and his replacement came as rather a shock to them. Now, for a time they thought that as far as the desert war was concerned they might be for the dustbin, too. It was with genuine relief that they soon heard that the new plan of operation was only a re-hash (though an enlarged one) of an earlier dish cooked up by Stirling, which had somehow been allowed to get cold in a remote pigeon-hole.

It was to be a campaign of lightning assaults on Rommel's supply depots, chiefly Tobruk and Benghazi. A big offensive was being prepared for late October and it was vital to throttle the enemy's communication at every available opportunity. David could not quarrel with this plan as it was his own initially, and Paddy was always happy when something was in the pot.

Benghazi, which by now had almost become the name of David Stirling's swan song, was to be the principal objective of this new thrust inside the enemy lines. It would need 20 men, 40 supply trucks and 40 jeeps, and in view of the recent bitter experience by the British of Rommel's mobility and strength it was an ambitious venture, but neither guerrilla leader doubted that they would pull it off. They had beaten Jerry many times, and would be only too happy to do it again.

The twin attack on Tobruk was to be led by Colonel John Haselden, an Arabist expert and undercover man in enemy territory. This was the man who, after an earlier talk with David Stirling, had built up David's original idea of the action. Two other raids were also included, one by the LRDG on Barce aerodrome and the re-capture of the Jalo depot by the Sudan Defence Force.

When Paddy and David were alone in Peter Stirling's Cairo flat, drinking liberally of the Scotch generously provide for them, they talked and talked for hours about this new programme which had obtruded so unexpectedly on their initial plan, hatched in the desert hide-away south-east of Benghazi.

The distances to be covered were immense. First, they would have to travel from Kabrit to Kufra at the south of the Great Sand Sea, a distance of 850 miles. From there to Benghazi was another 650 miles, and all the way it would be tough going, but Paddy had done it before and was ready for any troubles.

In mid-August he set out with the first convoy of twelve jeeps and six supply trucks, and followed the Nile up to Asyut where he headed across country to the oasis of El Kharga. There they rested for a night before driving westward to Kufra, which had taken on the size of a full-blooded military establishment. There was a pleasant enough oasis here, too, with its green palm trees and lakes and patches of cultivation. It also had an aerodrome, and its friendly population was made up of Arabs and Sudanese who had once been in the relationship of masters and slaves.

Here Paddy Mayne lingered for a few days, then, when David Stirling and Fitzroy Maclean flew in he packed his kit and headed northward, skirting the flank of his former base at Jalo (now enemy occupied) and then on up to the hilly Jebel country near Benghazi.

It was a journey worthy of Alexander the Great, but Paddy and his desert veterans made easy work of it. The other two convoys followed on, spaced apart by a day each, to reduce the risk of aerial detection and, finally, all three convoys linked up in the Jebel rendezvous. Captain Bob Melot, the Belgian Arabist, was there to help with language difficulties and general intelligence work. No better man could have been found for the job and Paddy fully trusted him. It was, therefore, rather a shock when Bob reported that a Senussi Bedouin, just back from Benghazi, had told him that the Germans had full information of the impending raid and were ready to hand out the toughest punishment to the attackers.

The native informant was known to Bob Melot and was thoroughly reliable. He spoke of a minefield and prepared ambush positions and also of the departure of the supply ships from the harbour.

Neither David nor Paddy was happy about the news. It was clear to both of them that against a forewarned and heavily reinforced garrison they would have little chance of success in doing destruction and none whatever of capturing and holding the town. It would be as if 220 Germans had tried to overrun Tobruk during the long siege.

Nightfall brought a fitful sleep to the commanders, who alone with Melot knew of the bad news. It had to be this way, as even with a strong, proved force like the SAS morale could be undermined in such circumstances if the story got around. The raid was scheduled for 13 September but David felt that a postponement was justified because of the grim warning. So he radioed HQ explaining the position and asked for further orders. Back came the tart reply: "Ignore bazaar gossip and proceed as planned."

The pattern of things had improved in the Alamein area by the beginning of September and Rommel had been heavily repulsed in his spirited drive into Egypt at Alam Halfa. Alexander and Montgomery, fully aware of the impending invasion of French North Africa, were but biding their time and soon Rommel would be on the run.

To the top planners at GHQ any weakening of the German frontline strength at this stage would be welcome, and a raider threat to Tobruk and Benghazi would certainly siphon off both men and armour from the Alamein area. Indeed, the more the Germans were alarmed about the coming raids the better it was for the planned main offensive.

So, the total destruction of the SAS guerrillas would be as nothing compared with the results to be achieved from a weakened and dispersed enemy, eh? It looked suspiciously like this to Paddy, and as he angrily remarked to David: "There's no use in keeping dogs and barking yourself."

Just after sunset on the evening of 13 September, Bob Melot and another man were detailed to destroy an Italian radio station in a small fort on top of the escarpment. Almost immediately afterwards the main force under Stirling and Mayne moved tortuously off down the escarpment and crossed to the tarmac road leading into Benghazi. A short distance along it the leading jeep ran smack up against a road barrier. Everything was strangely quiet and the post seemed at first sight to be unmanned. On either side of the road was barbed wire and here and there freshly dug up earth. It had all the appearance of a minefield. "Hey!" muttered Paddy, "Perhaps this is the minefield mentioned by that Senussi spy!"

Lieutenant Bill Cumper, the explosives expert, got out of the jeep to have a closer look, and seemed to decide that this wired and recently dug area was indeed mined. So, the vehicles would have to stick closely to the road. He turned to the lock on the roadblock and released it adroitly. But as the bar swung open a hurricane of gunfire burst upon them: machine guns, Bredas and mortars. There was only one reaction possible, that was immediate and furious retaliation and the SAS were adept at this.

They blazed back. Then Sergeant Bill Almonds, with reckless courage, drove straight at the shadowy figures ahead with all guns firing. He had cleared the block when his jeep went up in flames. Another one roared forward only to meet the same fate. Paddy shouted to those nearest him to fan out from the road (not too far, because of the minefield) and concentrate the fire on the discovered enemy positions.

"You, Bennett, get that bloody Breda!"

"Rose, get that machine gun there!"

All the time, Stirling, Maclean and Cumper circled around, shooting and also directing the course of this mixed-up battle. It looked, for a time, like the grand finale for the SAS group but then, gradually, the enemy began to wilt under the ceaseless onslaught. As a German prisoner, captured three weeks afterwards, said: "It was like fighting the furies of Hell."

It was indeed fury – white hot fury – that those Nazis and 'Eyeties' found themselves up against. Not the faint-hearted, quick-to-surrender Britishers that their own propagandists had told them about so often, but determined, savage men of iron.

Now someone reported German reinforcements coming up in the distance and David Stirling called to his men to break off the action and head for the hills. Paddy had left his jeep by this time and was lying up in a forward position lobbing grenades into the nearest enemy strongpoint when Sergeant Bennett drove up under heavy fire, shouting urgently to him to jump aboard. Suddenly with a bound Paddy landed on the bonnet of the jeep and Bennett jammed his foot on the accelerator and they were rushing into the night.

Daybreak came too soon and found Paddy with half-a-dozen others hanging on precariously in the overcrowded jeep still six or seven miles from the escarpment. In the distance, the pulsating drone of aircraft engines could be heard rising louder and louder. The jeep travellers could only hope that the dim dawn remaining would conceal them for a little longer and they ploughed on across the sand and stones.

Seconds later, they were listening to the ugly crunch of bombs, followed by the staccato bark of machine guns. "Some poor sods are getting it," said Paddy as they bumped and lurched along. How much time before they were spotted themselves? The minutes dragged on, and now the escarpment loomed large and comforting ahead of them. Were they going to make it, after all? Hardly had the thought crossed Paddy's mind when out of the sky somewhere behind them came the deafening roar of an aeroplane swooping at full throttle.

Quick as lightning, Bennett pulled the driving wheel over and the jeep swung violently to the side as a burst of machine gun bullets tore up the sand. One of the men aboard had been flung clear but Paddy shouted to Bennett to keep on. Now the escarpment was scowling down on them as they rushed headlong into its bosom. Another thunderous roar as the buzzard of the sky swooped again in quest of its prey and they quickly scattered into the nooks and crannies which abounded in the ravine they had just entered.

Paddy was nowhere to be seen, and Bennett wondered if he, too, had fallen off the jeep in its mad rush to safety. If so, he must go out and find him. He might be lying on the track desperately wounded and helpless. So Bennett set forth. As he moved down the ravine his eyes fell on a large man striding in from the desert beyond, with a limp figure hanging over his shoulders. It was, of course, Paddy bringing in the trooper who had fallen off the jeep. The moment that it had pulled up safely in cover he had gone to collect his missing comrade. This was so typical of him, always thinking of his men and responding to every emergency. It was the same with the wounded back at the rendezvous or the base camp. Food, drink or cigarettes, they could have his ration and few would ever know about it.

This poor fellow was coming round now, but talking bemusedly like a drunken man. Paddy stretched him out on a blanket and Bennett produced a flask of rum. In a few minutes he was alright again and thanking Captain Mayne for rescuing him.

All day they lay in the ravine and listened to the bombers and fighters and reconnaissance planes roaring about the skies like angry hornets, and they wondered how their comrades were getting on.

Paddy, Bennett and the trooper rested together under a cliff outcrop and chatted in a tired, desultory way between dozes. Once their peace was violently shattered as an unusually loud explosion shook the ground around them and sent rocks tumbling down from the face of the overhanging cliff.

"What the blazes, Bob," inquired Paddy, turning round to Bennett, "am I doing here in this bloody war? I'm a Northern Irishman and my country has no conscription[1]. Back home I could be fishing and

---

1 With one third of the population of Northern Ireland Nationalist, it was thought unwise to introduce conscription. Nevertheless, 38,000 men and women volunteered, and some 4,500 were killed. The Dublin Government of de Valera remained neutral throughout the War. Both Britain and the USA considered the seizure of Southern Irish bases, but Northern Ireland kept the Atlantic lifeline open. Winston Churchill was to sum up Ulster's contribution when he said: "But for the loyalty of Northern

shooting and drinking to my heart's content. So, what the hell am I doing here?"

"I really don't know, sir," replied Bennett. Then a roguish smile broke on his face. "Unless, sir, it's because you just love a scrap."

"Whatever it is, Bob, I'm thoroughly fed up with this bloody fly-infested desert and will be mighty glad to see the back of it."

What really puzzled Paddy was the lack of initiative shown by the enemy in regard to these raids. They knew how ineffective the bombing of their own airfields and depots had been, yet in seeking out the SAS raiders they seldom used land forces. Now, if he were in their shoes, he would drop parachutists to the rear of the SAS immediately after a raid and send ground patrols out to meet up with them, sandwiching the enemy in between. It was strange that a High Command that had led the way with airborne attacks on Crete should have failed to follow up in other places with the same effective tactics. Kabrit and Kufra, for example, were wide open for airborne attacks and, once taken, these battle bases could become instead a dangerous thorn in the side of the British and they could be supplied from the air regularly.

When darkness fell, Paddy and his men packed into the jeep again and struck inland for the rendezvous. By dawn they had reached it and were greeted with the news that about half of their unit had got back. Captain Bob Melot was severely wounded in the belly and legs but had accomplished his mission and destroyed the radio station.

In the later afternoon, enemy planes came droning overhead again and all the boys lay doggo under camouflage nets or in the scrub cover. This was an effective routine that always deceived the enemy and there was no reason for alarm now. The air scouts duly passed by.

But then one of the jeeps appeared, disregarding orders not to travel in daylight when aircraft were on the rampage. Almost at once, a solitary plane circling overhead spotted it and dived to the attack. It missed the target, and flew off.

But Paddy knew that within seconds the news of this one jeep (and maybe, of lots more) would be radioed from plane to plane and in almost no time at all they would converge on the wadi and strafe it from end to end. But there was nothing he or any of the others could

---

Ireland and its devotion to what had become the cause of thirty Government Nations, we should have been confronted with slavery or death and the light which now shines so strongly throughout the world would have been quenched."

do but stay where they were and just hope for the best.

His silent forecast proved right, and soon the hideaways were taking the pasting of their lives. It lasted for hours, and in fact it was sunset before they pulled out, leaving a trail of destruction behind them. Many were dead and many more wounded, some of the latter so severely that they had to be left there.

It was heartrending, but there was no alternative. Six hundred and fifty miles of moon-like terrain had to be covered and apart from the privations to which this would expose them, lying on the boards of open trucks, their presence would slow up the convoy and jeopardise the lives of the able-bodied and the lightly wounded.

The best that David Stirling and Paddy Mayne could do for these sad casualties was to leave a medical orderly and an Italian prisoner with them under instructions to drive into Benghazi under a Red Cross flag and summon help.

The air blitz had also taken a heavy toll of trucks and jeeps and when a roll call was taken that evening after the straggling remnants of the raid party had caught up, it was discovered they could only accommodate the men by chucking off the baggage. This was done, and at 10 o'clock they left.

Paddy, as usual, led the way. They were now heading for Jalo, nearly two hundred miles distant, which they sincerely hoped the Sudan Defence Force had wrested from its lately-arrived Italian garrison.

In his group he had six jeeps, and Sergeant Bob Bennett at the wheel of his own acted as pathfinder for the others. Unfortunately, Bob had some sleep to catch up with, and little over an hour later he nodded off at the wheel. How long he slept nobody knows, for Paddy and the other occupants of the jeep were also fast asleep, but suddenly they hit a boulder and they were all very much awake.

Bob backed away and then drove off as if nothing had happened but two hours of searching for familiar landmarks convinced him that he was hopelessly lost.

There was nothing for it but to stop and explain the position to Paddy and the others over a brew-up.

Out came the maps and compasses and a deluge of advice, but an hour later they were still off the beaten track and two young Guards officers in the rear of Paddy's jeep began to show clear signs of unrest. At the next halt one of them approached him.

"Captain Mayne," he began, "Lieutenant ---- and I have been discussing our present plight and feel that it would be better if we returned to the coast rather than drive on blindly into this abyss of sand and desolation where we can only meet death in the worst possible form."

"And what makes you think," inquired Paddy, "that you won't meet death on the coast? Don't you know that the Jerries and the 'Eyeties' are waiting there for you?"

"Well, sir, we might find the right track, and failing this, we could always surrender," stammered the young man, already noticeably wilting under the glare of the grey-blue eyes now watching him with hostility.

"Surrender, sir! How dare you talk of such a thing! This is a fighting British regiment, not a bunch of yellow wops! As for going back, you forget that we have only a limited supply of petrol, food and water. Now, Lieutenant ---, less of your belly-aching! Due south is our only course – and your only chance of survival."

The nervous, upset young man moved away mouthing confused apologies, and when he had gone Paddy turned to the cool, tough Bennett and joked, "Sergeant Bennett, remind me to have those two ladies-in-waiting posted back to their regiment as soon as we get back to Kabrit."

A little later one of the thoroughbred guardees was overheard remarking to the other: "I say, old chap, this big Irish gorilla is a bit of a bounder, you know. Prefers the company of his sergeants to gentlemen, but I suppose the choice is natural. Likes to likes."

If Captain Mayne had heard this criticism of himself he would have taken it as a compliment. For his own regular officers, sergeants and men were to him the salt of the earth and natural-born gentlemen, requiring no instruction on manners or deportment from the Brigade of Guards or the drawing-room set from Belgravia.

Paddy had no personal liking for the guardees. They were not to blame, however, for what he regarded as their superciliousness and snootiness, such was the mould in which they had been cast since nanny took over from nursie and public school matron had taken over from nanny, then right on down the unloving line to passing-out day at Sandhurst. Apparently (though not actually), only a soupçon of parental affection; nothing more of home life and its sweet intimacies than afforded by term vacations, in which they might very well find that Mother and Father had gone off on holiday to France, Switzerland or the Bahamas.

Paddy Mayne had a strange, real hate of this traditional set-up, a hate perhaps unreasoning because, after their own fashion, its members were for the most brave and honourable and many of them had already distinguished themselves in this war by deeds of outstanding valour. But to Paddy's dour, call-a-spade-a-spade mind the foppishness, affectation and seeming insincerity of some of this so-called "top level" was unendurable. Enough to make one heave the gorge, he was wont to say. The pity is that the stamp of their chilly upbringing proclaims them a race apart!

Well, they certainly did not belong to a comradely and socially democratic outfit like the Special Air Service. And their voiced apprehensions might well have stirred up some panic amongst those of the men who were new to the desert life. And there were far too many of those on this trip.

On through the dark night drove the small convoy of jeeps, with headlights blazing. Paddy, sitting beside the now alert Bob Bennett, had his eyes fixed a few feet beyond the front wheels watching anxiously for rocks or holes. Just at the first light of dawn they found the lost track, and a few miles short of Jalo they stopped to rendezvous with the other convoys. Then, they pulled off together.

Again, a bitter disappointment awaited them. When they reached Jalo they found when they approached their target, that the Sudan Defence Force had been confronted by a thoroughly alerted enemy, and bitter fighting had resulted. The Italian garrison was unusually defiant, and victory was not to be bought cheaply. The two British forces decided that it must be a do-or-die battle and were making dispositions when a radio message from GHQ flashed through ordering them to return to base, abandoning the assault.

But this time, there was good news too. The message went on to report that their combined operations over the past days had forced the enemy to divert from the front areas very large numbers of aircraft, transport vehicles and troops, and this had greatly aided the Eighth Army in certain counter-operations upon which it was then engaged.

The date was now 19 September, and the blueprint of the titanic history-making battle of El Alamein was being thoroughly and scientifically traced by General Bernard Montgomery.

"Strange," observed Paddy to Sergeant Bennett as they motored off to Kufra, "Strange indeed, how many generals in this desert Army are Irish! First there was O'Connor, then Auchinleck and Cunningham, then Dorman-Smith, and now Alexander and Montgomery. Three of them I know of come from my native Ulster. It seems that all we're good for is raising soldiers."

"Haven't you forgotten one important one, sir?" inquired the sergeant. "What about the big chief himself, Sir Alan Brooke? Isn't he one of yours?"

"You're right, Bob, damned right! Sure, he's a fine upstanding man from County Fermanagh, but he's not here, Bob. He's in London."

"But his brains are here," rejoined Sergeant Bennett, laconically.

Back in Kufra after the disappointment of Benghazi, Paddy Mayne allowed himself to relax. "El Hamdullilah!" he murmured to himself as he basked in the sun by one of the brilliant turquoise blue lakes. Praise, indeed, be to God for sparing him a little longer! The day was magical in this sleepy little medina of El Giof and as he rested on his elbow and surveyed his surroundings, in the sultry heat, his half-born thoughts drifted to and fro.

One minute he was transported far away to the bee-buzzing glades of his spacious family home nestling in the foothills of the majestic Mountains of Mourne, to that blue roof lighted by the dying sun, the gardens green with vegetation and light foliage, the sycamore and chestnut trees rustling and whispering in the evening breeze and, later, the purple velvet sky hung with a million magic lanterns. The next minute his mind with tenderness and love lingered on the memory of his dearest ones whom he longed so much to see again and talk with about so many things that pen and paper would not accept. And then, at times, Paddy's heart was torn with anguish when he conjured up again his leavetaking of his wounded comrades – brave, splendid soldiers, most of whom he would never see again in this world. Those last hours with them, so cruel and yet so heart-moving, were to live in his memory to the end. Out in the desert on the previous night, he had lain apart from the others and in solitude and during the early watches of the night he had heard their voices clearly in the orchestra of the sand, that weird and macabre singing and wailing that haunts the wilderness.

Perhaps it was the Djinns, the spirits whom the Bedouin feared but, if so, they spoke with the tongues of his comrades, dying and dead in that accursed wadi back in the wilderness.

How sweet to be back in this oasis, this place of mental calm and unhurried stocktaking! Here, when his friend David Stirling returned, they would settle down together for a brief time and work out their future plans. Lately, a sense of destiny had crept into his subconscious thought and he was sure that the fate to which he was now harnessed would be a truly exalted one.

In these silent, drowsy moments, Paddy gave full rein to his highly sensitive Celtic imagination. This day, he was for the most part happy, and for one dominating reason. The SAS had been through a tough drill of hardship and misfortune, and now it was a unit of the British fighting forces second to none. The credit for this, to Paddy's mind was all David Stirling's, although many men already sought to shift it to himself. But criticisms of his Commanding Officer by anybody passed him by, for Paddy was not of the envious type. He had affection and sincere respect for David, sentiments which he did not normally dispense out of hand; and both increased as time went on. Some of the staff officers in Cairo certainly thought, and perhaps piously hoped, that the ground was fertile for jealousy but in this they were very wrong. Unlike the traditional Irishmen of the Jonathan Swift type, whose unbrotherly rancours once prompted Dr Johnston to exclaim with heavy irony: "The Irish are a very fair-minded race; they never speak well of one another," Blair Mayne was devoid of this vice.

"True riches," he once remarked to Sergeant Bennett, "cannot be bought. One cannot buy the experience of brave deeds or the friendship of companions to whom one is bound forever by ordeals suffered in common. True friendship itself is an emerald beyond price."

In Kufra, he liked to drink wine and always laid up a store of it against the day of his return.

"My day," he would cite Khayyam happily,

"My day with long oblivion is gone dry;
But, fill me with the old familiar juice
Me thinks, I might recover bye and bye!"

And in his ring of friends Paddy's juice was for one and all. His generosity had to be experienced to be believed and the password to his company was a merry song or a sentimental ballad.

The natives of the oases, a strange mix-up of African races, watched these roisterings from afar, in a kind of bewildered wonderment. What an audience! Women with bold, dark, flashing eyes; lean, sinewy, brown and black skinned men with eyes hooded from smoking hashish; and children like children everywhere, jolly, friendly, and completely free and easy. They were just an innocent group of people caught up in terrible events which they could not understand. French, Italian, German and British were all alike to them, 'roumis' from distant lands with murder in their hearts and the love of Allah barred from their infidel souls. In Shaa Allah! God willing, they would depart one day and leave them in peace.

Paddy bestirred himself from his reverie as the familiar sounds of a jolly brew-up wafted across the cool waters. Bennett and Sadler, masters of the time-honoured English craft, were at it again and to their labour of love they brought a song which Paddy had taught them, "Come Back Paddy Reilly!"

It seemed most appropriate for the occasion. With happy laughing voices they sang:

> "The Garden of Eden has vanished they say
> But I know the lie of it still.
> Just turn to the left at the bridge of Finea
> And stop when half way to Cootehill.
> 'Tis there I will find it. I know sure enough
> When fortune has come to my call.
> Oh! The grass it is green around Ballyjamesduff
> And the blue sky is over it all,
> And tones that are tender
> And tones that are gruff
> A whispering over the sea."

And then the soaring chorus, loud and plaintive:

> "Come back, Paddy Reilly, to Ballyjamesduff!
> Come home, Paddy Reilly, to me!"

Every word of it, like all the words that Percy French had ever written, was sweet music in Paddy's ears and humming the words joyfully to himself he got up and made his way round to the lighthearted tea-makers, determined to give them a bar or two of 'Phil the Fluter's Ball' before they took their siesta.

CHAPTER 10

Singing in the wilderness

Although the Benghazi raid could never be described as anything other than a disaster the backroom boys at HQ in Cairo, whether anxious to justify themselves in spawning such a scheme or just being silly again, hailed it as a great success. David Stirling found himself most enthusiastically welcomed and received promotion to Lieutenant Colonel as reward. Paddy Mayne, too, got much warm shoulder clapping and rose to the rank of Major. The detachment itself was now to become a full regiment and had found a permanent place in the British Army.

Shortly, General Sir Bernard Montgomery's offensive would be launched and the SAS would be back on duty in its now accepted role of harassing the enemy behind his lines. This time it would not be skimped, as hitherto, of manpower.

David Stirling, restless and dynamic as ever, was impatient of the delay imposed on his plans by the massive, painstaking build-up for the big El Alamein onslaught and so he divided the regiment into two squadrons, A and B, and appointed Paddy in command of A. His orders to Paddy were to take his unit, via Kufra, to a base in the Sand Sea and then from there attack the Matruh railway line. The rear base camp would be near Kufra, where a section of the LRDG was operating and they would work as closely as possible together. This plan had been endorsed by General Montgomery, and so, to work!

On 7 October 1942, Paddy set off with eighty men and a transport column of jeeps and three-tonners. The forward base which he established was about one hundred and fifty miles from the railway target and he and his men settled in very quickly. Away from what he regarded as the 'Very-Top-Level Old-Chap' artificiality of Alexandria and Cairo, Paddy was happy again. Around him he had a nucleus of old friends who had campaigned alongside him in many parts of the desert. They could all be relied upon, he knew, to face an emergency and their courage, like his own, was dauntless.

Soon they were hard at it again; wreaking a trail of havoc along the coast roads, mining and blowing up long stretches of railway line and actually ambushing trains.

Paddy Mayne's own unceasing energy and his grim determination to get at the enemy's throat kept him forever on the move, and he frequently headed off into the blue on a roving commission. On one of these journeys he stumbled upon an apparently deserted – but in a strange way, a somewhat sinister – stronghold, and decided to investigate. But he did not feel justified in exposing the three troopers who were with him to any unnecessary risk. It was to be a one-man job, he resolved, and after instructing the others to cover him he left the jeep 200 yards away from the small fort and went forward on foot. Stealthily, he crept inside but drew back when he heard voices. Now, the mystery! In a dark passageway Paddy listened intently – and could just distinguish that some of the voices were Italian and the others English. The Italians seemed to be posing questions in strong, rasping voices, and were being answered in weak, plaintive voices, sometimes broken with sobs. He crawled nearer and listened on.

"For the last time…," growled a Latin voice, "Tell us why you came, or your eyes will be gouged out!"

Paddy burst open the door, tommy-gun at the ready. Eight undersized and unshaven Italians were standing around two dishevelled RAF flyers who were slumped in deck chairs. Several of the Italians had truncheons, others had pistols, and one held a stiletto.

"What the blazes is going on here?" shouted Paddy, an awesome sight towering above them, his red beard bristling with anger.

One of the RAF men's voices broke with emotion. "These dirty bastards have been torturing us," he croaked.

"Then," answered Paddy, tossing him his tommy-gun, and drawing his own pistol, "do what you like with them!"

From where he sat the RAF man blasted off his fire and seconds later the eight Italians lay dead. Paddy then told the two prisoners he had rescued to follow him to the jeep. But the one who had the tommy-gun told him that both his legs had been broken when their plane crashed, and that the Italians, who had captured them on a reconnaissance, had inflicted third-degree torture on them by lifting them up and dropping them on the stone floor for hours on end. This had been done to each in turn, and his friend was now only half-conscious.

Paddy listened in tight-lipped silence. Such barbarism made this savage war itself worthwhile. For if Fascism and Nazism produced such monsters as these, they must go – and go quickly! When Paddy's men arrived a little later they were sickened and disgusted by the affair. They blew up two armoured Lancias which were parked in the courtyard and then, having dynamited the fort, they were glad to get away from the plagued place.

Some will object to Paddy's action and say that these wretched Italians should have been made prisoners and handed over to a War Crimes Tribunal to be tried in court and, if found guilty, punished in whatever way seemed appropriate. But to the men of the SAS there was no moral issue involved. *Paddy was right, and the brutes got what they deserved.*

For the next six weeks success followed success for the SAS and Paddy became more and more satisfied with his squadron's achievements.

Even the new boys were cottoning on fast. One, a fellow Irishman and a brother officer named McDermott, went so far as to attack and capture an entire railway station. Another, David Sillito, was taken by surprise and attacked while mining a railway track at Tobruk. He became separated from his men but rather than surrender, which would have been justified in the circumstances, he chose to trek a distance of 180 miles across the desert back to Paddy's base and how he ever accomplished this remarkable feat of endurance without food or water passes one's understanding.

His own account of the ordeal is interesting in that it gives an insight into the mental make-up of a typical SAS crusader.

> "When I got back to where the jeeps were," he writes, "the other three had pulled out thinking I had been killed. So then I was on my own with no food and no water – just a revolver and a compass.

There were three things I could do. One was to give myself up to the Italians – but that was off! I could walk along the track through the German lines to my own front line – but I didn't like the idea of that. The only course left to me then was to walk to my own base on the Sand Sea.

They reckoned I walked altogether one hundred and eighty miles. It took me eight days. I knew the back bearing because I had navigated in the area on other raids.

The first night I walked as far as I could to get away from the Italians in case they came after me. I laid up the first few hours after dawn to watch out for spotter planes, but as none appeared I carried on.

The first day I just kept slogging on, with nothing to eat and nothing to drink. Occasionally, I came across piles of empty petrol tins upon which was collected dew, and was able to wet my tongue on them. There was not much of it.

Then, in a wrecked tank, I found a tin of bully beef but when I opened it and tried to eat the meat I found that I couldn't as my tongue had become like dry putty and mastication was out of the question. I threw the meat away but kept the tin.

It came in handy for holding my urine which I then started to drink. It stopped me from desiccating and drying out altogether. Of course, it was acrid and unpleasant but it was better than dying of thirst. I kept this up for seven days – marching on the bearing in daylight and using the stars at night.

During the hottest part of the day I used to lie on my back and use a greatcoat as a tent till that became too heavy to carry.

Eventually I hit a wadi called Hatiet Etla, which was the one we had rested in prior to setting off on the final stage to the railway and I knew that the LRDG had a store of emergency rations and biscuits, bully beef and water hidden in a broken down three-tonner they had left there.

I hit the northern extremity of this wadi – it was about a mile long by about one hundred yards across. At first I thought I was at the wrong place and followed some jeep tracks for several miles until I found a haversack. It contained nothing of use to me, so dragging my blistered feet I returned to the wadi. Just as I got there it began to rain. Oh, what a joy! What a relief!

I must have drunk half a dozen tins of water and then I went hunting for the hidden rations. Suddenly I heard voices and wondered if my exhausted and deranged brain was playing tricks on me. Then everything faded out and I sank into oblivion.

The next thing I remember was waking up and finding myself in a group of SAS comrades.

Fortunately for me they had been due to leave this wadi early in the morning, but because of some mechanical trouble they had been delayed.

To get back to base camp on foot would have meant another thirty or forty miles which I don't think I would have made.

They gave me a cigarette and some tomato juice, and dressed my feet as best they could. Then they took me to the main base in the Sand Sea where I was attended by Dr Pleydell. I stayed there one night and was taken back to Kufra and from there flown to Cairo. At my own request I was transferred from the Military Hospital to our own base at Kabrit. The doctor said I was suffering from physical and nervous exhaustion, but after two weeks in the exhilarating company of my buddies I was able to go up to the blue again on operations behind the German's Mareth Line."

Paddy's men were like that, the stuff of heroes one and all. Fortunately for them their forward camp enjoyed immunity from the air attacks. Both the Italian and German flyers were fighting shy of the rugged desolation that was the Sand Sea. It was thought that they feared having to make a forced landing and then having to undergo the ordeal of slow extinction in the blazing hell-fire of the desert. It is true that Kufra had been raided in the past and the same prospect should have been duly considered but, at any rate, for the time being, A-squadron enjoyed peace and quiet at its forward base camp.

Dr Malcolm Pleydell, the Medical Officer of the Regiment, was there in the thick of it, looking after the sick and wounded, and clearly he was deeply regarded and respected by his hard, tough charges. He, in turn, developed an abiding affection for every one of them, but Paddy Mayne was his hero.

"David, " he wrote, "had been the man with ideas, while Jock Lewis and Paddy were those whose efforts had helped to make them practicable and successful. They had worked in a sort of mortal symbiosis. And here we are now: Paddy with his own squadron in operation and reports being wirelessed back to base:

'Railway line destroyed at...Station, Officers and sidings blown up,' or, 'Road mined at...Telegraph lines demolished.'"

For Paddy this was but child's play and only when it was decided to bush-whack a train or convoy loaded with enemy troops was his blood really up. Then the cut and thrust of a man-to-man engagement was the challenge of the hour and he accepted it with a will. In the whole of the vast battle area of the Middle East there was no tougher band of fighters than Paddy Mayne's A-squadron.

His Second-In-Command was Captain Bill Fraser, about as rugged a Scotsman as ever wore a kilt, and the irrepressible Captain Bill Cumper, a Southern Irishman whose rough banter and high spirits were a comfort to all when adversity struck.

Then Sergeants Almonds, Bennett, Riley, Rose, Seekings and a host of others whose names were listed for every raid worthy of the name since the SAS was formed.

On 18 October, Major Mayne received a signal order from Eighth Army Headquarters to intensify his attacks and bring them as close as possible to the enemy's rear at El Daba. Road and railway communications were to be severed, and severed again and again as soon as they were restored.

It was a tough assignment. For the German and Italian armoured and motorised divisions were deploying in strength from the Mediterranean at El Alamein to the Qattara Depression and the German counterpart of the Special Air Service, the Brandenburgers, were ranging the desert on the same sort of errands as Paddy's men.

It was, however, an emphatic order for action and it was to be obeyed with resolution. The SAS regarded themselves, with proved justification, as an elite regiment and it would have been taken as an insult if they had been commanded to do something which the Home Guard could have done as well.

Both Captain Fraser and Captain Cumper were already on a raid elsewhere, so Paddy took Lieutenant Tony Marsh and twenty-five men with him in six jeeps and headed straight for the Egyptian border. Urgency was the key-note of the operation. General Montgomery was about to start his history-making offensive and the enemy must now be given no respite. Paddy was proud of the role he had been told to play. It was recognition at the highest level of the worth of the SAS.

Crossing the bleak waste beyond the Sand Sea they felt very exposed but they had to hurry on and just take their chance with enemy planes. Fortunately the RAF had now become the masters of the skies and there were few interlopers left.

Paddy's party crossed the Libya-Egypt frontier and kept on doggedly for five more days. On the sixth, they had their first encounter with the enemy, in the shape of a convoy of lorries. It happened at twilight and it was hard to estimate the convoy strength, but Paddy decided to attack anyway. His plan was swiftly outlined to his squadron: three jeep crews would attack the front section of the convoy and halt it, two would attack the rear, the other would stand off in case of emergency.

The enemy was not altogether unobservant, and suddenly the procession's trot turned into a gallop and in the following chase three trucks got away. The rest were captured, and now Paddy had 20 German and Italian prisoners on his hands and no means of providing for them. His mission was the destruction of the Mersa Matruh railway line and the coastal road. While he briefly pondered the problem some of the Italians wept unashamedly and begged for mercy. Had they known, they need not have bothered; Paddy Mayne was a crusading soldier not a bloodthirsty murderer. Still, they presented a real problem to him.

"If we leave them a truck," he remarked to Lieutenant Tony Marsh, "they'll beat it back to their lines and give us away. We can't take them with us because we may be going into action, and if we destroy their trucks and just leave them here then they may die of hunger and thirst. So what do we do?"

"Positions reversed," replied Marsh wryly, "there would be no problem. We would be dead ducks by now. Still, I've got your point. You are going to leave them here, aren't you?"

"Yes, Tony. You are right. If their buddies have any gumption they'll come back and look for them."

But leaving them was not so easy. The wailing of the Italians now soared into a symphony of self-pity and Paddy felt thoroughly embarrassed.

"The poor wee Jerries and 'Eyeties'," he wrote to his brother shortly afterwards, "they looked so pitiable! Eventually I had to take two 'Eyeties' with us and leave the rest with what grub they had."

The three captured lorries had to be finished with, and time bombs attended to this very effectively.

The railway line and the coastal road were now also attended to and then the squadron made for its base, known as Howard's Cairn, there to plan more depredations. On the way back, they came across a Heinkel bomber that had force-landed. The machine was intact but had run out of fuel and the crew were busy tapping out radio messages for assistance when Paddy appeared. A minute or so later they watched their bomber go up in a tongue of flame. This time, the captives had to be taken along with the squadron as they were beyond the reach of anywhere.

Still, life had its occasional compensations for the slings and arrows sometimes hurled around by a wayward fate, and now Paddy became the proud possessor of a German rolleiflex camera, a couple of pistols and a shotgun with cartridges!

The latter could – and did – prove very useful, for occasionally a deer would be sighted and venison in the wilderness was a feast fit for the gods.

In the desert it was not all the hellish clangour of war; indeed quite often life in it could be an experience of pleasure. The weather, it is true, veered from the extremes of heat to genuine cold. In summer, it was insufferable hammerstrokes of the sun; during the daylight hours the most odious form of steamroom in the Turkish Baths, and at nightfall a surprising chilliness. In the winter, it could be perishingly cold by day and worse still in the night. But in between the extremes there were also periods of delicious mellowness. Paddy Mayne relished these interludes, loved the rugged grandeur of the hillsides and ravines and the quaint aloofness of the wilderness.

Deep in his heart, too, was his admiration for the Arab nomads, strange and somehow noble in their own mysterious way, who wandered there from oasis to oasis following some primeval gypsy instinct. He felt that this was where he, too, belonged, that these Bedouins were his brothers and that henceforth his life and theirs would be entangled in a coil that would defy uncoiling. The heavenly bodies, too, took on a new significance, especially the moon and the stars, beacons to guide in the stilly night, lanterns to light and jewels to delight.

To Paddy, with his deep love of poetry, the varied canvases of the desert gave a backcloth of warmth and tenderness to the verses of Omar Khayyam, so many of which he knew by heart.

The lines cascaded through his mind:

"Here, with a loaf of bread beneath the bough,
A Flask of Wine, a book of verse and thou
Beside me singing in the wilderness
And wilderness in Paradise enow."

And then something about the wind along the waste willy-nilly blowing God knows where. But here the winds were elemental things with personality, tempers and idiosyncrasy befitting each.

"The stars are settling and the caravan
Starts for the dawn of nothing – Oh, make haste!"

On the night of 23 October, at precisely 2045 hours, General Montgomery had unleashed the greatest bombardment in the history of war and the desert shuddered as if struck by a giant earthquake. Paddy and his men driving through the cold, moonlit night were startled to hear this sudden cataract of thunder, and even at a distance of forty miles from the scene of it they felt the earth trembling beneath them.

For twelve momentous days the battle raged and, finally, the Axis divisions, having fought with splendid bravery against overwhelming odds, had to accept defeat. And then the rout began to spread from El Alamein to Fuka sixty miles away, and from there onward to the end of the story.

The German Commander-In-Chief, Field Marshal Rommel, though it was his defeat, obtained for himself a niche in the Hall of Fame and would be remembered for generations to come. Just now, with the arrival on 8 November of General Eisenhower and a force of 80,000 men in Algeria and Morocco, he realised that his famous Afrika Korps was going to be annihilated but before that happened he was determined to give a good account of himself. And to the end Rommel and his forces fought with true chivalry.

Here was a problem again, mental and moral, for Paddy. Living on his back under the stars he often wondered what in the end the destruction and hate of this world war would achieve. At times, he was genuinely afraid; afraid of a barbarism masquerading under crusading hypocrisy and brazen lying. He pitied the Germans and the Italians as well as those on his own side. They were all the same, basically, born with the same hopes and fears, saddled with the same troubles, and uplifted with the same blessings. The curse of Cromwell on this madman Hitler and his clique of cut-throats! The sooner the Black Camel of Death knocked on their doors, the better for all.

After six weeks of this nomadic living, A-squadron was ordered to withdraw to Kufra again and from there proceed to the oasis of Bir Zalten, one hundred miles south-west of Jalo. From this new base attacks would be made on the retreating enemy from Agheila in Misurata, and B-squadron would operate beyond this area to just west of Tripoli. David Stirling, with his men, left Kabrit on 20 November and motored by the coastal road to Agedabia, where it turned inland for Bir Zalten.

There Paddy was waiting, and soon David and he had spread out maps and photographs and were working out the most unpleasant surprises for the enemy forces already reeling under the might of the Eighth Army and now threatened on the rear by the American First Army which had landed in Tunisia.

Enemy encampments were to be the targets and Paddy's unit, with its usual (or most unusual) luck and determination, had soon run up another score of big success.

The B-squadron, operating in a populous section of Tripolitania, with hostile Bedouins here, was as unsuccessful as Paddy was the opposite. Several factors, apart from the unfriendliness of the local Arabs, may have contributed to this. One was certainly the considerable number of green recruits who had just arrived, and another could have been the narrowness of the coastal strip on which they were to go into action.

In fact, disaster struck when David was aiming for his forward base at Bir Facia, four hundred miles west beyond Paddy's base and new territory for the SAS. The ground became worse and worse for travel and the damage to jeeps became more and more serious. But there was no alternative route which they could take if their presence was to pass unnoticed.

They had been trying to get round the southern flank of the Wadi Tamit through an area recognised by those desert experts, the LRDG, as impassable, and now even the redoubtable David Stirling himself had to admit defeat and try the passage of the wadi itself. This, however, turned out to be even worse, and in the boulder-littered water-course the jeep axles snapped like matchwood.

Eventually, the base at Bir Facia was reached and they settled down in an adjoining wadi. David's plan was now to send out eight patrols to selected areas where they would attack enemy transports, plant mines, and do any damage that was possible such as the shooting-up of transport parks and encampments.

In theory, it was a sound plan: in practice, it turned into disaster. So many raids came to grief, and patrol after patrol was destroyed or captured. Rommel had become acutely aware of the demoralising effect of the SAS phantom attacks upon his troops and the word went out that Stirling and his men were to be hunted down and destroyed. At once, the chase began. On Christmas Day, Captain Street and his patrol were surrounded at Bir Facia and taken prisoner.

David Stirling himself was back at Headquarters during this period and did not realise that his squadron was disintegrating. Success was around everywhere else and the Eighth Army was grinding forward like an irresistible juggernaut. Agheila had been taken and the province of Cyrenaica liberated again. But weeks passed before reports trickled back to David of the disasters which had overtaken the SAS men, and then he decided to pull his forces back to Kabrit and prepare for fresh adventures.

For himself he reserved one final dangerous operation, and instructed three of his B-squadron officers to rendezvous with him in the Bir Guedaffia area.

On 10 January 1943, Stirling got away from Headquarters. He planned to deliver attacks on the enemy lines between Gabes and Sfax in Tunisia, an assault on Tripoli from the west to deceive and confuse the Rommel men, and last of all he himself would thrust his way through to the American First Army in Northern Tunisia. This latter project was characteristic of David Stirling, he was going to make his own mark on Eisenhower and his generals by leading the first unit of the British Army to join hands with the Americans in the desert. That would enlarge his own stature.

He set forth his ideas on a technical basis, though their purpose was strongly personal. He wrote:

> "My plan was to bring in my brother Bill's 2nd SAS Regiment, and to divide down my own regiment, which had grown far beyond the official establishment of a full regiment into the nucleus of a

third one. This would enable me to keep one regiment in each of the three main theatres, the Eastern Mediterranean area, the Central Mediterranean – Italian area, and the future Second Front Area."

David's ambition, quixotic but very understandable, was going to land him in a prisoner-of-war cage on 25 January, though several of his men were to win the distinction of being the first of the British forces to link up with the Americans.

Paddy Mayne had spent a chilly and uncomfortable Christmas at his Bir Zalten rendezvous. With him, safe and sound, were all his trusted comrades making the best of the foul wintry conditions. For them, the war in the desert was now drawing to a close and soon they would be on their way back to Kabrit and for a brief spell enabled to enjoy just a few of the creature comforts of modern civilisation.

Now, in farewell to these last hours of the old guard in the sandy wastes, it is fitting here to quote Dr Malcolm Pleydell again in relation to his CO:

"There was Paddy with his bushy beard and massive shoulders, giving way to the mood of the moment and joining with his unmusical singing to each song in turn. But he refused to sing a solo, contenting himself instead with reciting some of French's poems and becoming so enrapt with their spirit that even as he did so his brogue became marked enough for us to find the verses hard to follow. He showed an easy tolerance of sentimental jazz songs, and in reply to my criticism he pointed across at Shotton and said, 'Look at him! He's singing his heart out. Don't you see he is as happy as a skylark. Och! Never you mind, Malcolm, we'll have you singing 'Macnamara's Band' yet!"

Yes, Paddy was Irish alright; Irish, for sure, from top to toe, from the lazy eyes that could light into anger quickly, to the quiet voice and its intonation. Northern Irish, mind you, and he regarded all Southerners with true caution. But he had Southern Irishmen in his Irish patrol, they all had shamrocks painted on their jeeps, and I know that he was proud of them; he never grew tired of quoting the reply given by one of the Southerners in answer to the question: why was he fighting in this war? 'Why,' he had replied, 'Of course it's for the independence of small countries!'

There was something very rugged and forceful about Paddy's leadership. Although he lived and slept with the men, queued up behind them as he waited his turn for food and ate with them, yet no one would dare overstep the mark and become too familiar with him. For he could silence a man with a glance, could cut him short without a world; while everyone held a considerable respect for his physical capabilities. And yet, despite, or together with, these characteristics, he would be the first man to come up and try to discover why you were depressed at Christmas time. Such were a few of the qualities which made him so successful as a commander."

But for one class of people, Paddy Mayne reserved a special hate, and that was the Military Police. It was, in fact, a hatred that could well have cost him his command and very nearly did so, back in Cairo in late January 1943.

Just home from the desert, he met up with his old chum whom he liked very much, a Geordie named Tommy Corps who, like himself, had once been a more than useful heavyweight boxer. Naturally, they took some drink together, maybe a drop too much. As they walked down one of the main thoroughfares two red-hats approached them, a Colonel and a Sergeant. Paddy glared at them with mounting fury and then suddenly barked to his companion: "You take the Sergeant! I'll take the Officer!"

He immediately followed up with a fierce attack which sent his victim hurtling to the ground. The Sergeant, reacting a little faster, managed to clinch with Tommy Corps and almost immediately military policemen rushed in from all around. Tommy was arrested and taken to the local prison, but Paddy managed to escape and hurried off to Kabrit.

Later, the police got in touch with the SAS and informed Paddy that they were holding one of his men for assault and battery and were sending two officers to interrogate a very largely-built officer of his unit, who had also been involved in the affray. Paddy instructed them to bring back Tommy Corps to his own unit for punishment, and then disappeared himself from Kabrit on a seven-day excursion and naturally was not available when the interrogators arrived.

Tommy Corps had of course kept his mouth shut and Bill Fraser, deputising for Paddy, had no idea who the stranger could be. Perhaps he belonged to some other regiment. It was indeed regrettable that the Commanding Officer was away on operations. He certainly would stamp down on any unruliness of this kind.

The Commanding Officer, who had just been appointed to take over from the captured David Stirling, was none other than Paddy Mayne himself, now very much *persona grata* with General Alexander, who had followed his daring exploits with close interest.

For Tommy Corps there was no punishment. The SAS had been brought up on a tradition of absolute obedience to superior orders.

In his book, *The Desert My Dwelling Place*, Colonel David Lloyd Owen, DSO, OBE, MC, gives a pen picture of Paddy Mayne with whom he served for a time in this barren land.

> "Paddy," he writes, "an Irish Rugby International and a barrister [he was, in fact, a solicitor], was an enormous man with tremendous physical strength and an attractive Irish brogue. He was a most gentle and kind person who possessed all the qualities of leadership which made him so successful. He had an aggressive and ingenious brain which was always seeking new ways to harry the enemy, and he was the type of man who would never ask anyone to do anything that he had not done himself. He was a born leader and he flourished under the powers that he could exercise.
>
> Yet his gentle appearance and nature were sometimes deceptive and I would have hated to have found myself on the wrong side of Paddy Mayne. It took little to upset him and then it was very difficult to control him. As a fighter he was unsurpassed, for his very presence in the full flood of his wrath was enough to unnerve the strongest of human beings. I'm sure he would have forgiven my saying that many a Provost Marshal has had good cause to remember that it was hardly wise to upset Paddy."

In Civvy Street Paddy transferred his hatred of Red Hats to the Bobbies, and when under the influence of John Barleycorn he was wont to manhandle the odd officious member of the local constabulary a little too vigorously. Fortunately, these occasions were not numerous.

And now, although he did not know it, Paddy's war in the desert was over. It had ended in a mixture of madness and true nobility. Madness in the reckless and utterly irresponsible attack upon the Red Hats in

Cairo, which might well have landed him back where Stirling had found him eighteen months before – a detention cell awaiting a court-martial.

The nobility, inspired by deep patriotism, was provided by David Stirling, who, languishing in a prisoner-of-war camp in Italy, contrived to send code messages to the British War Office recommending Paddy as his successor.

CHAPTER 11

Intermission

It seems like taking coals to Newcastle but the General Staff felt that some token gesture might help to appease the Russians now fighting the most titanic battle in the history of the human race at Stalingrad. And so it was decided to send the Special Air Service regiment to the Caucasus.

Fitzroy Maclean, that most intrepid of soldiers, had been commissioned six weeks earlier to recruit and train special guerrilla units for operations in Persia in the likely event of the Germans taking Stalingrad and overrunning that country in a thrust to India. It was a terrifying but very real prospect and it had been anticipated by the British as far back as August 1941, when the German onslaught on Russia had been raging for little more than two months. It had forced them to do something which they disliked greatly but found necessary because of mounting Intelligence reports that the Germans were concentrating great numbers of agents and establishing a fifth column.

On 25 August 1941 British and Russian troops invaded Persia (modern Iran) and after four days of sporadic fighting the Shah capitulated.

The lightning victory achieved a secondary dividend by securing for the Russians a supply route for war materials. General Zahedi and some highly placed army officers and politicians, believing the secondary dividend to be the principal objective, were greatly embittered by this rape of their country and Zahedi, still in command of an army group in the South at Isfahan, commenced to intrigue with the Nazis.

In November 1942 his long-awaited moment of retribution seemed to be on hand. Fitzroy Maclean decided that the best way to deal with this troublesome gentleman was to put him out of harm's way and this he did by kidnapping him in his home, at the point of a pistol, and removing him to an internment camp in Palestine. And, strange to relate, the irrepressible general was to make the news again eleven years later when he staged a *coup d'état* that ousted the pro-Communist Dr Musaddig and restored the Shah to power.

Now Maclean, having accomplished this necessary first step, settled down to the training of his guerrillas on the same lines as those he had learned himself when serving with the SAS.

Meanwhile his friend Paddy Mayne was having the devil's own job, struggling with the top brass in Cairo, to prevent the liquidation of his regiment. The fight was long and exhausting and at times seemed hopeless. It was in fact so hopeless and discouraging that it was all he could do in the end to withstand the sirens' call that the detachment, having fulfilled the function for which it had been formed, should now be disbanded and its members absorbed into the Commando units where their experience would be invaluable in the training of new recruits. They had won their spurs, conceded the top brass with plummy self-assurance, and had fought the good fight. Now it was their turn to savour the fruits of their labours, and at the same time make a worthwhile contribution to the war effort.

It was undoubtedly very tempting and the prospect of easy living and junketing in the fleshpots of Egypt or Palestine might well have proved too much for a weaker man. But not for a fighter like Paddy.

As he pointed out again and again, with single-minded doggedness, eighteen months of hard campaigning and shared dangers had forged his men into a *corps d'élite*, whose courage and resourcefulness made it a striking force second to none.

At the fourth and final meeting with the staff officers, they pointed out that as the Americans and British were now routing Rommel's Afrika Korps, there was no area left where raiding was any longer necessary or desirable and the chairman of the group strummed the table impatiently, as if to indicate that the discussion had been unduly prolonged and should now terminate.

Then a lobster-faced brigadier, who looked as if his Indian Army career had been mainly occupied with polo and drinking, inquired casually if Mayne and his 'chappies' were prepared to go to the Caucasus to harry the Germans' lines of communication.

To Paddy this was a bolt from the blue. Russia he had never considered as a likely battle-ground for his sturdy voortrekkers, but if the alternatives were to be Russia or disbandment, he had only one choice.

"We will go to any place, sir," he replied tersely, "where we can get a crack at the enemy."

Ten days later he was advised that he was to transfer most of his regiment to the Middle East Ski-School in the Cedars of Lebanon for training. In the Semperamis Hotel in Cairo over many brandies, Paddy and Bob Melot discussed this 'stranger than fiction' order and its problems. First, it meant studying the Caucasian terrain very carefully from aerial photographs and selecting base-camps. Then it involved the recruitment of free Poles to overcome the language difficulty. Finally, there was the question of supply.

It was late January 1943 and the battle of Stalingrad was drawing to a close. The German Sixth Army under Colonel-General von Paulus was disintegrating and the threat to Asia Minor appeared to be over.

The myth of Nazi invincibility had been shattered. Why, then, were they being trained to fight in Russia? Admittedly, the Caucasus Army-group was still intact and the Germans were very far from being beaten as yet. But it did not seem likely that they would attempt a major putsch towards Persia and India with their northern flank exposed to the Red Army. Fitzroy Maclean, they knew, had just been informed that the Persian guerrilla plan had been abandoned and he was marking time in Cairo.

It all seemed very strange, but there was nothing for it but to get on with the job: and, as the strength of the regiment was being raised, there was certainly plenty of hard work ahead.

The following day, Paddy and Captain Melot flew to Beirut and were met by an army driver who had been sent down from the Ski-School in the Cedars of Lebanon to fetch them. He was an amiable talkative Cockney, who knew the country well and kept up a running commentary on its many points of interest. At first the road followed the coastal plain – a narrow sliver of fertile land, wedged between the sea and the mountains which in summer produced grapes, figs, olives, oranges, bananas and wheat, but now looked desolate. Then, after travelling for about forty miles, they turned into undulating foothills, beyond which they saw fold upon fold of snow-capped mountains, rising in the distance to pierce the grey wintry clouds. It was a sight of breath-taking beauty. After three hours of tortuous climbing, mostly in low gear, they came to Dimane, a picturesque little village with a market-square lined with trees, now stark and unfriendly. Here they stopped for refreshment and Melot talked happily to the *patrone* of the shabby little guest-house in French. The man was a Christian, a member of the Maronite Church (Catholic in its affiliation) and he had been educated at Tripoli. So pleased was he with Melot's breezy gossip, that he produced a bottle of Napoleon brandy and this infused them with a feeling of euphoria which had been sadly lacking in the long perilous journey through the mountains. Furthermore, it promised to fortify them for the next stage to Becharre, ten miles further up this precipitous road.

At Becharre, they drank *arak*, as clear and tender a wine as any to be found in the vineyards of France, and by the time they reached the Cedars, they were in merry pin. Night had fallen, but a large, radiant moon had pushed its way through the lowering clouds and illumined the wintry scene.

The Hotel des Cedres, a gaunt building with the dark outlines of twin cedars on the front terrace, looked less than inviting, but the SAS men were glad to be at the end of their long and terrifying journey. To sleep in their state of delicious tiredness would be a luxury.

The following morning Paddy awoke to find himself in an alpine paradise overlooking the grove of world-famous cedars, some of which, according to local legend, had been planted in the reign of King Solomon.

There was not time, however, for exploring his surroundings yet, for presently he had to make the acquaintance of the Staff of the Army Ski-School and arrange for the reception of his men. Several days later when he and Melot found time on their hands, they took over a jeep and started to explore this wild and diverse region. What they saw delighted and captivated them.

In a letter to his friend, Major Jack Finnegan, of the Royal Army Medical Corps (RAMC) at Geneifa, he wrote:

"In this land of Biblical enchantment, I feel translated to the seventh heaven. The air, though bitterly cold, is dry and stimulating and I have never felt better in my life. The solitude and loneliness give an air of unreality and absurdity to this business of killing. Up here time has stood still and the past is with the present. Why, only yesterday, in a village called Ma'Lulah old Bob Melot and I met peasants – simple and loveable – who spoke Aramaic, the language of Jesus. Melot is multilingual and understands most of these people and they certainly are a mixture. Strange how purifying and contemplative a ten thousand foot mountain can make one – even an old buccaneer like myself!"

In the earthiness of simple peasants with their sheep and goat herds and the patriarchal atmosphere of the high mountains it is easy to understand the soul-cry of this rugged soldier, so recently involved in the horrors of war. Peace and tranquillity were a rare experience for him and his spirit was quickened and sublimated.

On clear nights there was no escape from the awesome immensity of the heavens and no doubt he heard the voice, remote and mysterious, whispering across the aeons: "I am, always was, and ever shall be" and wondered about the world he had left, swamped in a deluge of hate, cruelty and fear.

This world of ours has its nights and not a few of them, as the Saintly Bernard observed. But still, if it were not for the nights, we would not see the stars.

Skiing Paddy mastered in two weeks and having settled in eighty of his men he returned to Kabrit on orders from GHQ. Two days later he was summoned to Cairo and informed that the Caucasian "Show" was off and he was now to assemble his men at Az-Zib, a small village in northern Palestine, hard by the Syrian border. There they were to prepare for island assault operations.

Cliff-scaling and route-marching were to have first priority and afterwards they were to practise beach-landing from light assault craft. It was to be a crash course and they were relying on Paddy to see it through properly.

A week later when all his troopers had been recalled to base, Paddy summoned them to a mass-meeting. He told them that there had been a change of plan; that now they were to be transferred to Az-Zib where they would receive special training as 'assault troops'. The military police in Cairo would probably have said that they needed no such training, judging by their experience of them, but this was one commanding officer who was very unlikely to canvas their views.

Among the veterans of the SAS there were few complaints, but after a few weeks of 20-30 mile route marches, carried out in harsh, hilly countryside, either under a blistering sun, or in the freezing cold at night – sometimes in a combination of both – some of the new men began to wilt under the strain. It was but natural. The spirit was willing but the flesh was weak.

But from their commanding officer, instead of sympathy, they received marching orders – back to the units from which they had come. It seemed harsh and unfair to men who had the guts in the first place to volunteer for a cloak-and-dagger outfit such as the SAS. Some of his officers told him so, privately, but Paddy explained that he had not got the time to coddle weaklings; that he was looking for supermen and had to find them in the shortest possible time.

Nevertheless, the criticisms passed to him did sink in and he decided that he would call the latest recruits together and explain the reason for the exceptionally hard regimen which he was set upon being followed.

"Gentlemen," he declared to them, "I suppose most of you feel that I am overdoing this square-bashing business and that the demands which I am making upon you are both unreasonable and senseless. At first sight it would seem to be so but perhaps if I illustrate from my experience as a rugby player, you will understand me better.

"Before the war, I played for Ireland and also for the British Lions. One would have thought that from the backslapping and flattery which my team mates and I were accorded that we were supermen, and I confess that for a time I deluded myself into thinking that perhaps indeed we were. We were lusty, well-fed young lads, mostly from well-to-do families who trained for an hour on Wednesday afternoons and played on Saturdays.

"Then, on a visit to Liverpool I was taken to a Rugby League match between Warrington and Wigan. It was the surprise of my life. Here were two professional teams demonstrating how rugby *should* be played and either one of them could have licked any one of our International sides and even the Lions themselves. The strength, speed, stamina, cunning and controlled ferocity which I saw astonished and bewildered me. How did they do it? What was the secret of such brilliance?

"Later, I was introduced to the Warrington coach and I asked him.

"He started by saying that a player must really get fit; fit enough to jog-trot for an hour and a half. Then he must be taught the finer points of the game, thoroughly. On top of this the player has to strengthen his body by weightlifting and a course of set exercises. All of these, the trainer concluded, were equally important to ensure success.

"So here it was. Fitness, physical strength and a sure knowledge of rugby craft had made these professionals what they were.

"It is the same with Air Commandos except that in place of rugby craft, you substitute weapon drill and field-craft.

"In the last analysis, it is better for those who do not reach our standards to be rejected, because those standards are essential to carry out the dangerous operations which we shall be called upon to undertake. It is by attaining those standards that you shall have a better chance of surviving the war."

After this, the number of rejections was reduced and the hardships of training were more cheerfully accepted, and when the ground-work was finished they took to the boats – light landing craft as they were called – and tackled the rocky coastland by night and by day, in all kinds of weather. Then they were transferred to the sweltering heat of Suez and embarked on the *Ulster Monarch*, an ex-cross-channel steamer that had plied between Belfast and Liverpool before the war.

The assault craft training was intensified and for five weeks they roamed the gulfs of Suez and Aquaba and staged mock attacks on the treacherous and desolate coastland of the Sinai peninsula, that very forbidding wilderness where God spoke to Moses and handed down to him the Ten Commandments.

Jack Sillito, who won his Military Medal for trekking 180 miles across the Libyan desert without food or water to rejoin his unit after he had been left behind in an ambush, recalls this period of training very vividly. Conditions were similar to living one's life in an oven. The heat was unbearable. Of his Commanding Officer, he has this to say:

"In the desert fighting, he was a born leader; there is no question about that. He led from the front, that is the main thing and whatever he asked you to do he could do or had done it himself.

That was why he commanded respect. He was truly worshipped by the men.

He didn't like bad language and would not tolerate it in his presence; he did not like women and was very uncomfortable with them. He was a quiet man – very gentle and withdrawn and shy of company. But when he was in the mess and had a drink or two, he became very boisterous indeed.

He was a strict disciplinarian. If you did anything seriously wrong there was no question of seven days CB[1]. You went straight back to your unit. The disgrace lay in being kicked out of the Special Air Service. Several men were punished in this way. It was a thing he was reluctant to do. A man might just not come up to his standards in physical endurance or have the willpower to carry on. His nerve might even fail him. In any of these circumstances he would be returned to his unit without anything prejudicial being recorded against him. But it was otherwise if he had misbehaved.

When training in the Red Sea, we were at first confined to the ship, except when mock raiding. This went on for a few days until Paddy decided that the confinement was bad for us and that we should have a route march. I don't know how far we marched. It must have been six miles out and six miles back at as quick a pace as we could go, in a temperature of 110 degrees. When we got back to the quayside, I halted the men and pulled them to attention. One man moved and Paddy was on him like a ton of bricks. That was when he appeared to be a bit unfair. But this was the discipline he was demanding and he insisted on having it."

It was a discipline and Spartan training that was to return them to their base the toughest and fittest regiment in the British Army and, although they did not know it, the call to action was at hand.

---

1 Confined to barracks.

CHAPTER 12

Spearhead

In the late Spring of 1943 the German and Italian High Commands knew that the Allies were going to invade Sicily, and the Allied High Command knew that they knew but there was nothing much that anyone could do about it, short of calling off the invasion for an indeterminate period. This the Russians would have regarded as a base betrayal, a stab in the back when they were fighting for their very existence – and few could have quarrelled with them for taking such a line.

But General Eisenhower was calling off nothing. Everything had been worked out with exceptional thoroughness and he was about to trigger the first large scale assault upon the Axis fortress of Europe. He had carried out, successfully, a seaborne landing in North Africa. This had not involved the American First Army in any massive combat but the subsequent fighting with the battle-seasoned Germans had given the General advance warning of what he could expect in Europe. Even the Italians, whose fighting qualities he had so often heard disparaged, had battled with singular courage and determination in a campaign which they were doomed to lose because of the early drubbing they and the Afrika Korps had taken from the Eighth Army.

The British had never forgotten the debacle of Gallipoli in the First World War and minor incursions such as Narvik and Dieppe in the current one had been less than encouraging. They had, however, noted the success of the German glider and parachute assault on Crete and had been training the same kind of striking force for several months.

The result to be achieved by using such units, while vital, was limited and the High Command decided sensibly that sky-troops could be best used as guerrilla forces operating behind the enemy's fixed coastal defences and harassing the mobile reserves which Field-Marshal Kesselring had concentrated near the suspected invasion points.

The conquest of Sicily was going to be no easy task, for Intelligence reports indicated that the island was engirdled with heavy batteries in steel and concrete emplacements. The RAF had been pounding this fortress ring for days with little visible effect and it seemed that the Allies would now have to take a chance with a mighty naval bombardment and risk losing quite a number of valuable ships.

The senior officer in General Montgomery's Staff remembered the Special Air Service, now training and regrouping in Palestine. A few weeks earlier in an after-dinner speech at GHQ, Major-General Laycock had said this about them:

> "I suppose, by and large, if I was asked to say which of the Commando Units that served under my command has been the most successful I should say that the record of the SAS under Lieutenant Colonel David Stirling in Libya was the best of all.
>
> For initiative and resource, for endurance, for faultless training and fearless action which culminated so often in grievous loss to the Germans of valuable men and material, I would put them second to none."

And now he inquired tentatively of his chief:

> "What's wrong with using these élite troops to spearhead the main invasion forces by landing under cover of darkness and silencing the coastal guns at the areas already selected by you and General Eisenhower?"
>
> "Nothing at all!" came the crisp reply. "An excellent idea."

And so Paddy Mayne, now the Commanding Officer of the 1st SAS Regiment, was ordered to embark with his troops on 6 July 1943 and sail aboard the Irish cross-channel steamer, the *Ulster Monarch*, to the island of Sicily.

Among the crew were many old friends from his native Ulster and despite the grimness of the task ahead Paddy found time to indulge in his now characteristic drinking and singing sessions with his men, and these other chums.

Ahead of his ship minesweepers cleared a channel and on either side two British destroyers guarded against submarine attacks.

For security reasons the regiment was officially named the Special Raiding Squadron (SRS), but no change of title could ever alter the *esprit de corps* of this quixotic band of daredevils.

Their giant Irish leader reflected the spirit magnificently. Throughout the voyage he stayed in jovial mood. A new thrill of elation filled his massive frame at the thought of action, and he was supremely optimistic about the plan.

To his friend, Lieutenant St John Coates (later Lieutenant Commander) he confided his pleasure in having so many Southern Irishmen under his command as well as Ulstermen and expressed great satisfaction that their small but virile company, despite its neutrality, was truly playing its part in numerous affairs that were shaping the destiny of mankind.

As they left the African coast, which they had been hugging for five days, and crossed the narrow straits beyond Tunis, he and his Company Commanders knew that they were heading for Capo Murro di Porco, a point on the south-east coast of Sicily where four big coastal guns pointed menacingly out to sea.

Paddy's orders were clear cut: put these guns out of action and pave the way for the waves of invading troops due to come an hour or two later. Then he was to use his discretion as to other objectives. The High Command of the Eighth Army was always very sanguine of Mayne's use of his discretion.

In this exercise Paddy and the other assault leaders were greatly assisted by the Copps (or more properly, the Combined Operations Pilotage Parties, as they were officially designated), who under the command of Lieutenant Commander Nigel Willmott, had been landing from submarines and surveying the invasion coastline for months. The information which they brought back saved thousands of lives.

Every shore had its natural perils: inshore rocks, sandbars and soft beaches upon which nothing mechanical can travel. Bad enough to have to run the gauntlet of shore batteries, but for landing craft to run aground on off-reefs or shoals and be sitting ducks for the 15 inch shells that would surely come was an unthinkable prospect.

And so it came about that, thanks to these intrepid men, every nook and corner and natural hazard was known to the Allied Command long before the planned assault and all commanders were supplied with detailed charts.

Now under a soft Mediterranean night sky, the warm zephyr seemed to augur well for a safe approach. Then, as if it were an omen, the stars were blotted out, the soft breeze freshened into a whining gale and the sea, which a moment ago seemed like a vast and silky violet ribbon, was transformed into a raging, unfriendly maelstrom.

Paddy, leaning on the deck rail, set his jaw. He remembered so vividly how a similar, sudden storm had wrecked the very first parachute raid in the desert. He recalled, too, the faces of the good friends he had lost that night because no one had given the order to abandon the raid.

Doubts nagged at his mind. Would his first operation as Commanding Officer on the new front be doomed before a single shot was fired? The whole operation was now nearly an hour behind schedule. It was 3.20 am, and daylight would soon be upon them. Lion-hearted though he was, Paddy's optimism was fading with every lurch of the ship. He turned to his Company Commanders, but was unable to answer the questions in their eyes.

"If this weather keeps up," he groaned, "I'm afraid the little boats won't be able to live in the water."

He was referring to the assault craft known as LCAs.

The coastline came into view. Even as Paddy gave the order to go the *Ulster Monarch* swayed, pitched and bucketed so much that it became almost impossible for his men to clamber into the small boats which were to take them to the shore. One trooper attempted to climb in, but the small boat rolled perilously. He missed his footing and fell into the sea; others were being violently sick over the side, some over themselves. Anything less like an invasion attempt was hard to imagine. No one, particularly the seasick soldiers, seriously believed that the job was really 'on'.

But, once inside the lee of the Sicilian coast, the water almost miraculously began to calm and Paddy could see the ghostly outline of the steep cliffs that had to be scaled before he and his men could get at the guns. Undeterred by the stormy weather, the RAF had been softening up the artillery positions by bombing and strafing. That part of the operation had gone well. But something had gone

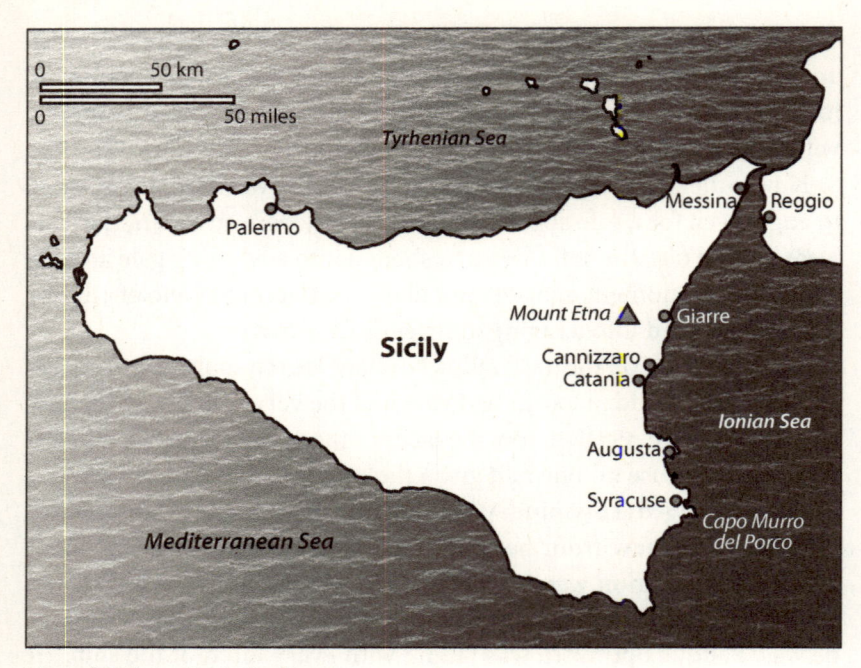

Map of Sicily and principal towns.

seriously wrong with the next part. An air armada of a hundred gliders containing troops and jeeps were supposed to have timed their landings to coincide with the arrival of Paddy's force at Capo Murro di Porco. But most of the gliders had been cast off by the towing planes about forty miles short of their target and the gale had forced others to drift hopelessly off course.

It was a pitiful sight to witness. The assault craft, with Paddy and his hand-picked crew in the leading one, sped for the shore. From all around came cries for help from survivors who were clinging to the wreckage of their crashed and crippled gliders. Should he stop to pick up the drowning and wounded glider troops? Or press on?

Paddy kept his eyes firmly fixed on the objective ahead, now looming clear and tempting. There was no possible switch. He had to drive forward if there was to be no hitch in the tight schedule, which was becoming more acute because of the unexpected delay. There was no question of stopping.

"It was a terrible thing to have to do," the huge Irishman wrote to one of his friends some months later:

"But a further delay of even a few minutes would have thrown out the timing of the whole operation. The main invasion fleet following us would have been at the mercy of these coastal guns and the casualties could have been enormous."

Those who knew Paddy understood how much heart-searching that decision must have caused him, for he valued the lives of men, and would spend many an hour planning an operation in meticulous detail, striving for ways and means to avoid any unnecessary waste of life. He would have died himself a score of times rather than see one of his valiant comrades fall victim needlessly to enemy fire.

Just now in this Dantesque inferno of noisy death and destruction Paddy was straining his eyes for the Copps who were to guide him in. They had landed earlier in a rubber dingy from a submarine and soon he spotted their flash-lamp signals and set his course accordingly. The Copps, a naval officer and a rating, having fulfilled their mission were to return to the *Ulster Monarch* in one of Mayne's nine landing craft, now grounding on the shingle and dropping their ramps.

In a matter of seconds, the SAS men were ashore, safe and well for the time being and truly relieved at having their feet on *terra firma* once again.

Now, glancing up at the cliffs they had to conquer, Paddy's men realised how accurate his briefing had been. It was all just as he had shown them with the aid of scale models, almost as if every man had been there before. One who thought so was Sergeant Bob Bennett, square-jawed courageous parachutist, who had stayed by his Commanding Officer's side through a dozen hair-raising exploits, yet still survived. He tells what happened next in the curious seaborne invasion:

"We scrambled straightaway up the cliffs," he recalls, "nervously trigger-happy, gasping for breath, wondering what lay in store for us at the top. Was there going to be an all-out battle? Had Paddy bitten off too much this time? Perhaps we were all too edgy, but once at the summit one of our chaps thought he saw the figure of an enemy soldier and opened up with his carbine. But it turned out to be a statue! Tense as we were, we couldn't suppress a chuckle.

They were the only shots fired. The RAF had done such a good job on the bombardment of the coastal defences that the Italians manning the guns had fled underground. Paddy shouted an order to the engineer section to lay the charges on the coastal guns to put them out of action. I took my troops down to the shelters to bring the enemy soldiers up. When we got down to the tunnels beneath the guns, I could hardly believe my eyes.

The Italians were cowering in a corner, praying for deliverance. Some were crying, and fell to their knees – others were grovelling in sheer terror and fright. They were like helpless children, shocked into submission by a terrific non-stop bombardment from the air, which must have lasted for hours. One could feel sorry for them, but this was no time for sentiment. I took what I wanted from them. They willingly unstrapped their watches with trembling hands and gave them to us. Others fumbled for bundles of grubby lira notes which they pressed into our hands. All they wanted was to be allowed to live and get back to their mommas, regardless of the cost or the humiliation."

In the desert many of them had been cowardly and cruel and the British troops reserved for them a special hate but Paddy was always chivalrous to a beaten foe. He also had a sincere respect for those brave Italians whom he had met elsewhere in combat. These cringing wretches he knew to be inferior garrison troops, many of them more than middle-aged. They had never wanted to be soldiers at all. Il Duce, Benito Mussolini, had forcibly recruited most of them for his grandiose and deluded adventures, but he had not the power to give them courage or the will to kill.

It was all right for the jack-booted professional Fascists to paint on house gables and public buildings the martial injunctions: "*Credere!*" "*Obbedire!*" "*Combattere!*" (Believe! Obey! Fight!), and reasonably expect credulity and obedience from a brow-beaten, bewildered people, but to tell them to fight was absurd. Fight for what?

The ordinary soldiers had only known penury, near-starvation, insanitary barracks and billets, and generally a surfeit of squalor and dirt. Civilians were even worse off on this Italian island. It was not surprising that their morale, along with that of the armed forces, was at rock bottom. Despondency and despair were, like the desert flies, everywhere.

At the first streak of dawn an enemy battery further inland opened up fire, and Paddy was alarmed to see that the gunners were firing not at the lately-landed invaders but out to sea. Fountains of water were rising dangerously close to several large troopships that had approached the coast.

Immediately, he rushed his men across country to this concrete emplacement and after a brief, brisk engagement the artillery was silenced.

Now Paddy led his force off in the direction of Syracuse to meet the British Fifth Division, which HQ had informed him would be on the coast road. En route, they attacked snipers and overran some garrisoned farms where they were able to rescue airborne troops who had been injured and captured when landing. Innumerable anti-aircraft guns and machine-guns were blasted to pieces.

By eventide, all enemy resistance in the region had been crushed and the weary SAS men lay down by the roadside and went to sleep.

Paddy was not so lucky. He had collected 500 prisoners-of-war on his journey and now as they squatted around, their large brown eyes followed him everywhere, searching his own with hungry self-pity. It was clear that they feared for their lives.

Paddy was dog-tired himself and wanted a bottle of Chianti before turning in, but he felt horribly self-conscious before this sea of roving orbs. Wearily he turned to Sergeant Bob Bennett and remarked in a polite, restrained voice:

"I'm fed up with this lot, Bob. Take them away and plonk them somewhere. They're harmless enough, and we've not got enough rations for them anyway."

Sergeant Bennett dutifully herded them together and led them into a field where he indicated by signs that they were to sit or lie down and remain there.

Some of them must have known about the atrocities of their German SS comrades – and expected a similar sort here. For an unearthly wailing arose and rent the night sky. Nothing that the Sergeant could do by way of gestures seemed to help. So he took to his heels and left them in their misery.

Next morning, the elusive Fifth British Division was discovered and Major Mayne, with obvious relief, was able to hand over both his wounded paratroopers and his prisoners.

The operation had been a cracking success and it was with a proud heart that Paddy returned with his men to the *Ulster Monarch*, now lying peacefully at anchor a few hundred yards off-shore. The blistering gale of two nights ago was now an age away and the sun shone warmly as they stretched themselves on deck for a splendidly earned rest.

CHAPTER 13

Augusta

THE RETURNED HEROES of the Special Raiding Squadron (SRS) were back aboard the *Ulster Monarch*, some sun-bathing on the decks, some sea-bathing off the side, and all in one way or another enjoying life on the twelfth of July – which for many Ulstermen was a national holiday – when orders came through that they were to attack the port of Augusta, about twenty miles further up the coast from Syracuse, that very day and in broad daylight too.

It was enough to break the spirit of Job himself, but with a few good-humoured curses and grumbles the boys soon set about getting their weapons and kits prepared.

In the wardroom, Major Blair Mayne conferred with his Captains, Harry Poat and Harrison, about the forthcoming assignment. It was not going to be an easy one. Augusta had been an Italian naval base until the Italians found that the British had left them without a navy. Now, our Intelligence reports said that its defences were the best in all Sicily, with reinforced bunkers, housing fortress artillery and anti-aircraft batteries. Added to this was a vast complex of heavy and light machine-gun positions linked together by subterranean galleries. It was bound to be strongly garrisoned, and reports had indicated that German as well as Italian troops were there.

The three officers got out their maps and aerial photographs and put on their thinking caps. But all the thinking in the world could not overcome the basic fact that they were going to steam into a strongly fortified harbour in daylight, in an ordinary cross-channel steamer with only a 12-pounder gun as its total armament.

Paddy himself loved the bubbling light-heartedness which was part of the character of his regiment. In the face of death they gritted their teeth and fought like devils but when the gunfire died down the laughing and singing started. And if there was beer or wine or whisky, or anything else as uplifting to the mood, they were all for it to a man. They were lucky in their Commanding Officer, and they knew it. He shared their tastes and, while forbidding familiarity, he could easily and graciously join in the fun.

Hitler had issued a directive to his Generals in which he described the SAS men as "dangerous" and had ordered that any who were captured were to be passed over at once to the nearest Gestapo unit for slaughter. It was a left-handed compliment which these tough fighters would hardly have appreciated if they had known of it, but certainly a chance visitor to one of their wide-ranging regimental messes would not normally have recognised this happy bunch of chums as dangermen. There was nothing of the dead-pan brutishness which showed in German SS Divisions such as the Hitler Youth and the Death's Head, but in the sparkling, cheerful eyes there was a liveliness and intelligence that promised resourcefulness and even cunning in a tight corner.

Every man was trained to be self-sufficient and to be a thorough craftsman in the killer art of war. And the training never stopped, as one experience piled upon another and the memory of it was exchanged freely over camp-fire chats and drinks. Thanks to the insight of their Commander, they soon came to realise that the more they knew about their trade the better was their chance of survival in it. Paddy emphasised again and again in pep talks which he often gave that they were much better alive as efficient soldiers than as dead heroes.

Now, as he meditated on the impending assault on the naval base of Augusta, garrisoned by Germans as well as Italians, he felt helpless in the grip of a GHQ set-up which he mistrusted but did not dare to oppose. His mind went back to that crazy plan to attack Benghazi for diversionary purposes when the High Command knew that Rommel was fully aware that the SAS were concentrating in the desert hinterland for action.

"We're only flags on a map to those backroom boys in Cairo," thought Paddy, "and we're expendable if the Greater Plan requires it."

He remembered how David Stirling had laughingly described that previous stunt at the time: "Pawns on a large chessboard." David, with his romantic Celtic fatalism, had accepted that the game should be played thus. Paddy was not so sure. The defeat of the enemy was paramount but in his view no risk should be taken unless the end justified it and he was not madly enthusiastic about the ability of GHQ Blimps being able to see the end result of anything.

In Paddy's mind, they had mucked up so many things in the past that the wonder was that the British were still holding the field in this day and year of grace. Still, the rigidity of his training and his strong sense of loyalty demanded blind – or perhaps it would be better to say, half-blind – obedience to Command orders. In short, Paddy's reservations were real, but privately held.

Now, over the loud-hailer boomed the curt call to arms: "Action Stations!" Paddy and his two fellow officers went up on deck and joined their squadrons, the men of which were already bustling around their assigned landing craft.

The sea was calm and the sun was still warm. On the port side a British cruiser supported by three destroyers, hove in sight and began to signal frantically. The Captain wanted to know if the Captain of the *Ulster Monarch* had taken leave of his senses? This wasn't Southend-on-Sea on an August Bank Holiday! Back went the laconic answer:

"Am going in to land troops."

A silence followed this declaration of lunacy and then another signal came flashing over that made Major Mayne and all souls aboard the *Ulster Monarch* feel proud, intensely proud, to be British.

"In that case you will need all the support that we can give you."

Ahead, the port of Augusta began to take shape and presently the harbour installations and adjoining buildings and houses came into focus. Major Mayne, scanning the waterfront with his gaze, could at first see no sign of life. Easily identified was the citadel, and as his eyes rested on this there was a loud bang and a flash like a mirror reflecting the rays of the sun. A hundred yards out to sea a fountain of water rose and on the instant the cruiser and the three destroyers opened up fire together. The *Ulster Monarch*, which was about two miles off shore, joined in shelling with its 12-pounder.

As this symphony of gun thunder rose to its height the LCAs were lowered, and quickly they headed for the shore. Shortly afterwards the *Ulster Monarch* turned away and steamed out to sea, and, hopefully, out of range. Now the Special Raiding Squadron was on its own with a hail of machine-gun bullets beating against its armour-plated craft and kicking up the water all around. Peering through a spy-hole, Major Mayne picked out the heavy guns that were blazing away – and watched with pleasure the unavailing efforts to get these ranged down far enough to bombard his flotilla of LCAs. Then the British Navy began to get a more accurate bearing, and one by one the enemy batteries fell silent.

This session of sightless suspense was the worst soul-sapping experience for all the men inside the LCAs but under cover they had to stay, not knowing the second that they might be blasted into eternity. Even to these seasoned veterans it was an ordeal they would have gladly missed.

But now they were almost there. Five seconds! Four seconds! Three seconds! … A shudder, and a crunch, and the ramp was crashing down on the wet shingle.

"Let's go!" shouted Paddy, and he charged down the ramp and hared straight for the shelter of the sea wall, quickly followed by his squadron. The time was 7.35 pm and they had all landed safe and well; safe and well, that is, for the time being, anyway, for nobody knew what to expect next.

Then Paddy was up and over the sea wall and on his way into the town of Augusta. This is built on a spit of land joined to the mainland by a bridge. The population had fled and apart from some scattered sniping a blanket of silence had come down on the port, an eerie calm that baffled the Special Raiding Squadron, which had never expected to get this far – or even to land at all. But once they had got ashore, house-to-house fighting seemed to be inevitable.

In Rome, Benito Mussolini, whom Winston Churchill had branded as "the Fascist hyena", was boasting in a radio speech that Sicily was to be another Stalingrad and that his valiant soldiers would fight with fanatical fury to defend their Fatherland. Some did, but the vast majority were sick of Fascism and sick, sore and weary of the war and anxious to have done with it.

Many of them liked the British, and none of them liked the Germans. Their alliance with Germany was a tie-up of dictators, not one of the people. In the industrial northern Italy the workers were seething with discontent and were violently anti-Fascist. Many were Communists, with affiliations with the USSR and the hour in which to strike a blow for their own ideals was fast approaching.

When Hitler's Germany was winning all along the line in 1940, Mussolini had remarked to his son-in-law, Count Ciano: "It is humiliating to remain with our hands folded while others write history."

Italy was now writing history, but it was not a history that Mussolini, or his companions, would have wished. It was a tale of ignominy and treachery that would remain with her for many years to come.

What had happened in Augusta? Where were those Italian coastal divisions and the German gunners? And why had the really big guns never come into play? Only one battery of coastal defence artillery on the west of the town had opened up, and from the north of the peninsula, where Mayne knew from Intelligence that many of the big guns were sited, only machine-gun fire had come. Now all this had been silenced and only the snipers remained. Soon they would be winkled out and the town would be entirely in the hands of the SAS. Some Stalingrad!

And here the element of mystery enters into the story, for three days earlier the German naval unit, which had been operating "E" boats from the harbour, had suddenly packed up and gone north. The German High Command was unaware of this proceeding and so was the local Italian Commander, Admiral Leonardi, who was afterwards to be condemned to death, *in absentia*, for cowardice.

It was a mystery that was never solved but its effect on the Italians was highly demoralising and shortly afterwards they began blowing up perfectly sound fixed defence and gun positions. Only a few gun crews decided to fight it out, and their resolution wavered and broke when the British warships opened up and found the correct range.

Lucky indeed were the SRS that all this happened for they had been dispatched on a collision course that spelt another Dieppe and annihilation.

Mustering his men together and ignoring the temptation to look his latest gift horse in the mouth, Major Mayne pressed on into the town square and sent forward patrols to seize the bridge leading to the mainland. When this had been done, and it was reported back to him that the enemy was heavily concentrated beyond the bridge, supported by 4 inch mortars, heavy machine guns and three light tanks, he decided to consolidate his gains and hold the town and harbour against any possible counter-attack. To do this he sent up a troop with mortars and machine-guns to the bridge and ordered them to dig in and set up covering strong points.

It was near nightfall and he called his troop commanders and their sergeants together in the apartment quarters he had taken over. They wondered what for, at this stage of operations, for now all was quiet and their immediate objective had been gained.

"Gentlemen!" he said, "Gentlemen! I have summoned you here to give you what you will take if I don't, a licence to loot. But in doing so I am attaching one condition, and that is, that whatever you do you do it in two hours. Anybody who flouts this order will be punished, and punished severely at that! Understand?"

They understood all right, but were astonished at what he had said. All of them knew that their Commanding Officer was highly unorthodox but they didn't think he would be so rash as to give his licence for looting. It could mean a court martial for him and ruination.

Sergeant Bob Bennett asked permission to speak to him privately and the others withdrew from the room.

"Well, sergeant", inquired Paddy, "What can I do for you?"

"It's about the lads up front, sir," replied Bennett, "What about them? Are they to get nothing?"

Paddy grinned, Bob Bennett was a good soldier and a good fellow, the life and soul of any party, the sing-song specialist. It was typical of him that his first thoughts would be about his comrades up front. He got the answer.

"You had better shop for them, Bob!"

And Sergeant Bennett was gone, and shortly afterwards was passing on the oddest message that he had ever delivered in his whole career in the army to men who were already doing secretly what the Commanding Officer was now permitting. In a sense, it was a half-disappointment for them to find that loot was now theirs as of right. As Oscar Wilde had put it:

"I love taking Bovril in secret. It seems almost like a vice."

To Major Mayne there was no moral self-reproach. These brave men had been pitchforked into a suicidal operation a few hours earlier. If the expected resistance had occurred most of them would have been killed or wounded. Some would have been maimed for life, others blinded. It had been no bed of roses out here for any of them and he could not see why they shouldn't have a few hours of current pleasure and some little knick-knacks to take home to their loved-ones, if ever they did get home from this damned war.

In any case, there was little they could loot in a bomb-shattered Sicilian port, where poverty had dwelt so long even in the days of peace.

One thing there was plenty of, and that was wine and, for one and all, Paddy hoped that this would ease the tension and lift their spirits and warm their hearts on this bitterly cold night. It had to be laugh and be merry tonight, for tomorrow one might die, or even worse, be crippled forever.

As darkness fell, the SRS began to beat it up in style and the bars were packed to overflowing. Some were to be seen wearing top-hats and tailcoats; others had sombreros and coloured shawls. In the middle of one street a jolly, high-spirited trooper was hammering away at the keys of a piano, with a discordant group of harlequins around him.

This piano was to find its way to the *Ulster Monarch*, and be presented to the Captain with the compliments of the SRS.

Major Mayne found himself a Royal Engineers sergeant and together they went off to the bank. What they got there, nobody ever knew.

The carousal roared on all through the night, but Paddy was satisfied with just a few glasses of wine and fairly soon, hopelessly tired, rolled into bed. Next morning he woke up to find the bay packed with ships and the town chock-full of troops. A messenger informed him that an officer of the Army Provost Marshal's Department wished to see him. A few minutes later this worthy was shown into the apartment and he came to the point immediately.

"Major Mayne, I observe that there has been considerable pilfering by your men in this area and I would like to have your explanation before submitting my report. Do I make myself clear?"

"You certainly do!" snapped Mayne, a cold glint showing in those grey-blue eyes of his.

To those who knew him the red-for-danger signs were being switched on, but the stuffy type who confronted him saw nothing. The next moment he was seized by the scruff of the neck and swiftly and unceremoniously bundled through the door.

"Get out, you mongrel dog!" roared Paddy, "If you don't want your stupid neck broken!"

Sergeant Bennett, who had ushered the worthy into his CO's room and heard all that had taken place, now stepped forward and steadied the shaking Captain, on whose face was riveted an expression of sheer horror. Sandhurst Academy for the training of officers and gentlemen had not prepared him for this.

"It's all right, sir!" said the sergeant. "The CO's a bit overwrought. Things have not been easy for him or any of us lately."

It was no good. The Captain pulled himself together and strode out of the house into the morning's sunshine, muttering something about making "that savage pay dearly for this".

At the APM's Headquarters in Tunisia somebody must have decided that Major Blair Mayne was indispensable, for nothing further was heard of the affair.

No 3 Troop of the SRS, which had been having a prolonged gun-battle with the enemy all night and morning, was relieved and replaced by an armoured battalion supported by a heavy artillery unit.

The regiment had now fulfilled its task and was ordered to embark on British and Greek destroyers which were lying in the harbour. Motor boats ferried out, loaded down as they were with their booty.

Hardly had they got aboard when they were attacked by four German bombers and the destroyer commanders decided that Augusta, for the time being, was not the most salubrious place to be. Accordingly they all steamed off down the coast at full speed for Syracuse. When they got there the SRS was transferred to its floating base, the *Ulster Monarch*. The spoils of war went with them and soon the bartering started with the Royal and Merchant Navy men aboard. It was like an Arabian bazaar with all the shawls and silks laid out on the decks and the noisy chatter of buyers and sellers filling the air. For the Royal Navy boys it was all up hill, as their paltry pay was very much less than that of the merchant-men, and this for a time created some bad feeling. The wine however acted as a solvent for brittle rancour and the SRS troopers distributed it free of charge.

In the end everyone was happy and this was how Paddy Mayne wanted it.

On 14 July hangovers were quickly washed away in the warm, clear blue Mediterranean and the men splashed around like a happy bunch of sand boys on Brighton beach. Amongst them, equally exuberant, was their Commanding Officer.

Next day, the idyll was shattered as news whizzed around that Major Mayne had been summoned to HMS *Beatrix* on a matter of extreme urgency. Rumour had it that the SRS was to be flung in against the crack Hermann Goering Division, which was blocking the advance of the Eighth Army at the town of Catania ahead.

Aboard the *Beatrix* a high-powered conference was going on between Major Mayne and two Commando leaders on one side and three Staff Officers representing General Montgomery on the other. The rumour was right, and the proposed plan was to send in the Commandos to the north of Catania to form a beach-head and then the SRS was to pass through them and fight its way down the coast and attack the Germans' rear.

It was a good plan in many ways and Paddy would have been the first to admit it, but he also knew that there were 230,000 Italian and 40,000 German troops in Sicily, easily re-inforceable, and his own rear and his landward flank would be wide open.

It would certainly provide a magnificent final exit for the SRS which might well live in the memories of men, alongside the historic charge of the Light Brigade and other such splendid military epics, but as the French General exclaimed on that occasion: "C'est magnifique, mais ce n'est pas la guerre." ("It is magnificent, but it is not war.")

The time was now 4.30 pm and the pros and cons were being constantly paraded, as they had been for the past two hours, and Paddy was beginning to get bored. He was a combat warrior, not a strategist, and through his mind came flooding back the memorable lines which he had learned as a boy at Regent House School in his native Newtownards:

"Theirs not to reason why.
Theirs but to do and die."

Across his thoughts came the steady hum of well-bred voices in the torpid heat of the late afternoon. His reflection was: "Whatever these stuffy wallahs decide. I shall have to carry through – while they pack their bags and fly off back to Tunisia. Kismet! What odds! I cannot live forever."

Now his opinion was being sought on certain details and he roused himself and joined the discussion. It seemed that the Big Three had decided that the plan was sound and were now getting down to operational items.

"The boys won't like it when I break the news to them," he mused, "but Hell! there's a war on, and that's what we're here for, anyway."

A sudden knock on the door, and a messenger was shown in. He was from Signals, and handed a slip of paper to one of the Staff Officers who read it hurriedly and then addressed himself to the others.

"It's off, gentlemen! The situation at Catania has improved and a break-through is expected at any time."

Paddy felt like shouting "Three cheers!" but maintained his mask of impassivity as he took his leave and hurried off on the tender that was waiting to take him back to the *Ulster Monarch*. Now he knew what a death-cell reprieve meant, and how the condemned must feel on such an occasion.

Back aboard his base ship his news swiftly got around and the old rum ration got a knocking. As usual, these moments of jubilation were short-lived and that night they were bombed again. Sleep was denied them as the terrific din of countering AA gunfire blasted the night skies. The next night and the next, encore performances were laid on by the tensed-up Germans and Paddy decided that it was time to go ashore and find a more secure shelter. Sooner or later, they were bound to cop it out there on that familiar target in the harbour.

So, as darkness fell, they pitched their tents in a peach orchard on high ground overlooking the port. Again the Luftwaffe visitors came as before. It was like a milkman's round, 10.00 pm and 4.00 pm on the dot. And they must have known something, for the peach orchard had a near miss.

The following morning Paddy and co moved to another camp further away from Syracuse. Then came the news that the Eighth Army had won the battle of Primasole Bridge and the SRS was ordered to entrain for Cannizzaro, north of Catania and not far from that quiet little mound called Mount Etna.

On the 20 July, word came through to Major Mayne that he had been awarded a Bar to his DSO for his part in the initial landing at Capo Murro di Porco and the capture of Augusta; that his fellow officers and friends, Harry Poat and Wiseman had both won Military Crosses, and that his boys had collected seven Military Medals between them.

This was, indeed, timely recognition and very heartening news. So they were not just ciphers, after all, to the backroom boys at GHQ. To Paddy, gongs meant little, he had seen too many deeds of valour pass unrecognised and he knew in his heart that the greatest credit was due to the average, unspectacular infantryman who bore the brunt of all the big, set battles. These were the spine of the army, but their numbers clothed them in anonymity.

Still, they would be pleased back in Newtownards, and he could see his sisters, Babs and Frances, walking down the High Street, seven foot tall.

The camp in Cannizzaro was a pleasant contrast to the arid emptiness of the desert. Here were people; here were trees and shrubs and a great variety of living things. And, above all, they were unplagued by flies.

Paddy knew well that he could never tell the hour when the High Command would call upon them for further action. So he took full advantage of the present restful atmosphere and thoroughly relaxed. To his brother, Duggie, serving in the RAF as a pilot, and to all other members of his family he buzzed off letters, enjoining everyone to reply as soon as possible with the fullest news of home.

He, like all his men, was lonely, and sometimes he was very, very lonely. Three years had passed since he had seen his family and it was a long time in the life of a young man of twenty-nine years of age. And with Blair Mayne his family came first, especially his mother. Shy, solitary and melancholy when not with his drinking companions, he suffered deeply through being separated from his loved ones.

All his life he had been afraid of women (truly, his only fear). Perhaps it was his massiveness that gave him this strange, self-conscious complex, a feeling of ungainliness and gaucherie in their company. But it was there, and during his university days he was always to be found lurking in the background with men, at dances or any other social functions which he was obliged to attend.

Why he should have felt this way about himself, nobody knew, for nature had endowed him with a magnificent physique and a fine head and many a pretty girl's heart went a-flutter when she saw him striding into a dance hall or crowded drawing-room. He was so easily recognised as a man amongst men and, on top of this, he had a lively brain and outstanding athletic prowess.

In Ireland, a rugby international is regarded as something of a hero, and when he is a boxing champion as well there can be no barrier to the flood-tide of flattery which he gets. With Blair Mayne, the laurels of sport rested lightly on his brow and a night out in jolly company meant more to him than all the adulation of sycophants. To his law studies he gave a desultory interest. Just enough to carry him through.

Now events over which he had no control had revealed the man's inner genius. Here was a natural born guerrilla leader, maybe the best the British Army had ever possessed and every soldier in his regiment knew and backed it with his heart.

Reports of the progress of the Eighth British and the Seventh American Armies reached the camp daily and they were not altogether indicative of the blitzkrieg promised by General Montgomery after they had successfully landed. German armies would never allow themselves to be booted around as a rabble. The iron discipline and formidable military tradition would not permit it and Montgomery was foolhardy in his boasting.

On 14 July, Mussolini, writing in his diary about the struggle for Sicily then taking place, was more foresighted and analytical in his outlook. He wrote:

> "At four days remove from the enemy landing in Sicily I consider the situation exceedingly delicate and disquieting though not yet wholly jeopardised. We must make a short analysis of the situation and decide what must and should be done. The situation is critical –
> a) Because after the landing, penetration in depth took place with enormous rapidity;
> b) Because the enemy possesses a crushing air superiority;
> c) *Because he possesses trained and special services troops (parachutists and airborne troops);*
> d) Because he has almost unopposed command of the sea;
> e) Because his Staff are showing decision and elasticity in their conduct of the campaign."

Mussolini went on to note that the reasons for the rapid fall of Syracuse and Augusta must be inquired into with thoroughness so that a proper evaluation of the prospects of defending the approaches to the Straits of Messina could be made. He then listed a litany of doubts and misgivings about the war in general. How different were his private thoughts from his radio heroics!

While he was writing, Messina and Reggio, on either side of the Straits, were being systematically razed to the ground by the Allied bombers and the morale of the Sicilian population was deteriorating rapidly. All the vainglorious propaganda that Il Duce pumped into the local press was unavailing. The starved and wretched folk had heard it all before and it meant as much to them as obscene scribblings on a public lavatory wall.

Everywhere the atmosphere of defeat and despair pervaded. And yet, despite this, the Germans continued to resist with exceptional valour. Their High Command had spotted the danger of the twin thrusts then being made by the 50th and 51st Highland Divisions of the Eighth Army on the north-eastern sector of the island and had quickly moved its crack divisions from Western Sicily to meet the threat to Catania and the network of airfields on the Catanian Plain. Possession of the latter would enable the Allied air force to hammer the enemy ground forces and disrupt their communications in the rear, and also the bombers could be effectively screened by fighter planes. The 51st's job was to turn the enemy's flanks and thus enable the 50th to drive on up the coast to Messina.

At Catania, the 50th had run up against a stone wall in the shape of German Colonel Wilhelm Schmatz and his brigade of shock troops, including the famed Hermann Goering Division, and parachutists. Advance against such formidable fighting men was well nigh impossible and it was not until 3 August, when they were ordered to withdraw slowly to newly prepared strongholds north of Catania, that the Eighth Army was able to occupy Catania.

On the other side of the island the Seventh American Army was progressing favourably and on 22 July, Palermo, on the north coast, was taken. On 16 August, after a gruelling struggle, Messina was reached and the conquest of Sicily was complete.

The German Army, however, had carried out a masterly withdrawal and was now re-organising across the Straits in Calabria on the Italian mainland.

Partly because of the Royal Navy's dislike of entering narrow waters, and partly because of poor finishing by the Eighth Army, the enemy had been allowed to escape and now the penalty had to be paid by way of a long, bitterly-fought Italian campaign that was to exact a heavy toll from both sides.

CHAPTER 14

Bon Viaggio!

Away from the bloody battlefields of international war, in the corridors of power another battle was raging – one of recrimination, which would end in civil war.

On 24 July 1943, the Grand Fascist Council met in Rome and Il Duce, Signor Benito Mussolini, was very much on the carpet, lamely trying to explain his part in his country's misfortunes. Marshal Badoglio and the dictator's own son-in-law, Count Ciano, were in the forefront of his accusers and the outcome was public denunciation of Il Duce and, later, his arrest.

So, after twenty-three years, the tyrant of the New Italy had crashed, and everywhere throughout the land there was great jubilation and a genuine clamouring for peace. Partisan bands, who had been fighting underground for years, now emerged into daylight and, as they did, sympathisers rallied around and their numbers surged upwards.

For the Allied Armies there was no halt. The invasion of Europe was here – and it must drive onward until the Nazi hordes had been destroyed! The chances of a speedy victory were bleak, but in Russia, anyway, the tide had turned since the dedicated defenders of Stalingrad had thrown their invaders back in utter defeat on 2 February 1943. That was now nearly six months ago and though, to few, was the ultimate outcome in any doubt, much blood-letting was still to come before the half-mad Adolf Hitler cried "Enough!" and took his own life in the Berlin Chancellery bunker two years later.

Resting under canvas at Cannizzaro, Paddy Mayne waited and

longed for the next call to action. But it was not until 1 September that he and his squadron found themselves clambering aboard two LCIs (Landing Craft Infantry vessels) again at Catania bound for Bagnara, on the Italian west coast, twenty-five miles beyond the Straits of Messina. These fairly large raider vessels, which carried ack-ack and other artillery and had twin ramps on either side of the bows, afforded reasonable shelter for the troops aboard.

The hour of departure was 2.00 pm, and four hours later they put into Riposto for the night.

The following morning one of the crafts was unable to leave because a propeller had fouled a cable and the other took on her complement. Then more trouble happened, and in the end one LCI and five LCAs sailed off late in the evening of 3 September.

At 4.00 am the next morning, in the grey shadows of approaching dawn, Major Paddy Mayne and his SRS invaders swept on to the beaches of Bagnara, guns at the ready and eyes on the alert for the enemy. They had not long to wait, and soon all troopers were engaged in heavy gunfire with the defenders in different parts of the town.

The official objective given to Major Mayne was "to capture, occupy and hold Bagnara, Calabria, Italy," and he was granted 243 men of all ranks to carry out the operation. It was, as usual, a tall order, but Paddy was used to such orders and accepted them cheerfully. Now that he was on the job he was resolved to do it with his usual ruthless determination. First, he had to set up a headquarters, and this he did in a terrace house in the town centre – after personally clearing out a nest of enemy machine-gunners who were quartered there.

North of the town, No 1 Troop straddled the main highway in order to hold back any reinforcements that came that way, and at the rear of the town a section fixed a mortar in a dried-up river bed. No 3 Troop moved through the streets and took up a position on the southern outskirts.

In seven hours the SRS had firmly established itself in a town that had been garrisoned by a German Grenadier regiment, supported by Italians and artillery and sapper units. The fight for final possession was far from over but Paddy was confident that his men would make it, despite the heavy mortar and machine-gun fire which they were almost everywhere encountering.

Here, unlike the townsfolk in Sicily, the local inhabitants stayed their

Southern Italy in 1943.

ground and even walked the streets while the fighting raged all around. It was a bizarre sight, the black-veiled women of the medieval town, gliding along with pitchers on their heads while their ragged mensfolk lounged around, doing nothing. Some of the latter spoke bits of English after a fashion (probably they had been sailors) and were quick to greet the *Inglesi* with smiles and words of encouragement. It seemed that they too, like their Sicilian neighbours, desperately wanted to end this senseless war into which they had been flung against their wishes.

Paddy believed them to be sincere and truthful in this. They were a poverty-stricken, still primitive people whom the modern world seemed to have somehow passed by and they had almost no knowledge of current events outside their local fringe. In their rocky fortress, time moved as it had always moved, as slowly as the sure step of the mule or the mountain goat. They mistrusted and disliked the highly organised and efficient Germans, probably because these strangers were impatient of their slothful ways and treated them with ill-tempered brusqueness and annoyance. Whatever it was, the *Tedesco* had overstayed their welcome and found themselves engulfed in an atmosphere of lightly-veiled hostility. As for that Fascist who had sold himself to the Nazis, everywhere the cry was "*Mussolini Finito!*" and finished he was for the time being.

Night followed day, and still the SRS had effective control of Bagnara and slowly but surely all enemy resistance was being crushed. On the morning of 5 September, Major Mayne boarded an LCA and withdrew leaving his men to hold the town. From the south the main Allied armies were advancing and on the 6th they entered Bagnara to a heroes' welcome.

Major Mayne had been recalled to prepare plans for the biggest operation yet assigned to the SRS – a combined assault with the 3rd Commando and 4th Royal Marine Commando on the town of Termoli almost half-way up the Adriatic coast of Italy. He was back again on the *Ulster Monarch* with old buddies and feeling truly relaxed and happy.

On 8 September came the news that Italy had capitulated unconditionally and was being accepted as a co-belligerent with the Allies.

The armistice had, in fact, been signed on 3 September, but for political and military purposes it was decided that General Eisenhower and Field-Marshal Badoglio would broadcast, simultaneously from Algiers and Rome at 6.00 pm that the Italians had surrendered. It had been arranged that (i) at 11.00 pm on the same date American airborne troops would land near Rome and that the city would be seized by Italian divisions; (ii) the Italian Army would take over the coastal towns of Taranto, Brindisi, Bari and Naples; and (iii) at 4.30 am on the following day the Allies would land as follows:

a) The Fifth American Army at Salerno; and
b) The Fifth British Corps at Taranto.

It was shameful treachery on the part of the Italians, but from the Allies' point of view fair-seeming enough for it split the massive enemy

Axis right down the centre. It did not work out quite as planned, for German Intelligence had long ago been alerted for such a turnabout and swiftly the German Army disarmed the Italian troops in their areas. But some were already beyond their reach and these the Allies accepted for the policing and defending of ports and lines of communication.

General Montgomery had described this switching of sides by the Italians as the "biggest double-cross in history", and few people will quarrel with his tough assessment of it.

In Italy there was widespread speculation as to the whereabouts of the deposed Il Duce, Mussolini, and nobody was more curious than the German Intelligence. Field-Marshal Badoglio, the new head of the Italian Government, was not talking and his security services were demonstrating how efficient they could be. Later, it was revealed that the fallen dictator was first held prisoner on the island of Ponsa, then transferred to the island of Maddelene, off Northern Sardinia, and from there removed by sea plane and motorcar to an inn at the foot of the funicular railway which leads up to the skiing hotel, Campo Imperatore, perched on the towering San Grasso in the Appenines. Here he was held in custody until rumours of German activity in the area persuaded his captors to move him up to the Hotel Campo Imperatore for greater security.

Isolated 3600 feet up in that mountain fastness, Mussolini seemed to be beyond the reach of his German friends and everyone concerned with his detention relaxed. At the hotel there were some tourists, but, as their distinguished fellow 'guest' dined with the guards, they saw little of him.

Then, on the cloudy afternoon of 12 September, a German squadron of gliders swooped from the sky and landed on the mountain top. Quickly the occupants leapt out, fully armed, and made for the hotel. At their head, with a pistol jammed against his spine, the Italian Police General Solito ran forward shouting loudly:

"Don't shoot! Don't shoot!"

The military police guarding Mussolini were so petrified with fear that they were unable to fire a single shot. Colonel Otto Skorzeny, who commanded the raid, stood outside Mussolini's window and with his men chanted out again and again the words:

"*Viva Il Duce!*"

As this rescue demonstration was taking place a little Storch aeroplane had landed on a small plateau a little way down the slope, and, eventually, Mussolini and Skorzeny boarded it and took off, landing later at the German air base at Pratica di Mare, sixteen miles south of Rome. From there he was flown to Vienna, and after one night there he was taken on to Munich to meet Hitler.

On 13 September, Skorzeny spoke on the German radio and announced:

"I liberated Mussolini."

It was like a fairy tale composed by Hans Christian Andersen and the world on either side of the battlefront stood up and applauded.

Colonel Otto Skorzeny of the German SS had passed into the Hall of Military Fame and Legends, and even his enemies could not grudge him admiration.

In many ways he resembled Major Blair Mayne. Both were men of great stature and powerful physique. Both were determined and ruthless fighters, and both could be as gentle as lambs to defeated foes.

Paddy was cruising on the *Ulster Monarch*, off the Sicilian coast, when the news of Skorzeny's fabulous rescue of Mussolini came over the radio and he was much impressed.

"Why didn't our bright boys at HQ think of something like that?" he complained. "It would have been just our cup of tea."

It surely would have been helpful if they had for, as everyone now knows, Il Duce re-established himself at Salo and danced like a marionette on the end of a string for his master, Adolf Hitler. Romantic though his liberation was, it brought in its wake much unnecessary bloodshed and prolonged the Italian campaign by many months.

Eventually, the wretched puppet and his mistress, Clare Petacci, were shot by vengeful partisans near Lake Como and exhibited in the Piazza Loreto in Milan transfixed on meat hooks and strung up head downwards.

CHAPTER 15

Termoli

THE LAST, AND the most ambitious, operation carried out in the Italian campaign by the trouble-shooting Special Raiding Squadron was now coming up. Since the Bagnara battle it had been resting at various bases and on 2 October 1943, was encamped at the small port of Manfredonia on the Adriatic Coast, about twenty miles from Foggia, the inland Italian Air Base, which had recently fallen to General Montgomery's advancing army. That day, Major Mayne was ordered by HQ to embark with his troops on LCI 179 and, together with the 3rd Commando and the 60th Marine Commando, to sail north to the port of Termoli, land there and capture it and the adjacent town bearing the same name.

He was advised that the enemy was holding high ground overlooking the River Biferno, south of the town, and planning to put up the maximum resistance to the advancing British 70th Division. The SRS was to attack the enemy's rear and create chaos amid the defence positions.

The LCI in which Paddy and his men sailed was a fairly large vessel, capable of carrying two hundred men and their armed equipment, and had to tow a number of LCAs which would take them into the shallows and on to the beaches. The plan of action was for the 3rd Commando to go in first and build up a beach head, through which the 60th Marine Commando and the SRS would follow.

At 2.45 am on the morning of the 3 October, Paddy received a signal from the 3rd Commando that a footing had been secured and at once he ordered his men ashore. The LCI 179 had unfortunately run aground about fifty yards off-shore and it was well, indeed, that he and the Commando leaders had arranged to bring along the LCAs. Now he took over the first one to be cast off from the mother ship, and they sped landwards.

Jumping from his craft, Paddy led his men to the top of the beach ridge, across a railway line and then on to the northward Termoli-Vasto Road. Here, the three troops of his squadron separated. One under Captain Harrison was instructed to move inland with mortars and set up a position in the hilly woodlands from which it could overlook any German retreat from Termoli. Another troop was to head for and then straddle the Sampomarino Road.

The weather was wet, cold and stormy and the enemy resistance was truly tough. Farmhouse after farmhouse had to be wrested from the Germans the hard way, and casualties on both sides began to mount.

In the town of Termoli, the Marines and the Germans were engaged in heavy fighting, with many a bayonet struggle. Soon, prisoners were being herded to the shore and taken aboard the LCIs. Then came a thunderstorm of enemy aircraft bombings and shootings which went on for thirty-six hours. By wonderful luck, during the initial blitz all the assembled ships, and others bringing in reinforcements and supplies, escaped utterly unscathed. But the following day the air onslaught was intensified and some of the LCAs were sunk.

Then a full-scale counter attack on land was launched and field guns and howitzers started to rain shells on the brave Marines and SRS desert veterans. Their side hit back, and that day and night the maelstrom of death and mutilation went on and neither side was prepared to budge an inch.

Paddy Mayne, after encountering and killing twelve German parachutists single-handed, captured a farmhouse, which he established as Squadron Headquarters. Soon, disquieting reports were coming in. Captain John Tonkin, with his entire section, had been encircled and taken prisoner by troops of the First German Parachute Division.

Tonkin was to have a strange experience. After being moved from place to place, and, always treated well by his captors, he was taken to their Divisional Headquarters where he was seen by General Heidrich in the presence of an interpreter. To his astonishment, he was invited to lunch by this stocky, blue-eyed warrior and given a very pleasant lunch indeed, chicken, wine and cigars. They talked of Russia and Crete, where Heidrich had commanded a parachute division, and he expressed the sincere hope that peace could be reached between the two great Western Powers so that a bastion could be built against the Asiatic hordes.

Altogether, he was a pleasant fellow and John Tonkin felt that his life was safe in his hands, but later in the day an English-speaking officer warned him that the Gestapo might wish to see him sometime and if they did there was nothing the army could do to ensure his life. So, next day, he took leg bail from a German lorry taking prisoners up north and eventually, after many adventures, got back to the British lines.

While John Tonkin was collecting these experiences Paddy Mayne and his men were, like the Marines and Commandos, taking severe punishment. The Germans realised the importance of Termoli to their general strategic set-up and had summoned the 26th Panzer Division the whole way from Naples across the mountains and had also brought several pieces of heavy artillery into position. It won them nothing, however, for although they succeeded in breaking through here and there the breaches were swiftly sealed and they found themselves bashing against an impregnable rock of valour.

On the night of the 5 October, the Eighth Army advance units and tanks arrived in the area beyond Termoli and in the later afternoon next day Paddy Mayne and his squadron were relieved and able to take up a billet in a monastery in town. It was cold and desolate, and they were happy to leave it the following morning for a private house. There, with his usual flair for music in adversity, Paddy requisitioned an old gramophone and soon the tune was alternating between 'Lili Marlene' and an obscure Italian record which he had collected somewhere.

Around the party flowed rumours of a massive German counter-attack and from private radio reports Paddy knew that there was more than a grain of truth in them, but his men were battle-weary and wine and song were needed.

In the early evening an SOS came through for volunteers to fill a gap in the front line, and three lorries drew up in the square outside the monastery (it had obviously been picked as the right location!) to take them to the threatened positions. It was to be a long and bloody vigil lasting over two days. Casualties were high, and Paddy was asked to send a relief force immediately.

Again, he called for volunteers and, again, the response was superb. Thirty husky young men crowded into a lorry in the cobbled square next morning. As they did so, the eerie whistle of a shell rent the stillness of the noon calm and in one devastating moment they were wiped out, all but one man who was flung clear by the blast.

Paddy, usually so hard-bitten in battle, was genuinely shaken by this tragedy. He thought the world of his men and it was hard to believe that these merry-hearted young companions of the night before, who had been singing and drinking together with him in merry abandon, were now forever still.

He said little, but rage mounted within him. "I'll make up for this," he said and went off on a raid of his own. Nobody knew where he went, or what he did, but some say that he personally repaid the enemy for what they had done.

He certainly exacted some effective local revenge. Before leaving he sent off another lorry load of men to the front and organised a search party to comb every building in the square.

"That shell hit was no fluke," he growled.

There had been too many like it in this square although this was the first one involving his own men.

After he left, the search party found a German spy in the clock tower. He had been signalling to his own guns – and taking a double risk, one from those very guns and another from the friends of his victims on the ground below him. He was a brave man doing his duty, but unfortunately for him that day the SRS was not in the mood to take prisoners.

By this time, the Eighth Army was sweeping forward with irresistible force and the enemy was everywhere pulling out, demolishing roads and bridges as he went.

The SRS had proved its valour but the price was high. Of 201 who had landed, twenty-one had been killed, twenty-four wounded, and twenty-three were missing. To all who remained it was a bitter blow, more so than if they had been members of a bigger outfit, such as a division, for in the closely-knit, happy-go-lucky atmosphere of this regiment every loss was bound to be that of a friend and, in most cases, a close companion.

On 10 October, Lieutenant-General MC Dempsey, the Corps Commander, paid a special tribute to the SRS (which was about to resume its identity as the SAS) in which amongst other things he said:

> "The landing at Termoli completely upset the Germans' schedule and the balance of their forces, by introducing a threat to the north of Rome. They were obliged to bring to the East Coast the 16th Panzer Division which was in reserve in the Naples area. They had orders, which have since come into our hands, to recapture Termoli at all costs and drive the British into the sea.
>
> These orders, thanks to you, they were unable to carry out. It had effects though. It eased the pressure on the American Fifth Army and, as you have probably read, they are now advancing."

Termoli was to ring down the curtain on the SAS's Mediterranean campaigns. Soon they would be returning, at long last to Great Britain, there to equip and organise for the invasion of Northern Europe. Before doing so they went to Molfetta, 175 miles further down the Adriatic coast, and from there to Philippville in Algeria, where they spent Christmas. On Boxing Day they left for home.

CHAPTER 16

Tempered steel

In the Spring of 1944, the German armies were being driven back through Poland by the Bolshevik Russians. As the snow had defeated Napoleon during his invasion of Tsarist Russia in 1812, so again it had been the major ally of the Russians, no less than their own ferocious courage and almost incredible tenacity.

All but the most fanatic Nazi German began to see that the writing was clearly appearing on the wall. Stalingrad had proved impregnable. The years long siege of Leningrad had been lifted.

And elsewhere, encouraged at last by the hope of a crushing German defeat, resistance groups in all occupied countries were becoming bolder and more aggressive.

In the Mediterranean theatre, too, the fortunes of war were on the ebb for the Germans. El Alamein had become a part of history, and they had been hounded out of Africa. Now a victorious Allied army of many nationalities was sweeping up through Italy, preparing to thrust its way into Austria and Southern France. And Britain and the United States were completing their plans for a final death blow to the Hitler regime.

Still the Germanic fortress of Northern Europe was far from crumbling, and the British, with sad and bitter memories of Dieppe, realised thoroughly the magnitude of the task ahead.

Paddy Mayne fumed impatiently at his training base in Darvel, Ayrshire. He and his hard core of desert veterans felt their current job of training recruits to the SAS – now raised to brigade strength – might be very important. But renewed action was what they themselves most urgently sought.

Commando training provided some sport for the adventurers, but playing ducks and drakes with village constables and the Home Guard was pretty tame stuff for men who had experienced the real thing.

As for their mansion headquarters, well, that merely provided the baronial luxury which Major Mayne and his colleagues regarded as no more than their just and rightful due.

Servitors ran back and forth with cut glass decanters of Highland Malt on Georgian silver trays. The dull and regular diety which the severely rationed civilian population were tied to raised no problem for the officer gentlemen of the SAS Salmon, poached or otherwise, was ready for their table. Game, whether in or out of season, usually followed. Our lack of trading communications with Portugal seemed not to interrupt an apparently endless supply of the choicest Cockburn. But while these amenities pleased Paddy, his devotion to the main cause of the day, battle, was his overpowering passion. As long as the enemy held the field he was surging to get to grips with them. And he was under no illusions as to how long, and how bloody, the remaining struggle was likely to be.

Parachute jumping, cliff scaling, mountain climbing and all-night manoeuvres were exercises that were calculated to build-up top physical endurance amongst men in their prime of life. Such exertion did not interfere either with their capacity for all-night revelry nor their ability to get on with the job the following day and night.

Typical was the incident involving the Reverend Fraser McLuskey, newly appointed chaplain of the 1st SAS Regiment. He arrived at 8.00 am one morning, tired and travel-stained, after a night in a crowded war time train from London.

Shyly, he made his way into the Great Hall, hung with stags' heads and ancestral portraits, and littered with paraphernalia of well-attired officers. With nobody in sight, he made his way into the adjoining drawing room. There, in front of a roaring fire, he saw a strange company of gentlemen in various stages of disarray, and all in a somewhat stuporous condition. The less drowsy were still glass in hand. A tin-pot gramophone blared out music.

Fraser McLuskey was a big man, but he was over-shadowed by the huge figure of the fair-haired giant with blue-grey eyes who unwound himself from the recesses of a wide armchair and came towards him.

"What the Hell do you want?" growled Mayne.

"I'm your new chaplain," said McLuskey with some alarm noticing that his interlocutor wore the insignia of a lieutenant-colonel.

"Who sent you?" demanded Mayne.

"Brigade Headquarters."

"By God, sir! Why am I not informed of these things? It's typical of those bull shitting apes! Have a drink anyhow." And then noticing the padre's obvious fatigue, "By the way, have you had breakfast, old chap?"

Paddy tugged at a silken bell pull, and a Mess orderly in battle-dress appeared within seconds.

"Breakfast, sharpish, for our new Padre," ordered the Lieutenant Colonel.

And Paddy was quickly at some pains to explain that all-night drinking sessions, while not exactly the exception, were most decidedly not the rule. The previous night's party had been in honour of his Royal Air Force brother, Douglas, and his bride Pat, who had come to Darvel on honeymoon.

Over the porridge with thick fresh cream, bacon, eggs, kidneys, mushrooms and sausages, the seeds of an inseparable military comradeship and subsequent friendship were sown.

The new padre had neither a parsonic voice nor traditional parsonic mannerisms and although he declined the invitation to drink, he looked what he was, a man's man.

At the start he was frankly somewhat bemused by the new surroundings in which he found himself. As a man of the cloth he held dear, and unquestioningly, certain life-long principles which he found it difficult to compromise.

The SAS men were engaged in a form of training which was very hard to equate with conventional morality – even the morality of dealing in wartime death and destruction.

It was not McLuskey's prerogative to engage in inward theological disputation about the rights and wrongs of it all, but here were these chaps training with a purpose to become guerrillas and saboteurs. A tough mob of men they were, few of them given to arguing the finer philosophical or moral points of their behaviour in arms. If they argued at all it was to justify their sometimes libidinous sorties into the surrounding countryside. Men are human beings after all, eh? And if they don't do human things, why, then they'll do inhuman things, won't they? More importantly, if they were being trained in gangster drill in the interests of fighting for their country, who was likely to assail them for the minor peccadilloes which they could now engage in, most of them for the first time in their lives, without fear of chastisement?

On a somewhat more sophisticated level, Colonel Paddy and his fellow officers appeared to have scant respect for the civil law – in so far as they were at all concerned with it.

How could a contemptuous disregard for the inhibiting influence of ordinary society square with the lesson which the man of God felt it was his first duty to impart?

McLuskey found the answer quickly. The giant *esprit de corps* of the SAS was something which the Parachute Padre (as he became known) had never experienced before. Mayne had the rare gift of combining an easy familiarity with his men and an understanding of them together with a capacity to enforce an iron rule of discipline.

Padre Fraser McLuskey was a man whose opinion of the SAS can be taken as a pretty reliable one. As a cleric, he brought to the officers and men with him the sort of help they truly needed in the desperate situations which they were to face later. As an army man, his own high personal courage won him a Military Cross for gallantry in enemy-occupied France.

Later, after the war, he wrote of the loyalty between Mayne and his men:

> "Men were individuals and everyone mattered. It wasn't a large regiment – about 350 strong at this time – but everyone knew each other, and everyone seemed to be friends.
>
> There did not seem to be a great deal of discipline in the ordinary sense, but no unit in an army ever possessed a greater degree of loyalty to the CO or to the regiment."

There were other reasons why Mayne and McCluskey got on so well together. About one in five of the SAS men were Irish. Under Paddy Mayne's magical influence they found themselves at home and blossomed forth as a family, giving full rein to the flow of Irish *joie-de-vivre* and to the singing of Irish ballads and rebel songs. The English, not quite as strong (or clamorous) in a similar tradition, were delighted to find themselves in such jolly company and took their Celtic comrades to heart, adopting stage Irish on the way as an idiom of their own.

Paddy had no great singing voice, but he loved to hear others who had the touch of melody delivering the most rebellious of Irish ballads. He was splendidly impartial about their origin. Whether it was the Sinn Féin 'Kevin Barry' or 'Soldiers are we, whose lives are pledged to Ireland', the Orange 'Sash me father wore', the Irish-American 'Boston Burglar', or the Australian 'Wild Colonial Boy', Paddy Mayne would buy drinks all around him as long as he could get somebody to perform them.

Sergeant Bob Bennett, who had served with him since the early Kabrit days, and who had a fine tenor voice, was always a willing choirboy. Paddy often engaged in a duet with him, especially enjoying the 'South Down Militia' and 'The Foggy, Foggy Dew'.

But no matter how late the revels, or how much hard liquor had been downed, Paddy was up and about the next morning (it was often that very morning!) performing his duty with an alertness and thoroughness that surprised and sometimes disturbed his men.

He personally checked the quality of the inflow of both officers and other ranks who were posted to the SAS. Once he had accepted a man as suitable material for training he gave him the same loyalty as he expected to receive. There were some failures – though not many – who were sent packing, without loss of time. But whatever failings anyone showed, no mention of these ever appeared on their official records.

Offences were dealt with summarily, and not always with the velvet glove. But there were no spites, and no remonstrances. The man who behaved like a fool, and repeated his follies, was out – but that was all. Mayne saw little purpose in punishing men who were not going to serve the SAS's requirements. The fact that they had volunteered for such a unit satisfied him that they had a good heart. If they didn't measure up to the standards required, the fault was not theirs.

If, on the other hand, they did prove themselves up to scratch then there was no point in recording the minor scrapes they got into.

A reasonable understanding such as this was not lost on Mayne's men. One of the toughest he ever picked – and who was later to become one of his most trusted – was another thickset, broad-shouldered Ulsterman from Newtownards named William Hull, who had joined the Royal Ulster Rifles at the age of seventeen, then volunteered for the

6th Airborne Division. He was accepted but while stationed at Bulford, on Salisbury Plain, he overstayed his leave and was placed in detention.

It so happened that Colonel Mayne arrived from Darvel just at this time to interview recruits for the SAS and somehow met Hull, who wanted to join his unit. Hull informed Mayne that he came from the Shankill Road region of Belfast (tough Orange quarter) but was now living in Newtownards. Mayne's eyes lit up, and he continued to be pleased when Hull told him that he boxed and played football.

Then Mayne's eyes turned to Hull's boots and gaiters, which were scrubbed almost white instead of being the camouflaged green.

"Why are they scrubbed white?" he asked.

"I am in detention, Sir," replied Hull, with sinking heart. "Will this ruin my chances?"

"You will hear soon enough," came the curt reply, and he was dismissed from further interview.

But later he was accepted and ordered to join the SAS in Darvel. Neither he nor Paddy Mayne ever regretted it.

Paddy's spirit and his superb brand of loyalty infected his officers as well, and created an all-round atmosphere of camaraderie which very few ever saw fit to befoul. But, characteristically, he was even more severe in the tests which he applied when selecting or rejecting the officer material assembled before him.

Two young Guards officers arrived among a batch one morning. They had heard of Colonel Mayne's reputation and were rather overawed by it. The first to be shown in to him, an old Etonian, sported a uniform which was the very acme of St James's Street foppish elegance. His manner matched his togs – it was one of affected, aristocratic arrogance, blended with a derisory inquisitiveness about the unit named the SAS

Sergeant Bennett was standing in the background, waiting to take the new arrival to his quarters. Mayne, who had asked very few questions, but some very pertinent ones, spoke to the Sergeant.

"Don't bother to unpack this gentleman," he said. "Show him out, he won't be remaining with us."

It was time for the morning tea break, but Bennett knew that following the previous night's libations, Mayne would stand badly in need of something stronger than tea. He also knew that Mayne was far too thoughtful and kindly a person to knock back hard liquor in somebody else's company without offering them a portion as well.

Furthermore, he was no hole-in-the-corner toper, but a most convivial drinking companion.

So, Bennett whispered to the next Guarder candidate, who looked very apprehensive, just before he went into the Colonel's presence:

"If the Colonel asks you to have a drink, take it!"

"But Sergeant, I don't drink," replied the unhappy subaltern.

"No matter, take what you are offered," urged Bennett. "If you don't you'll be sent straight back to your regiment like the last gentleman."

As Bennett showed the young officer in, Mayne said: "Bennett, bring some Scotch, will you? And make it two glasses."

The order fulfilled, Sergeant Bennett withdrew discreetly, "Have a drink, my good fellow," said Mayne.

Duly alerted, the young officer mustered as much false confidence as he possibly could, and accepted eagerly. Mayne swallowed his own drink at one gulp in his anxiety to rout his monumental hangover. Not to be outdone, the gallant Guardee followed suit, under the mistaken belief that this was normal practice.

"That's better," said Mayne, pouring two more stiff shots.

The subaltern's tongue, loosened under the beneficent influence of the second glass, began to wag. He found himself getting on with Mayne like a house on fire.

Within half an hour, bumpers had been recharged several times, and the decanter was empty. As the Colonel pressed the bell to bespeak a further supply, the subaltern fell flat on his face. To Bennett, as he entered, Mayne said:

> "Take him and hose him down with cold water!" Then added, "And take his baggage to his quarters and see that he is comfortably fixed up. He has all the makings of a good SAS man."

CHAPTER 17

Nemesis

After the fall of France in 1940 and the Armistice that followed, France was divided into two separate Zones. The French State comprised roughly about two-fifths of the country with its northern boundary running irregularly from Poligny (in Jura) almost to Tours (in Indre et Loire) and its western boundary running south from Tours through Orthaz to the Pyrenees, was set up under Marshal Pétain and ruled from Vichy. The remainder of the country, with Paris as its centre, was directly ruled and occupied by the German under a Military Governor. Almost immediately a junior French General, Charles de Gaulle, who had escaped to Britain, broadcast an appeal to all patriotic Frenchmen not to accept the surrender of the French forces and to rally round him to continue the fight until the last German should be expelled from France. A few Frenchmen in England and some in France (the latter making their perilous way through Spain and Portugal to Britain) joined de Gaulle, but the vast majority of French people, whether in Vichy France or German-occupied France, stayed in their homeland either to carry on their lives amid the privations and humiliations of a defeated country in war time or to initiate a clandestine struggle against the conqueror.

The British and Allied Governments recognised General de Gaulle as the leader of those Frenchmen who were determined to carry on the fight against the Reich but, due to the initial paucity of de Gaulle's supporters and to the demoralisation and fierce divisions of the French people after the surrender, neither the British nor their allies were prepared to make a substantial contribution to the programme planned by the new French leader. Indeed, they made it quite clear – perhaps too brutally clear, thus accounting for subsequent bitterness and hostility – that they were reluctant to trust him or any Frenchman alive. Hence the early British plans for the infiltration of France in preparation for the eventual assault on the continent were formulated independently of de Gaulle and without any reference to him or to any other French leader.

In July 1940 the British set up SOE – the Special Operations Executive – a secret Service designed for the conducting of subversive warfare. The fall of Chamberlain's Government in May 1940, the evacuation of the British Expeditionary Force in June and the collapse of France brought about an urgent and thorough reappraisal of British strategy and out of this, amongst many other things, came the SOE.

The Germans brought to the task of subjugating and occupying France their efficiency and ruthlessness of administration. SS men and Gestapo agents were everywhere and unhappily, as occurs in every oppressed or occupied country, a certain number of French people, inspired by the most selfish and sordid motives, or simply lacking the moral fibre to endure the harsh restrictions and privations of a defeated country, collaborated with their German masters, thereby causing greater miseries and fratricidal strife in a country where life was already hardly endurable. Between those who resented the indignities of the occupation and sought to resist the conquerors at every turn and those who either stoically accepted the inevitable or basely sought to profit by the situation there soon arose the most vicious hatreds. When eventually there was added a fanatical rivalry among the best and most patriotic for the control of the general movement to resist the enemy, France became a most unhappy, divided and dangerous country.

The German strategy of occupying many European countries had naturally led to the inception of many movements of bitter national discontent. These movements were at first characterised more by zeal and frustrated rage than by intelligent organisation and military effectiveness.

The British Government, led since May 1940 by the pugnacious Churchill, quickly perceived the enormous importance of harnessing, arming and directing these earnest, if ineffectual scattered, patriotic efforts. The Allies had begun, after Dunkirk, to build up a war machine for the eventual invasion of Europe and the destruction of the Axis powers' domination.

Not the least important part of their war preparations was the creation of a service whose function would be to seek out, contact, co-ordinate, arm and sustain the various natural underground movements in Europe and elsewhere which were even then, and later would much more effectively, hamper, tie down and even destroy great masses of Axis troops, equipment, supplies and communications and thus prepare the way for and eventually assist the Allied assaults that would one day be launched against the German-Italian fortress in Europe.

Thus the British Special Operations Executive came into being and remained in existence until 1946. It was quite a vast organisation with ramifications all over the world. Six of its sections were exclusively devoted to organising the war in France. Now harnessed to these was the SAS, the Special Air Service – a brigade of some 2,000 picked men, many of whom were veterans of North Africa, the Middle East, Sicily and Italy.

The SAS, unlike the other sections of SOE, was not intended to go into France until Overlord – the invasion – began in June 1944. Then its members would be dropped into France, miles behind the German lines, to make contact with the Special Agents already operating there and particularly with the Maquis and begin the work of large scale sabotage and disruption for which they were specially trained. This programme would (and did) prevent the Germans concentrating their full attention and resources on the Allies in numbers and intensity sufficient to repel the sea-borne onslaught.

It was principally with the Maquis that the members of the SAS were able to make contact in France. The Maquis were originally numbers of young Frenchmen who took to the hills in preference to reporting to the compulsory labour service set up by the Germans. In the beginning individuals and small groups hid out in the woods and mountains rather than work for the enemy. These men had to live in rough, primitive conditions and had to resort to stealth and brigandage to survive. This mode of life made them hardy and resourceful and at the same time increased their bitterness towards the Hun.

Soon they were joined by other men with strong patriotic feelings and it was inevitable that the idea of carrying out guerrilla activities against the Germans should spread among those outcasts. The leaders of the patriotic section of French people, both inside and outside France, soon realised that the Maquis were an ideal nucleus for a national insurrectionary movement. The SOE also quickly perceived that the Maquis were one of those spontaneous, undirected forces which it was its duty to seek out and use, and soon SOE agents were circulating among the Maquis, gathering information about their numbers and locations and transmitting this to London. Also the SOE was arming and instructing the Maquis and welding them into one large national force which would, when the time was ripe, be galvanised into a vast series of guerrilla activities against the Germans all over occupied France.

But while the Maquis, by virtue of their hardihood, numbers, organisation and expert local knowledge, were to play an important part in the destruction of the Wehrmacht (unified German forces) up to and after D-Day, they also, by virtue of their haphazard method of recruitment, proved time and again a menace to the activities and personal safety of the brave agents and forces of SOE. The reason for this is easily seen. Many of those who took to the hills rather than obey the harsh German labour laws did so for no very creditable reasons. Every country has its criminals, its spies and malingerers. The Maquis were no exception. Furthermore, pre-war France was bitterly divided politically and the warring factions did not always achieve brotherly amity by reason of the occupation. Indeed, the presence of the Germans, with the opportunities it gave of denouncing one's rivals and currying favour with the conquerors, made far more bitter antagonisms among these highly individualistic people. In times of civil commotion some take to looting or levelling old scores.

So it was in the French underground. Some thought only of personal gain or the working off of old grudges and some brave patriots and foreign agents were betrayed or robbed or abandoned in their hour of need and sent to a cruel death or (if lucky) into later life with the bitterest thoughts about the Maquis. But generally the Maquis were reliable, hardy and brave men without whose co-operation, resources and local knowledge the work of the SOE would have been, if not impossible, infinitely less efficient and memorable.

Their divisions and dissensions were indeed very embarrassing to the Allied Command in the Spring of 1944 and agents everywhere were told to spare no effort to dampen down these Gallic passions.

The Armed Services in Britain were now buzzing with talk of invasion of Europe. Fighting men everywhere have always complained that they, the people most directly concerned and to whose lot the hard and dirty work falls are always the last to hear what fate, in the person of the military brasshats, has in store for them.

May 1944, was no exception. But the preparations which were on hand, and the feverish comings and goings of the brasshats indicated to the most dim-witted in the Services that something big was afoot.

Towards the end of the month, the idyllic existence of the SAS at Darvel was abruptly ended. The regiment moved southward to quarters in a high security sealed camp on an airfield at Fairford in Gloucestershire.

Within days, small reconnaissance groups were being airborne for parachute drops into central France. Their assignment was to get in touch with the Maquis and Resistance movements and to select the best bases for the SAS squadrons which were to follow. British Special Agents, already in France, had alerted the French Underground Movement about their arrival.

In Gloucestershire, the whole regiment was strictly confined to the camp. But it was noticed that Mayne was making mysterious disappearances, then turning up again a few days later. The deepest secrecy surrounded his movements.

Only after the war did it become known that he made at least ten cloak-and-dagger trips to France, dropping in by parachute at night, meeting Colonel Buckmaster[1] and other British Intelligence Agents, coming out again in small boats from the coast of Brittany two or three days later, and being picked up by submarines at off-coast rendezvous.

These trips were made at his own insistence, and in the teeth of fierce opposition from certain Whitehall warriors who wanted him to remain in Britain.

But Mayne had heard of treachery by the Maquis in some areas, of suicidal feuding inside the movement because of jealousies and petty personal spites. He knew himself of brave men and women, working for Free France and Britain, who had been betrayed to the Germans in some inner Maquis attempts to settle scores with which the victims were in no way concerned.

He was determined to see that his own men were not going to be

---

1 Colonel Maurice Buckmaster was the leader of the French section of SOE

squandered for such ends. He had set their landings for one express purpose – to cause the Germans the utmost possible harassment behind their lines. And the only way to do this, he felt, was to prepare the way himself.

These personal missions fulfilled, SAS squadrons were parachuted into France nightly at carefully selected dropping zones. Their function was then to sally forth from their concealed bases in armoured jeeps (which had been dropped with them) and also on foot, to blow up bridges and railways, mine roads, shoot up enemy convoys, and engage in armed combat when the most favourable moment arrived.

They were to radio back to HQ any information which they could gather about enemy movements of men and armour. If radio contact became difficult or impossible, pigeons were to be flown off to Fairford with any news it was imperative to convey.

Not the least significant of this was intelligence about the fighting spirit and morale of the Maquis and the Resistance. It was vitally urgent to get accurate reports on this so that the British High Command could decide whether it was safe to supply them with arms, ammunition and vehicles which would not be used for their own private vendettas.

It was here that Mayne showed himself possessed of a degree of organising genius which few had suspected. Indeed, he was at pains to conceal this talent lest he was borne off to a desk-bound job in GHQ and separated from his beloved SAS men.

The first problem was to furnish the troops already in France with vehicles, arms, supplies and provisions. Next, petrol and ammunition. New personnel had to replace casualties, and additional jeeps were needed to replace those which were knocked out in combat. Landing zones had to be found, and made ready for arrivals. Split-second timing was necessary for night parachute droppings. The zones had to be lit up at the exact moment when the planes were due to arrive overhead, avoiding the German night fighters which were waiting like vultures to swoop on the RAF transports.

All this called for the closest liaison with the Royal Air Force Command, and this was effectively carried out. Now, the SAS had not only to find targets for their actions – concealed German aerodromes, petrol dumps, and ammunition depots not normally detectable by air reconnaissance – but they had also to radio back information about them to RAF Intelligence.

It says much for Air Force navigational technique that their planes seldom failed to arrive bang on time, or to deliver their payloads to their destination despite the hazards of ack-ack batteries and roaming night fighters.

It is true, however, that this precision planning did not always guarantee the safe delivery of goods to the people to whom they were consigned. Sometimes the Germans were waiting at the address. More often peasants, suffering the deprivations of war, were quick to seize anything and everything useful and saleable. Local girls bedecked themselves in Parisian style confections made from parachute silk which their boyfriends had thus "discovered". This caused no great heartbreak to the SAS, but it was galling that the items which had been attached to the parachutes – petrol, food and clothing, above all, turned up in due course in the local black market.

The equipment dropped along with each new man parachuted in was much sought after. It contained sixty-nine separate items, including such handy marketable commodities as binoculars, blankets, food packs, clothing, drugs and cigarettes, all unobtainable in France except at famine prices.

On 6 June 1944 the Allied High Command launched Operation Overlord, the long-awaited and daily-expected invasion of north-west Europe, and all along the coast of Normandy hundreds of thousands of brave and desperate men were locked in mortal combat.

Two days later Colonel Paddy was briefing twelve of his men for a mission which was to rival and outshine Otto Skorzeny's rescue of Benito Mussolini the previous year. They were to be taken by RAF transport to Dourdan, near Paris, and dropped by parachute. There they were to ambush and blow up a German troop and munitions train, supplying Rommel's army in Normandy, and simultaneously destroy a large, camouflaged arms dump about which the Maquis had given detailed information.

The plan, inspired by Paddy and approved by his brigadier, was truly spectacular but it seemed doomed to failure. And nobody knew this better than the chosen twelve. Only too well did they realise what they were up against and none of them expected to survive.

Still withal there were no complaints. They had voluntarily chosen danger and if the price had to be paid they were able, ready and willing to pay in the only currency they had to offer – their lives. All they, or any of their other comrades in the SAS, had ever asked for was to be afforded an opportunity of giving a good account of themselves, and now as they took their briefing for this kamikaze-style venture they hoped that in the kaleidoscope of swift-changing fortunes their contribution to ultimate victory would do the regiment proud.

Their leader was Captain Pat Garstin and all of them were personally known to their Colonel. Four were in fact fellow Ulstermen.

After the raid they were to 'hole up' for two days until the heat cooled off and then rendezvous with a Douglas bomber, which would land on an enemy airfield at night and take them back to England.

It was so incredibly daring that it worked.

After destroying both train and arms dump and fighting a running battle on the runway with three lorry loads of German soldiers they all made the aircraft and got back safely to base.

It was indeed an incredible feat of daring. With enemy strong points all around them they had signalled the pilot in with Verey lights and, as if to outdo their audacity, the pilot himself had turned on his lights as he came in to land.

If such an episode were shown on the silver screen, most cinemagoers would shrug it off as sheer fantasy, designed to provide light entertainment for an hour or two. But the bullet-riddled Douglas and an injured trooper – big 'Tot' Barker from Ulster – were grim reminders that fact is sometimes stranger than fiction.

It is difficult to visualise the Germans landing on an RAF aerodrome, near London, and snatching up twelve saboteurs, dropped in Richmond Park or Kensington Gardens, in similar circumstances. Perhaps if they had been given more to such enterprises the outcome of the war might have been different.

Let us be thankful, then, for Teutonic stolidity and Anglo-Irish madness!

CHAPTER 18

Vive la France!

THE PRINCIPAL AREA of operations for the Squadrons of the First Special Air Service Regiment was an eighty by fifty mile rectangle ninety miles south-east of Paris with Dijon at one end and Nevers at the other. It was a wooded hilly area and was well chosen for guerrilla warfare.

At first the Germans reacted both swiftly and savagely, and several of Colonel Mayne's groups took severe drubbings. One such was B-squadron, led by Captain John Tonkin, which was dropped on D-Day in the Limoges-Poitiers area where he promptly set about blowing up bridges and roads. Unfortunately, a Maquis traitor betrayed their hideout to the Gestapo in Poitiers and, on 3 July, they were surrounded and attacked. Of a force of fifty-one officers and men only eighteen, which included Tonkin, escaped. Thirty of the prisoners taken were afterwards shot by the SS and three who had been badly wounded in the action and taken to hospital were later removed to an unknown destination and have never been heard of since.

Unlike the desert, guerrilla casualties were high in France, but this was to be expected as one of the most titanic struggles in the history of war was now being waged. Paddy and his men were proud that the Supreme Allied Command had selected them for this important task and they were determined to give a good account of themselves.

Major Bill Fraser was the officer commanding A-squadron, and was one of Mayne's most intelligent – and courageous – leaders. He had come with his squadron on 11 June, and he was to stay there

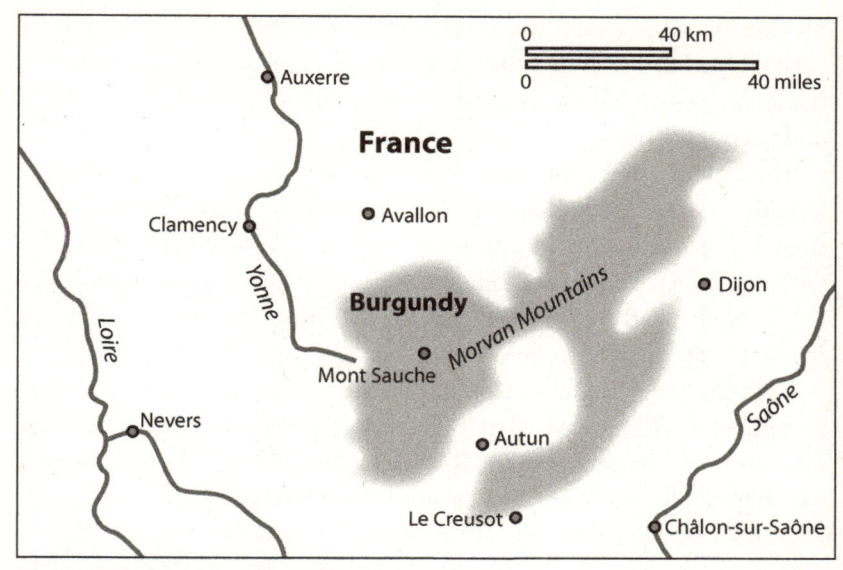

Map of the Burgundy region of France.

until replaced on the 5 September by Major Tony Marsh, DSO and C-Squadron, having had it rough and tough all the way.

Here it should be noted that a squadron was divided into sections which operated from separate camps and it was rarely that they combined to fight as one unit. The reason for this was that the chances of detection by the enemy were greatly reduced when operating in small groups, but when an opportunity did arise for a big-fisted strike it was gladly accepted by the wily and pugnacious Fraser.

The local French underground group with which this distinguished officer went into action was known as the Maquis Jean, and doughty fighters its members proved to be. Their camp, however, was too close to Fraser's own first hideaway and this led the Germans on to it, and gave him a pretty close shave. It was only shortly after he arrived that his camp was attacked by a German patrol and although they were beaten off he decided to shift his quarters. Padre McLuskey and the Brigade medical officer, Captain Michael McCready, were with his section and their services were required to deal with two casualties, the highly experienced Sergeant-Major Reg Seekings, who had caught a bullet in his neck, and a member of the Maquis who had a leg wound.

All through the night the Germans and the Maquis kept it up with machine-guns and mortars and it was dawn when Bill Fraser and his men slipped away. When they had covered a couple of miles through the forest he decided that it would be wiser to lay up there until nightfall and then push on.

They made their new camp about eight miles further on, close to a hamlet named Mazignen and in a small copse. Here Fraser and his men had to hang on in appalling weather conditions, hoping that Colonel Paddy would send relief soon. Eagerly they scanned the night skies and listened with cocked ears for the throb-throb of the Stirlings. But nothing came, and the situation was getting very critical.

Back home in England, Colonel Paddy was equally desperate since he appreciated full well what Bill and his boys were going through. But he could not persuade the RAF to tackle the flight in such suicidal weather. All he could do was to study the weather charts closely, and hope for a break. Eventually, it came and he immediately sent off three planes with supplies and three armoured jeeps. They were due over the dropping zone at 2.00 am and arrived on the dot. The parachutage that followed was successful and the misery of three dreary weeks was soon forgotten.

A section under Captain Alec Muirhead had established a camp at Mont Sauche, seven miles south of the original landing zone, on the day after A-squadron arrived and was undetected and undisturbed throughout the full period of its stay in France. Captain Wiseman was despatched to an area forty miles away and ten miles south of the important rail junction town of Dijon, to wreak what havoc he could on the many targets within easy but dangerous reach. He did his job well and became the most accomplished train-wrecker in France.

After the Paris-Dijon railway line had been cut one night, a Frenchman in British employ was sent out next morning to see the extent of the damage. He enquired of the workmen who were mending the line how long the repairs would take. They asked him if he was particularly interested and on replying in the affirmative, deplored the fact that he hadn't cut the line a bit further up where the damage would have been more effective. They then proceeded to draw a diagram for him to show exactly where next to plant the explosive to cause the most trouble.

Needless to say, when the opportunity presented itself, Captain Wiseman granted their wishes, and not satisfied with these mostly delaying exploits, he switched to another line and decided to attack a train carrying men and supplies to Rommel at Caen, where he was being very hard pressed.

The train was a big one and as it chugged along three hundred miles behind the front line, troops on board smoked, played cards and ate their rations, just as British troops would have done travelling from London to Dover. Some sang 'Lili Marlene' and other soldiers' songs.

Approaching a clearing in the Forest of Orleans, the driver sounded his whistle and all seemed well on this warm and sunny day. For a few hundred yards ahead a road ran parallel with the rail track. Then, suddenly, three jeeps appeared and ranged alongside the train. In the back seat of each a British gunner swung round a twin Vickers and began to rake the train from end to end with incendiary bullets. Soon the carriages were blazing and exploding violently as the ammunition boxes in them were hit. And, finally, the engine reeled off the track and overturned.

The SAS had become the scourge of Rommel, but now he believed that he did know how to hit back against these shadows. In the desert they had plagued his life and demoralised his army. Again and again they had cut his life-lines and here once more they were using the same tactics. Ah! But wait! In the desert they had the vast wilderness to swallow them up in its bosom, but surely in a heavily populated and strongly garrisoned country like France they could not escape detection! A network of ruthless SS killers would swiftly close in on them – and that would be the end! Little did he realise that the impossible was but a challenge to these supermen saboteurs.

Within three months they had killed or wounded 7,753 Germans, had captured 4,764 prisoners and caused 1,800 under General Elster to surrender to the Americans at Issoudan by cutting off their line of retreat. They had destroyed or captured hundreds of vehicles, including a great number of tank transporters, destroyed or wrecked many trains and blown up 164 railway lines. A synthetic oil refinery had been mortared and destroyed at Autun and at Malaine a gasoline factory had got the same treatment.

Flying bomb factory and assembly areas were located and the RAF duly alerted. Even the location of Rommel's headquarters was passed on. It is a small wonder that the half-demented Hitler shrieked and ranted at his Gestapo chiefs for not tracking down and exterminating these British Pimpernels. Even the brilliance and cunning of his army engineers was exposed and reduced to nought.

For a long time after the Allied Air Force had taken command of the sky and systematically destroyed all the bridges over the Seine which they could see, it was observed that the Germans were still somehow getting across the river.

It was a mystery which baffled the High Command in July 1944, until Bill Fraser discovered that pontoon bridges were being submerged during daylight. This information he immediately sent off to the British and American Air Force Headquarters, giving the exact position of these bridges.

Meanwhile, despite the objections of his Brigadier and others at HQ, Colonel Mayne reckoned that it was time he paid a visit to his men, and if a morale boost was required, this was just the thing they needed to hear since their CO was to all of them the very heart of the SAS Before he came, Captain Roy Bradford, a Devonian with a flair for adventure and boundless courage, lost his life in an encounter with an armed convoy and the news of his passing came as a bitter blow to this brotherhood of heroes, although the roll of honour was steadily growing and no one knew the hour when his own turn might come.

The moment seemed opportune for Colonel Paddy to speak directly to all his men, encamped in various parts of France, before taking off to see them. This he did in a broadcast from his base in England on a secret wave-length.

In his quiet, even voice, with just a trace of Celtic emotion coming through, he assured them that their sacrifices and deeds of courage were not passing unnoticed in Britain and he wound up by saying that he hoped to be with them soon. The broadcast was heard by all and a wave of excitement surged throughout the far flung posts of A-squadron.

In a sense these men were a forgotten army, just as the Fourteenth Army boys in Burma (they included those other splendid madcap raiders, Orde Wingate's Chindits) once felt they were. The smallness of their numbers sometimes made them feel rather insignificant and yet the Germans feared them more than any other unit of the British or American Forces. They had suffered at their hands in North Africa, Sicily and Italy and now, here in France, like a nest of scorpions they were in their midst again.

Herr Hitler, for whom neither the conventions of Geneva nor any of the gentle curbs of humanity had any application, had issued a secret directive to his commanders on 18 October 1942, that no quarter should be shown to enemy commando raiders operating in any theatre of war. Its exact wording ran:

> "From now on, all foreigners brought to battle by German troops in so-called commando operations in Europe or in Africa, even when it is outwardly a matter of soldiers in uniform or demolition parties with or without weapons, are to be exterminated to the last man in battle or while in flight. In these cases it is immaterial whether they are landed for their operations by ship or aeroplane or descend by parachute. Even should these individuals, on their being discovered, make as if to surrender, all quarters is to be denied to them on principle."

Only twelve copies of this diabolical order were printed, and we know that several Wehrmacht Generals, including Rommel, refused to obey it but there is no doubt that in the hands of the SS, the Gestapo, or the Hitler Youth Division, it was carried out to the letter.

The SAS suffered greatly in France because of this secret directive, which was called the *Befehl*, and of which they knew nothing. They were well aware, of course, that the Maquisards were tortured and shot, and that hostages also had been taken and shot as reprisals. They expected no better treatment themselves and yet, with traditional British honour, Mayne's brave men would not descend to such acts of barbarism on their side. The Maquisards believed in an eye for an eye and a life for a life, and they seldom spared a prisoner. Torture was a regular expedient for them and their enemies and the character of the prisoner was irrelevant.

In such a vicious circle of inhumanity it was not surprising to find that the Germans only surrendered to British and American forces.

On the night of 4 July, D-squadron led by Captain Pat Garstin was sent to the Forest of Fontainebleau, only to find that it had been betrayed by a Maquisard who had been captured by the Gestapo in Paris. 'Betrayed', in the circumstances may be the wrong word, but the result anyway was disastrous for D-squadron and only a very few of the twelve men who had been dropped survived, and one of these was crippled for life.

They had come across from Keevil Aerodrome in England in a Stirling bomber punctually at the dropping zone chosen by Colonel Paddy himself. Their hearts were no doubt pounding with the prospect of action as they floated down gently to a large cornfield surrounded by trees.

As the first stick landed they were confronted by a group of men in civilian clothes who greeted them with cries of "Vive la France!" and followed up with a murderous burst of gunfire. The SAS men swiftly reacted and returned the fire but four of them fell wounded. Steel helmeted German soldiers moved in from all angles and reinforced the others in plain clothes.

The set-up was hopeless for the parachutists but in the ensuing melee three of them somehow escaped and eventually reached the American lines. The wounded and five others were taken prisoner and driven on a lorry to La Pitié Hospital in Paris, where the former were admitted.

Captain Pat Garstin was one of them and, instead of having his wounds attended to, he was subjected to cruel and prolonged torture by the Gestapo.

The others were taken to Gestapo headquarters in the Avenue Foch, in the centre of the city, and there they were given three days of brainwashing and third degree treatment supervised by a very unpleasant person known as Dr Otto Schmidt. But neither the mental nor the physical torture broke these five men and they were consigned to a shabby hotel in the Place des États-Unis which had been converted into a prison.

The next day they were joined by Captain Garstin and Trooper John Barker. The first-named was in a pitiable state from shock and loss of blood but his captors were unheeding.

On 8 August, they were paraded before a sergeant-major of the SS and informed by him that they were going to be exchanged for some German agents who were being held in London. "As you are going via Switzerland, which is neutral, you will have to wear civilian clothes," he said with an unctuous smile. It seemed fair enough, but some of the men were suspicious until reassured by Captain Garstin.

An hour after midnight the prisoners were handed into a lorry with two SS men as guards. One of them spoke French and Corporal Serge Vaculik, a Czech who had been brought up in France, tried to engage him in friendly conversation but all to no avail.

Through the canvas flaps they saw they were being escorted by two car loads of SS men. It seemed such a waste of petrol at a time of scarcity and Vaculik's suspicions were heightened. He asked the French-speaking guard if they were really going to Switzerland, and was promptly told to shut up and that he would learn soon enough.

And soon enough he did! His worst fears were confirmed when the convoy suddenly halted and then turned into a field through which it travelled for two or three hundred yards. The guards then opened up the tail-piece of the lorry and ordered them to get out and line up. From the cars the SS men spilled out, automatics in hand. Vaculik in despair, turned again to the guard to whom he had spoken earlier.

"Are we going to be shot?" he inquired.

And back came the answer short and harsh: "Of course you are going to be shot! What did you think this was, a picnic?"

Quickly he passed the dread news round. Captain Garstin whispered to Corporal 'Ginger' Jones to make a dash for it when he shouted "Now". To Vaculik on his right he whispered the same instructions and the word went down the line.

Meanwhile, the Germans were moving into position, with their sten-guns at the ready, to put into effect Hitler's damnable directive regarding such captives, when a Gestapo agent in civilian clothes stepped out in front of them and proceeded to read out something in German. Then a Gestapo sergeant took the paper from the other man's hand and read it out in English. It started like this:

> "For having wished to work in collaboration with the French terrorists..."

The utter callousness of the situation is almost beyond comprehension. Here was a man representing an arm of the German Forces and representing also the national leader of a presumably civilised people, reading out in a toneless and casual manner a death sentence, veiled in words of legality; here this macabre massacre was being enacted in the grey light of early dawn and in a lonely part of a country where all concerned were really strangers – the condemned, heartily welcome, and the executioners, just invaders and tyrants. Seven men on the brink of eternity, with a new day breaking, the rooks cawing, the cocks crowing and no doubt the local peasants awakening for the morning chores. But it was all just another job for Hitler's very special butchers, trained and held in reserve for inhuman service of this kind. With merely seconds to go, no doubt each one of the potential victims thought of his loved ones far away – but there was little time for thought.

The Gestapo thug was still reading:

"...and thus to endanger the security of the German Army you are condemned to the penalty of death and shall be shot."

As soon as he uttered "shot", Captain Garstin shouted "Now!" and everyone except himself sprang forward and bolted towards the cover of the trees.

On the instant, ten sten-guns opened up and five brave men lay dead on the damp, leafy earth. Two escaped, Corporals Jones and Vaculik, and after ten days they came together again through Maquis contacts and were hiding in the village of Hermes when the Americans liberated it.

The two corporals were back in England on 28 July, reporting the whole sad episode to Colonel Paddy Mayne who listened with tight-lipped tension, clenching and unclenching his huge fists in his agitation. To him the satanic evil of the Gestapo in arranging for the clothing switch of their prisoners in order to save their faces later if they should be caught was loathsome. But everything about these hideous murders was utterly loathsome and Paddy really felt ill hearing and thinking of them – all those fine comrades with whom he had shared pleasure, danger and hardship, now dead and gone, not in fair soldierly combat but foully murdered – four of them fellow Irishmen; three, in fact, fellow Ulstermen, the fourth being Captain Garstin from Southern Ireland. The Ulstermen were Trooper Joe Walker from Moira, Trooper John Barker from Cookstown, and Trooper Billy Young from Randalstown.

Billy Young was a lovable young County Antrim rogue who used to poach Lord O'Neill's demesne, and had a little earlier been before Paddy for overstaying his leave.

"It was this way, sir," he tried to explain, "I was goin' down the oul' lane from me home when I turned from the wind to light a fag an' the next thing I knows 'am back in me house again."

There was no harm in poor Billy, just fond of a good laugh and a mug of beer, and that seemed to be about all he wanted out of life. Another Ulsterman, Lance-Corporal Lutton, who had been wounded in the wheatfield, died in La Pitié Hospital shortly afterwards. What magnificent men they were! The stuff of heroes, each and all.

Serge Vaculik and Ginger Jones were to meet again some of those responsible for this foul deed – this time at a War Crimes trial at Wuppertal, in Germany. It was February 1947. Six SS men sat in a military court composed of a Guards Colonel and five other officers. The wheel had turned full circle and now they were fighting for their lives. The pity was that the arch fiend, Dr Otto Schmidt, was not there too, but he had died in Russia.

The trial dragged on for two weeks, and in the end all were found guilty of murder and four of them were sentenced to be hanged. The others were sent to prison.

CHAPTER 19

Blood and guts

"Cowards die many times before their deaths
The valiant never taste of death but once."[1]

THE BARD MUST have had some pre-vision of Major Ian Fenwick of the Special Air Service when he composed these lines. Commander of D-squadron, he was sent by Colonel Mayne from England to France shortly after Captain Pat Garstin and his troops had been betrayed and later foully done to death. His sphere of operations was to be in the south-west of Paris and he was to operate from camps in the Forests of Fontainebleau and Orleans, and his primary object was to be sabotage on a large scale.

Ian Fenwick had not been long with the regiment, but long enough to become one of its most popular officers. A gifted cartoonist, employed by a national daily newspaper before the war, his extraordinary and amusing topical sketches adorned many a billet, but even more diverting was his lively wit, sparkling like champagne, and throwing off shafts of good cheer to all who came within range of his striking personality. He, with a stick of parachutists, dropped from a cloudy sky on the night of 13 July 1944, south of the town of Pithiviers. They formed the advance guard of the squadron, which within days was to be swollen up to its full strength by other parachute landings in the same area.

Without any fuss or ado, Ian Fenwick established a base in the Forest

---

1 William Shakespeare – Caesar Act 2 Scene 2

of Orleans and set about the major task entrusted to him by his friend and Commanding Officer, Paddy Mayne. Railway lines were blown up on all routes leading to Paris; enemy convoys of motor transports were ambushed and destroyed and then, flushed with success, Fenwick boldly switched his attention to trains carrying troops and war material and these suffered a like fate.

At first he and his men had to operate on foot but when the jeeps came floating down in the dark and they became more mobile the range of their activities was greatly enlarged. Soon they were roaming the *routes nationals* at night, seeking out targets and pressing home their deeds of destruction with such striking success that the Germans quickly came to realise that a deadly enemy was right in their midst.

But finding this elusive danger-gang was not easy, for rarely did the SAS patrols work in daylight and at night they were even harder to distinguish from the German motorised units which were camouflaged with green foliage, a ruse quickly adopted by the SAS.

The sheer audacity of these British raiders was for a time their best defence, for the Germans were slow to believe that an enemy group would be so recklessly brave as to drive along the main highway, with their headlights blazing, in and out of convoys of tanks and heavily armoured cars, and even getting past manned roadblocks. But this Colonel Mayne's men did, and with signal success. It would probably of course have been impossible if the Germans had operated proper security regulations, such as road checks or identity cards and the proper examination of all vehicles passing the roadblocks. But chaos was swirling all around, and a prize problem was who was who.

All the while they kept the closest possible liaison with Resistance groups in their areas and from them received great assistance, mostly in the shape of information as to the enemy dispositions.

On 24 July, a report arrived of an intended enemy attack by a powerful force from Orleans and it was decided to disperse the troops of the squadron to various hide-outs northward in the direction of Paris. One group was sent to a picturesque chateau near Thimory, south-west of Montargis; another to a wood outside Pithiviers; and yet another to the Forest of Fontainebleau on the outskirts of Paris.

At this moment, GHQ in England was planning a major airborne attack on the German rear in the vicinity of Paris and the SAS had an important mission to fulfil, organising a reasonably safe reception for these sky troops and generally preparing the way for them by contact with the local Maquis and Resistance. It was now imperative to be wary and out of sight until the big drop actually took place. Unfortunately, once again unreliable elements of the Maquis were talking and the enemy was listening.

On 7 August, Sergeant Bunfield of the Signals Section received a message that Colonel Mayne was dropping that night if a landing zone could be laid on. Before this could be arranged, however, the Germans attacked the Fontainebleau Forest camp in strength at three o'clock that afternoon and a bloody and desperate battle raged for the next seven hours.

Lieutenant Riding was in charge in the absence of Major Fenwick, and he was determined to make the enemy pay dearly for any advantage gained, but by midnight he realised that the position had become hopeless and decided there was nothing else he could do but break the cordon and move to a new locality. This he accomplished, but not without suffering fairly heavy casualties.

Ian Fenwick was at this time in another sector, well out of harm's way, but when he called in with a unit at Nancray-Sur-Rimarde he was informed by members of the Resistance that a blood bath was taking place at the Fontainebleau Forest base; that Lieutenant Riding, Sergeant Almonds and many more were dead, and there was little hope left for the rest of the base unit.

The reaction which this news had on Fenwick was instantaneous. He checked his firearms and, taking four men with him, set off at once in his jeep for the base. It was still daylight and an enemy plane soon spotted him and signalled an ambush party at Chambon to be at the ready. Rounding a bend Major Fenwick, who was driving, was stopped by a French peasant woman and warned about the ambush.

"Thank you, madam," he replied, "but I still intend to attack the Boche." And he drove on, accelerating to maximum speed.

Approaching Chambon, he ran smack into withering cross-fire and was killed instantly. The jeep, now out of control, crashed into some sapling trees. Two of his men were killed outright and the other two were knocked unconscious by the crash and taken prisoner. One, Sergeant Dunkley, was later handcuffed and taken away by SS troops and has never been seen or heard of since.

The other, Sergeant Pat Duffy, with the luck of the Irish, and the help

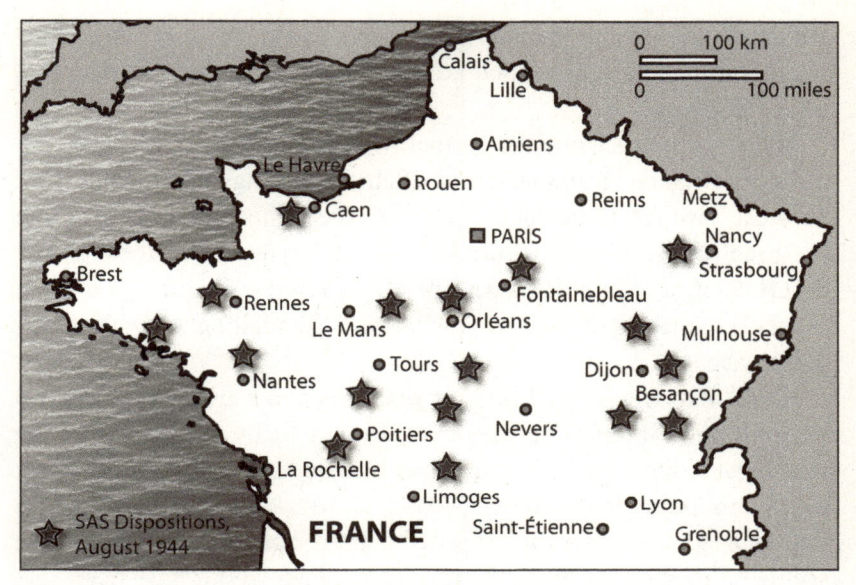

Distribution of SAS dispositions in France.

of a patriotic French nurse, who provided him with a German Officer's uniform, escaped from a hospital at Fontainebleau and, after a very perilous journey, in the end reached the safety of the American lines. For his daring and courage, he was awarded the Order of the Purple Heart, one of the highest awards for bravery given by the American Army.

Colonel Mayne had by that time landed at Captain Alec Muirhead's camp at Mont Sauche. From here he went on to Bill Fraser's HQ at Mazignen where he heard the news about Riding and the tragic death of Fenwick.

Paddy now decided to make his way to the Forest of Fontainebleau to re-organise the remnants of Riding's party and put some heart back into the men. The welcome which he had just received from the squadrons of both Muirhead and Fraser was tremendous. For some strange and unaccountable reason his very presence seemed to throw a protective screen around his men and their morale soared immediately.

He had come across from Muirhead's rendezvous to Fraser's in a black Citroen car, which he drove himself and drove well, with the aplomb and nonchalance of a country squire encircling his ancestral estate. Now Fraser's squadron was off to receive a parachutage and

Paddy decided to stay at camp and rest for the morrow. The night was warm and balmy and he took advantage of this to sleep in the open under the stars.

What a change from the formality and the exaggerated spit and polish of Brigade Headquarters at Chelmsford, England! What a relief he must have felt to be back again with these thoroughly wholesome brethren of his, most of whom he had soldiered with all through the desert, Sicily and Italy! This was the life he loved – the life of a combat guerrilla harassing the enemy at will – and then falling away like a will o' the wisp.

Speed of movement, cunning in planning and fearlessness in action were his natural gifts, and they made him virtually indestructible. He was, in fact, rather superstitious about his good luck and (typically) not fully conscious of the soldierly genius with which he was endowed. To a man of lesser character the proposed trip to Fontainebleau might have seemed a pilgrimage of death, and such a man would have been cast down and even petrified to inaction through fear. But never Colonel Paddy Mayne. Once a decision had been taken, action must follow – any thoughts of temporising were out of the question.

Earlier in the evening he had remarked to Bill that his squadron had been overworked and needed a rest. Bill, although knowing this to be true, still reckoned that there was plenty of fight left in them, but the casual thought in Paddy's mind had now crystallised into a firm decision and he announced that preparations for replacement by C-squadron should start as soon as he had time to arrange it.

On the morrow he was gone at cockcrow, and on 6 September C-squadron motored into Mazignen, led by the ubiquitous Paddy himself and that dashing swashbuckler, Major Tony Marsh, the Commander of the relieving column.

All of these men came from the American lines behind which C-squadron had landed, on Colonel Mayne's instructions, from Dakota air transports. This was much more pleasant, as one of the team said with a grin, than dropping on a rigged landing strip in the stillness of the night with hostile Germans within hailing distance.

A-squadron set off on the reverse journey in a blaze of glory riding in a couple of captured troop-carriers and other assorted vehicles escorted by heavily armed patrols of C-squadron. It is significant of the local appreciation of their work in France that the villagers of

Mazignen turned out in strength and cheered the large motorcade to the echo.

Bill Fraser and Padre McLuskey pressed Paddy as to his mission at Fontainebleau, and learned that when he got there he established a base and then went on foot chasing up the dispersed troop. Eventually he found Lieutenant Riding and most of his men. Many of the latest recruits were, in fact, beginning to crack up under the strain and this was very understandable. They had been operating for weeks on the enemy's doorstep and each and every one of them knew that torture and death was his lot on being captured and, of course, death in one form or another was forever stalking them. But, as McLuskey wrote, Paddy inspired confidence in the men and when it became known that he had arrived their morale soared.

His presence also helped to dampen the rebellious and unruly inclinations of the Maquis, who in this area were little better than a band of cut-throat brigands. To quote from a contemporary report made by Lieutenant Riding:

> "Their main desire seemed to be to get arms and hold the local farmers (or anyone against whom they had a grudge) to ransom. They had no discipline or organisation and went to pieces when attacked."

In fact, for the most part, they were a thoroughly unwholesome lot and Paddy gave them short shrift when dealing with them and they feared him greatly. Tommy Corps was, nevertheless, especially vigilant when these gangsters were around for he knew only too well that they would think nothing of jabbing a knife into his Commanding Officer's broad back if a suitable opportunity occurred.

The passing of the loveable Ian Fenwick was sadly lamented by everyone in the regiment, but all took pride in the manner of his death. He was a true hero of the SAS and his name will be forever immortalised in the regimental records. But in the summer of 1944 there was little time for sentiment and sorrow and the ugly business of total war had to go on.

For Paddy there was no respite. Troops had to be somehow ferried across the German lines, and he passed back and forth in the jeep and every day took his life in his hands and walked the razor's edge.

So, too, did his friends Tommy Corps and Captain Mike Sadler, who accompanied him everywhere and shared his danger. They were to him a genuine source of inspiration and when he was awarded a second bar to his DSO some months later he protested that these two men should have been similarly decorated. The official citation reads:

> "Lieutenant Colonel R. B. Mayne has commanded I SAS Regiment throughout the period of operations in France. On the 8th August he was dropped to the 'Houndsworth' base located west of Dijon in order to co-ordinate and take charge of all available detachments of his Regiment and co-ordinate their action with a major airborne landing which was then envisaged near Paris.
>
> He then proceeded in a jeep to the 'Gain' base near Paris making the complete journey in one day. On the approach of the Allied forces he passed through the lines in his jeep to contact the American forces and to lead back through the lines his detachment of 20 jeeps landed for operation 'Wallace'.
>
> During the next few weeks he successfully penetrated the German and American lines in a jeep on four occasions in order to lead parties of re-inforcements.
>
> It was entirely due to Lieutenant Colonel Mayne's fine leadership and example and his utter disregard of danger that the unit was able to achieve such striking success."

There can be little doubt that the decoration was well earned.

Apart from passing through enemy lines on several occasions and leading back large reinforcements to various bases in the general Paris area he had to travel hundreds of miles over roads and lines used and sometimes patrolled by the enemy and at any moment a fate similar to that which overtook poor, brave Fenwick awaited him. But whereas Fenwick's impulsive chivalry had made him throw caution to the winds, Paddy's foxiness and sixth sense for danger, which had developed of necessity in the desert, saved his skin and that of his comrades again and again. Even when surprised, his lightning quick mind took in the set up at a glance and on the instant action was taken.

On one occasion, when hurrying along a dusty lane close to the ever-changing front line, he and his companions heard the sound of an approaching motor engine and before they had time to turn back or drive off the road for cover, an armoured car with gun pointing menacingly forward swung round a bend. Things looked grim as they were out-gunned and the ammunition they carried could not penetrate the armour of the enemy.

"Pull up quickly," Paddy shouted, and they looked round to see where the voice came from, but he was gone.

Seconds later the armoured car slowed down to a halt and as the hatch lifted a loud explosion thundered out, and up went a sheet of flame where the enemy vehicle had stood.

Paddy had leapt from the moving jeep when danger had threatened and had positioned himself, under cover of the hedgerow, just where he expected the enemy to stop. Two hand grenades did the rest, and he casually jumped back into his jeep and was on his way as if what had just occurred was a mere bagatelle.

Such incidents were part of Paddy's daily routine in Central France and were to be repeated again and again, adding lustre to a reputation already legendary.

While the SAS were operating in this twilight world the massive British and American armies were steadily breaking their way out of their Normandy beachhead. July had been a critical and bloody month but it ended in the exhaustion of the German forces so necessary for the sweeping successes of August and September.

The First Canadian and Second British Armies were now sweeping along the North of France in full cry for the key port of Antwerp and they achieved their objective on 4 September.

The First and Third American Armies were thrusting through the centre of France towards Paris and from the south General Denvers' Sixth Army Group was advancing steadily, almost without opposition, towards its rendezvous with the American Third Army near the Swiss-German border.

General Eisenhower held the view strongly that Paris, like Rome, should be spared destruction or grave damage. It was a jewel of western civilisation, and it was his plan to besiege it and force the German garrison to surrender.

The French Resistance, however, wanted to jump the gun and claim the credit for liberating the capital of their country (not unnaturally!) and so, 18 August, the Liberation Committee issued an order calling for general insurrection. Three thousand gendarmes joined up with the Resistance fighters and a furious battle began.

General Eisenhower was taken completely by surprise. His Third Army, which was intended to by-pass Paris and complete its encirclement, was re-grouping on the Orleans-Chartres-Dreux line. The Sixth Army Group, which had landed in the South of France only on 15 August, was nearing Dijon, one hundred miles from Paris.

The undisciplined rabble of Paris were no match for the iron-regimented Germans and the day following the uprising the Resistance leaders had to beg for a truce. The Military Governor, General Choltitz, who had disobeyed Hitler's orders to devastate the city, agreed to this and an armistice was proclaimed on the twentieth.

The terms were that, in exchange for non-molestation of their withdrawing troops, the Germans would treat the Resistance guerrillas as belligerents (ie recognised regulars). This meant that if taken prisoner they would not be shot.

It was a splendid gesture on the part of Choltitz, but it was thwarted by the Communists who, continuing with their attacks, brought furious retaliation from the Storm Troops and the French militia men.

Bloody street fighting followed and General Omar Bradley, commander of the American First Army Group, had to reverse his plans and send in two French divisions on 22 August, led by the legendary General Leclerc and General Gerows. To these upright soldiers the German Governor surrendered and all effective enemy resistance in Central France came to an end.

The big air drop, for which the SAS had been preparing the way, was now no longer needed but Mayne and his men continued to harass the Huns.

By mid-September, the Allies had driven them back to their frontiers in the North and to the banks of the Moselle in the South. The Russian summer offensive had swept the Germans in one flood tide from the Dneiper to the gates of Warsaw. In the Balkans, the Russians had occupied Romania and advanced to Hungary. And yet, despite the inevitability of defeat, the fighting spirit of the German soldiers remained high and many a hard battle still lay ahead before final victory was achieved.

Units of the SAS were now dispersed to many fronts, and for a time their new role was to move ahead of the conventional forces and seize war criminals and SS generals. They were officially attached to Field Security, but with French and Belgian squadrons in their midst Paddy

Mayne could not resist the temptation to return to guerrilla warfare.

On 5 October, Paddy moved to Brussels where his Belgian friend of the desert, Captain Bob Melot, awaited him. There was work to be done and these were the two men to get it going. Not for the only time, Adolf Hitler's intuition was right. These men were certainly dangerous. All of them, but none more so than Robert Blair Mayne.

CHAPTER 20

Operation Irish Terrier

IN FRANCE COLONEL Mayne's troops continued to hound the enemy-on-the-run, and their sorties were still under his direct command.

The Chelmsford base was like a vast nerve centre, with code and other reports flashing back and forth night and day.

On 6 October, C-squadron arrived in Brussels where its Commander, Major Tony March, was already installed. It was instructed by Paddy to suspend operations so that it could reorganise and re-equip. Meanwhile, other units were serving with such success that they earned special notice by the Germans. One document read:

"2nd Panzer Division.
IC No. 294/44 Secret   GEF .ST 1710 1944
   On the 16.9.44 members of the SAS were arrested near Pexonne approximately 3 kilometres south of Badenvillor.
   The questioning rendered the following details. A group of SAS is active in the area of Baccarat approximately 25 kilometres south-east of Luneville, Department Meurthe. The strength of the group is not known.
   According to statements of the prisoners, sabotage activities were intended in the area between St Die and Strasbourg.
   The intention was:
a) The interruption of the railway lines Luneville-Strasbourg and St Die-Strasbourg.
b) The blowing up of bridges, traffic junctions and telephone communications in the Bezirk Nordvogesen and Elsass area.

> For the maintenance of communications with England the troop is fitted out with two-way sets.
>
> According to coinciding statements of three prisoners there are at the moment three SAS Regiments which belong to the 1st SAS Brigade. The Commander of the Brigade is a certain McLeod [Mac Cloud]. The Commander of the 1st SAS Regiment is Colonel Kaine. The Commander of the 2nd SAS Regiment is Colonel Fanks. The Commander of the 3rd SAS Regiment is not yet known to the prisoners. The strength of the respective Regiments to which the prisoners belong is judged to be 500 men.
>
> The employment of similar troops in various numbers is anticipated in the same area. Experience gained in the campaigns in Italy and France shows that members of the SAS are specially trained for this type of work. *Their activities are extremely dangerous.* The presence of SAS units is to be reported to the divisions concerned."

The Colonel 'Kaine' above referred to was, of course, the redoubtable Paddy Mayne himself, whose true identity his men would not reveal, even when 'questioned' by the Gestapo. Now cast in the rôle of Scarlet Pimpernel he was at the enemy's door itself, preparing for the final incursion that would complete his mission of No 1 guerrilla of the Allied Armies. His regiment had become the bugbear of the German Army, as witness the following extract from another secret document by the General-kommando on 14 November 1944.

> "Subject... Appearance of SAS Troops in the Army Area.
>
> From captured enemy orders and papers it has been learned that the enemy intelligence service has tried to infiltrate single agents and teams to build up resistance-groups in the rear of the present German front (that is to say, in Alsace-Lorraine, and also in the Saar and Rhineland) in the same way as it did in France and Belgium during the years of the occupation. In this work, the SAS troops will share the principal role with the special espionage units.
>
> By SAS troops (Special Air Service) are meant especially trained parachute troops."

Then there is a long rigmarole about SAS combat methods and the directive winds up:

"On the landing of the SAS troops in France, it was learned that every member of the SAS had a pass in French and English. This stated that the bearer of the pass was a regular member of the Allied Forces under the command of General Eisenhower and that he was to be given every kind of support, information, means of transportation, care and lodging. It was signed by the leader of the Resistance groups in the area of France. The pass is a means of recognition for the introduction of SAS units in connection with the local resistance groups, partisans, escaped POW's etc.

Units in this command will immediately report all observations pointing to the presence of such SAS troops in the Army area.

Captured SAS members are to be turned over to the AOKI.
For the Army High Command,
Chief of the General Staff."

David Stirling's brainchild had certainly developed into something more than the happy band of adventurers whom Colonel Vladimir Panikoff so severely censured in his book *Popski's Private Army*; it had become public enemy No 1 for Hitler's Nazi regime and the special scourge of the skulking SS murderers, now seeking desperately to lose their identities.

Some of Mayne's troops were at this time in Holland linked with General Montgomery's Second Army and acting as cloak-and-dagger men, seeking out war criminals. Two SS Generals had already fallen to their guns, and for many more time was running out.

For several months these SAS men remained on active service before returning to England in March 1945. Others were working in close liaison with the American Army, and all were doing a splendid job, so splendid indeed that it was publicly recognised by the Supreme Commander, General Eisenhower, in an Order of the Day to Brigadier McLeod:

"I wish to send my congratulations to all ranks of the Special Air Service Brigade on the contribution which they have made to the success of the Allied Expeditionary Force.

The ruthlessness with which the enemy have attacked Special Air Service troops has been an indication of the injury which you were able to cause the German armed forces, both by your own efforts and by the information which you gave of German dispositions and movements.

Many Special Air Service troops are still behind enemy lines; others are being re-formed for new tasks. To all of them I say, well done and good luck."

Now they were poised to spearhead the invasion of Germany itself and again Colonel Paddy Mayne was given the personal duty – and to him, great honour – of leading his troops into battle.

Towering like a Goliath among average men, Colonel Mayne strode restlessly up and down the rain-swept quayside at Tilbury. Dawn was still three hours away on that murky night of Friday, 6 April 1945, but sleep was out of the question for the dashing leader of the Special Air Service. The mere thought that he was on his way once more to unleash his massive frame of combat hatred against the unsuspecting Germans sent tremors of excitement racing through him. He lived only to fight, and he would fight to die.

In a quiet, yet authoritative, compelling brogue, escaping his lips in short bursts, Colonel Paddy supervised the loading of supplies aboard two landing craft. The two squadrons of highly specialised troops over which he had taken personal command were completely self-contained in transports, equipment and rations, and also had a small 'Q' rear echelon. Every hitch and hold up on the dimly lit quayside brought another grunt of irritation from Paddy. He smoked cigarette after cigarette, softly cursing the stretch of water that lay between him and action.

"Look at 'im," whispered one trooper, leaning over the rail of the LCI "Like a cat on 'ot bricks. 'E can 'ardly wait! Rather 'im than me!"

Anyone who knew Paddy, and most of them did, having followed him across half-a-dozen battlefields, realised the reason for his impatience and unrest at moments such as these. They had witnessed many times before his sullen resentment at being kept away from the throat of the enemy. On the last occasion, in the Spring of 1944, he had been commanded by Higher Authority to stay behind in England while his men parachuted into France to help the Maquis blow up bridges and trucks, trains and convoys on their way to the front. He had become almost unbearable, almost impossible to live with until, at last, he was given permission to drop behind enemy lines and join his men in the thick of it all. It was not only his insatiable thirst for action which sparked off this feeling of inadequacy inside him, but rather more than that, it was the desire – almost lust – to share their risks. He was not a man to stand back and watch others do the dirty work. He always preferred to lead the way into danger, and would never ask any man to do anything which he would not do himself.

When he finally re-joined his troops it was like a scene from a James Bond thriller. Paddy, a massive Martian figure in his parachute harness, had a squeaky old portable gramophone strapped to one leg and a bottle of Irish Whiskey strapped to the other. "It's worth at least ten hand grenades," he used to say. The jeep which was dropped with him had a bullet-proof windscreen, machine guns in the nose and tail, and smoke canisters to blind and bewilder his Nazi pursuers.

Now the scene had changed. The guerrilla war waged by the SAS in the wooded hills east of Paris had disorganised and disrupted the Germans, and enabled the Allies to gain a toe-hold and later, a firm foothold. Every week that passed saw the Boche invader winkled from towns and villages which had lain under their mirror-polished jackboots for years, until they were pushed, squeezed and hurled back inside their own frontiers.

Paddy's own position had changed, too. A new Brigade Commander had been appointed who had a reputation almost in the same range as his own. This was the ex-Chindit 'Mad Mike' Calvert, credited with killing more Japanese in the jungle hand-to-hand fighting than any other man in the Burma campaign. The two battling giants did not particularly like one another at first sight, but Paddy was in full agreement with Mike's sentiments. In an Order of the Day he had called upon the regiment for one final effort to hand a knock-out blow to the 'Hun'. If a punch like that was to be thrown Paddy wanted to be there in the ring.

There was, in fact, less than a month to go before the Germans chucked in the towel, but only the most over-confident or optimistic overlord would ever have thought so when taking into account the ferocity of the enemy's rearguard. As Paddy motored towards the Nijmegen area, where the main Canadian Army Headquarters was based, a message was flashed that the situation was becoming critical. There was a real urgency for his two squadrons to move into the troubled area.

After driving all day, Paddy arrived at the Army HQ, to be met by a worried-looking brigadier. Facing their troops, and fighting still

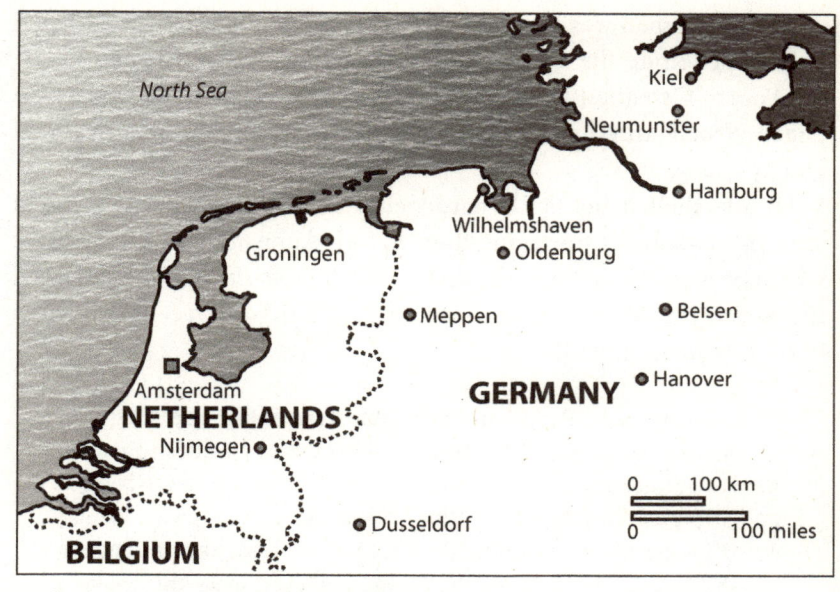

Netherlands and north-western Germany.

with almost fanatical zeal, were the remnants of Hitler's prize fighting paratroops. Little or no progress had been made against these zealots and the nature of the terrain was such that it was getting more and more difficult to win even an inch of ground. Paddy's face cracked into a huge grin. "Well," he chuckled, "we'll have to see what we can do then, won't we?"

When he studied the topography of the area in which he was to operate with his two squadrons his face hardened, and he began to ponder on his previous show of confidence. Almost entirely, the field of action was crossed and re-crossed by canals and dykes, making it very difficult for jeeps to get around with any degree of freedom. It was impossible for vehicles to drive off the roads, and here were very few places where they could reverse or turn around. Further, there were innumerable bridges and culverts which had been prepared for demolition by the enemy. Most of the fields around them had been turned into quagmires by drenching rainstorms, and would have been boggy even in dry weather. Conditions for an advance could not have been worse and Paddy could sense the uncertainty, which almost everyone shared, in the voices and actions of the men he had come to join.

The broad plan was for Paddy's two squadrons to leave the Meppen area to penetrate the German lines, then force a gap through which the Fourth Canadian Division could later pass. It sounded so easy on paper. Now Paddy had to make it look just as simple with deeds of glory.

He marshalled his battle-hardened veterans in a thickly wooded area just outside the town, and then delivered one of those pep talks for which he was renowned in the desert. One of the officers who attended the parade that late afternoon, Captain DH Harrison, recalls the words of his Commanding Officer:

> "Tomorrow," said Paddy, his steel-blue eyes emitting the kind of signals that augured ill for anyone who dared to question what he was about to say, "the Canadian Fourth Armoured Division is going to push to Oldenburg, that's about sixty miles away. We are going to operate on its left flank. After we have reached Oldenburg we shall push up north to the Wilhelmshaven area and make a real nuisance of ourselves. Now, is that clear?"

"After we have reached Oldenburg..." No 'ifs' or 'buts' about it. Failure, or the possibility of defeat, did not enter into his calculations. Yet before Mayne and his men could ever hope to reach their target they had to carve their way through thousands of heavily armed and desperate troops fighting a last-ditch battle for their Fatherland. He knew them of old in the desert, in Sicily, and in Italy, and he respected their valour, but the idea that they could in any way prevent him from reaching his objective never crossed Paddy's mind, or, if it did, he brushed it aside, as he would a fly on his forehead.

Anyone who expected Paddy Mayne, a resplendent warrior leader with a DSO and two bars strung across his mighty chest, to plunge rashly into an ill-conceived, daredevil action regardless of loss of life, was utterly mistaken. He always weighed up, very exactly, the possible consequences before allowing the men under his command to take unnecessary risks. He treasured his comrades as real folk, not merely as army numbers, or 'bodies' to be thrown in at random to plug a gap, and he worked out the operation with studied care to avoid useless bloodshed.

The detailed plan he finally decided on was for B-squadron of armoured jeeps, led by Major Bond, a close friend of Paddy's, and C-squadron, led by himself, to fan out along two parallel roads in the Pappenburg region, contacting one another at pre-arranged rendezvous points, and protecting each other with cover fire if the emergency arose. Before the attack really got under way, however, Major Bond and three others in his jeep hurled round a bend, straight into the line of fire from paratroopers hidden inside a shell-scarred mansion house. Bond lay dead, shot through the head.

With that small forward group was Corporal William Hull, from Paddy's home town of Newtownards, in County Down, who vividly remembers his CO's reaction when the news was flashed to him.

"He arrived on the scene in a white-hot fury," recalls Billy. "He quickly sized up the position and ordered me to go upstairs in a deserted cottage and cover him with machine gun fire from the rear window. He was determined to get the Germans inside that mansion house for killing his friend. He told me to start firing at the house as soon as his jeep swept round the bend in the road and headed for the 100-yard drive-way up to the house. Seconds later, his jeep swung round racing for the driveway entrance. Once inside, German tracers spat at him. They looked as though they were going right through Paddy's head. 'The guv'nor's copped it this time,' I thought, but I kept on firing at the German strongpoint just as he ordered me to."

Paddy's jeep roared right up to the door of the mansion house, Vickers guns blazing. In a flash, tommy-gun in hand, he darted through the door and the old building echoed with the non-stop chatter of a tommy-gun fired in anger. Within a few minutes a terrible carnage of ten Nazi paratroopers lay strewn around the rooms, the war very much over for them. Paddy, the ruthless avenger, emerged unscathed, tight-lipped and silent, but satisfied that his close friend, Major Bond, with whom he had fought, drunk and sung through many a doughty campaign, and would have nodded his approval at the debt that had been more than fully paid.

It was to be a memorable day for Paddy, for he won his fourth DSO, and became the most decorated hard-combat soldier in the British Army. The official citation gives both a graphic and detailed picture of what happened, and we print it here in full:

THIRD BAR TO THE DISTINGUISHED SERVICE ORDER
Lieutenant Colonel (temporary) Robert Blair Mayne (87306)
DSO 1st Special Air Service Regiment, Army Air Corps.

On Monday, 9th April, 1945, Lieutenant Colonel Mayne was ordered by the General Officer Commanding, 4th Canadian Armoured Division to lead his regiment (then consisting of two Armoured Jeep Squadrons) through the British lines and infiltrate through the German lines. His general axis of advance was north-east towards the city of Oldenburg, with the special task of clearing a path for Canadian armoured cars and tanks and also causing alarm and disorganisation behind the enemy lines. As subsequent events proved, the operation of Lieutenant Colonel Mayne's force was entirely and completely successful. This success, however was solely due to the brilliant military leadership and cool, calculating courage of Lieutenant Colonel Mayne, who by a single act of supreme bravery, drove the enemy from a strongly-held key village, thereby breaking the crust of the enemy defences on the whole of this sector. The following is a detailed account of Lieutenant Colonel Mayne's individual action, which called for both unsurpassed heroism and cool, clear-sighted military knowledge.

Lieutenant Colonel Mayne, on receiving a wireless message from the leading squadron reporting that it was heavily engaged by enemy fire and that the Squadron Commander had been killed, immediately drove forward to the scene of the action. From the time of his arrival until the end of the action he was in full view of the enemy and exposed to fire from small arms, machine guns, sniper's rifles, and panzer-fursts. On arrival, he summed up the situation in a matter of seconds and entered the nearest house alone, and ensured that the enemy here had either withdrawn or been killed. He then seized a Bren gun and magazines and, single-handed, fired burst after burst into a second house, killing or wounding the enemy there. He then ordered a jeep to come forward and take over his fire position, he himself returning to the forward section where he disposed the men to the best advantage and ordered another jeep to come forward. He got in the jeep and with another officer as rear-gunner, drove forward past the position where the Squadron Commander had been killed a few minutes earlier, and continued to a point a hundred yards ahead, where a further section of jeeps were halted by intense and accurate enemy fire. The section had suffered casualties in killed and wounded owing to heavy fire, and the survivors were unable at the time to influence the action in any way until the arrival of Lieutenant Colonel Mayne. He then continued along the road, all the time engaging the enemy with fire from his own jeep.

Having swept the whole area very thoroughly with close-range fire, he turned his jeep round and drove back again down the road, still in full view of the enemy. By this time the enemy had suffered casualties and had started to withdraw. Nevertheless they maintained an accurate fire on the road and it appeared almost impossible to extricate the wounded, who were in a ditch near the forward jeeps. Any attempt at rescuing these men under those conditions appeared virtually suicidal owing to the highly concentrated and accurate fire of the Germans.

Though he fully realised the risk he was taking Lieutenant Colonel Mayne turned his jeep round once again and returned to try to rescue these wounded. Then, by superlative determination and by displaying gallantry of the highest degree, and in the face of intense enemy machine-gun fire, he lifted the wounded one by one into the jeep, turned round and drove back to the main body. The entire enemy position had been wiped out, the majority having been killed or wounded. The squadron, having suffered no further casualties, were able to continue their advance and drive deeper behind the enemy lines to complete their work of sabotage and destruction of the enemy. Finally, they reached a point 20 miles ahead of the advance guard of the advancing Canadian Division, then threatening the rear of the Germans who finally withdrew. From the time of the arrival of Lieutenant Colonel Mayne, his cool, determined action, and his complete command of the situation, together with his unsurpassed gallantry, inspired all ranks. Not only did he save the lives of the wounded but also completely defeated and destroyed the enemy.

As if that were not enough, Paddy entered into the fray again, with renewed vigour, ever-thirsting for enemy blood. Some days later his squadron were operating from an inaccessible area somewhere along the road to Oldenburg. All of them were out on offensive patrols except Corporal Billy Hull and another trooper. They were brewing up a mug of tea when, quite suddenly, Paddy appeared.

"Hurry up, boys!" he snapped. "Get into my jeep. We have work to do."

With no time to gulp down their tea, they were being driven by Paddy at break-neck speed down the main road, then wheeled off to a lane lined with cedars. Some way down the lane they came to a small wood, or plantation, beyond which was another main road. Between this and the wood, was a narrow strip of tall undergrowth. Paddy ordered Corporal Hull to lie down alongside the jeep and train his Sten gun on the road. Within minutes the metallic rumble of Nazi half-tracks could be heard approaching.

"Hold your fire," hissed Paddy, "until I open up."

Trundling into sight came a convoy of troop carriers, each containing about thirty Germans. Paddy let the leading one go past, then opened up, and his two companions followed suit. A tornado of screams and shouts rose from the Germans. Their trucks began to blaze. Bodies were scattered everywhere. The ambush had thrown them into an utter panic.

Paddy thought at first that he might be able to send for reinforcements, but quickly decided that there was no other course but to withdraw for the moment. To do this, he had to reverse his jeep down the narrow lane for fifty yards before he could turn round, a tricky operation with the Germans firing wildly back at them. But all three returned safely. Next day, they went back again to survey the debris. Several troop carriers were completely gutted, and seventy corpses lay by the roadside.

From that moment, until 4 May, when the German Reich surrendered unconditionally, Paddy Mayne and his squadron continued to engage the enemy in hard and savage combat, supporting the Canadian tanks and armoured cars with such élan and effectiveness that the Canadians affectionately referred to them as "Our little friends in the mechanised mess-tins."

One remarkable incident is worth recalling here, if only to show how far the long arm of coincidence can stretch. In the Libyan desert two German officers, one an eminent surgeon in Berlin before the war, landed a light reconnaissance plane two hundred yards from some scrub where Paddy's unit was hiding out after a raid. Both were unarmed and it seemed their descent was innocent enough. Their own explanation was that they wanted to exercise their legs and have a quiet chat, and although it was farfetched and odd, to say the least of it, any alternative theory was equally unappealing. They were of course quickly rounded up and their plane was destroyed.

At first their presence was an embarrassment, especially as they would not give an undertaking not to attempt to escape, but after a few days they won Paddy and his troopers over by their charming manners and witty conversation. Then one night they took off, and soon the episode was forgotten. No one begrudged them their patriotism.

The scene now changes to North Germany where Colonel Mayne's marauding columns have just rushed a small town, six or seven miles from Oldenburg and taken a large number of prisoners. The wounded on both sides are numerous and amongst them is Paddy's sergeant who is badly injured.

The SAS were too far ahead of the Canadian Armoured Division to have Red Cross support and had therefore to rely upon the Germans for medical aid. It was given without stint.

As Paddy hurried about disposing his armour and establishing strong points in case of counter-attack, he suddenly came face to face with his former prisoner of the desert – the Berlin surgeon.

Recognition was mutual and instantaneous. Minutes later, after a brief exchange of courtesies, they reached the school house which was being used as a field dressing station, and hurried to the litter on which the sergeant lay, in a deep coma with the grey, sickly pallor of death on his face.

A major operation was necessary, explained the surgeon, but the patient would have to be removed to Oldenburg where there were proper hospital facilities. Several others whom he examined required similar attention.

"Very well," said Paddy, "Take them all and your own badly wounded too; but let me give you this warning, we shall be in Oldenburg tomorrow and if I hear of any ill treatment or neglect you will answer to me personally, and God help you. Understand?"

The doctor's countenance hardened.

"You need have no fear," he replied stiffly, "I am a doctor, not a butcher."

"We shall see," observed the big Irishman, whose trust in his fellow men had been rudely shattered by his experiences in France.

The next day his prediction came true and Oldenburg fell to his squadrons. At the hospital he found the surgeon, now in white overalls and very much in the thick of it, and he was glad to shake his hand in admiration and friendship.

Elsewhere, some of the other men had very unique experiences. At Belsen, D-squadron of the 1st SAS was the first to arrive and what they saw was to horrify not only them but the entire world. Although the wretched place was never intended as an extermination camp it had become, through the criminal and inexcusable neglect of its administrators, a cesspool of disease and plague. And with the approach of Allied forces panic seems to have seized the guards and, in a state of nervous hysteria, murder became a commonplace occurrence.

It was, in fact, on 12 April, that the German military Commander at Bergen approached the Commander of Allied Forces in that area and asked for a local truce in regard to the concentration camp compound at Bergen-Belsen. He explained that typhus had broken out and was in danger of spreading.

Lieutenant Gunning and Sergeant-Major Bob Bennett of the SAS were sent to investigate, and the memory of what they saw will live with them for ever. Forty thousand men and women in an advanced state of starvation and emaciation, many of them suffering from typhus, and thirteen thousand unburied corpses. To them, it was the symbol of the rottenness and vileness of the Nazi regime and their tempers were none too sweet when they confronted the Commandant, Josef Kramer.

While Gunning talked to him in German, Irma Grese, who had recently arrived from the dreaded Auschwitz camp[1], leaned against a hut and sneered. It was more than Gunning could endure and he slapped her hard.

As Gunning and Kramer talked, some weird skeleton forms emerged from a hutment close by and whimpering like animals, dragged themselves forward, to a heap of rotten, evil-smelling turnips. Clawing and snarling at one another, they started to fight as they sought to devour this rubbish. Then two jackbooted guards rushed up and lashed them with whips. An SAS trooper in a jeep shot these devils dead, on the instant.

Shortly afterwards, D-squadron drove into Kiel. All resistance had ceased, but the Germans were armed and as Major Tonkin had only one hundred SAS men at his disposal, he decided to proceed cautiously and avoid unnecessary friction.

Half an hour later, however, Sergeant-Major Bennett who was

---

1 Irma Grese was a high-ranking concentration camp warden, later executed for war crimes.

patrolling the canal bank in a jeep, saw a large boat pulling away from the quay. With him sat Sergeant Ridler, who spoke German fluently. Quickly the latter asked a passer-by what was going on, and the answer he got sent them rushing to the quay with the twin Vickers firing over the ship's bows.

In a few seconds the ship was back and several hundred concentration camp internees of many nationalities were being unmanacled. They were the fourth batch destined that day for a watery grave. The incriminating evidence of Gestapo savagery, it seemed, was in the process of being destroyed.

It was a situation which in any other circumstances called for swift and terrible retribution but Tonkin had to pause and think hard on the position of his squadron and its isolation in a city crowded with enemy troops.

Nevertheless, on information received from the reprieved wretches, they dashed off to two concentration camps at nearby Ochtumsand and Neumunster, and to the local prison and released all the inmates. There were 'incidents' of course and some SS guards got hurt but it was only to be expected that the SAS men in their prevailing mood were not disposed to use kid gloves.

The war was now over, but when Paddy got first-hand reports of these hideous camps and the monsters who ran them he was sickened to the marrow. Enemy fighting soldiers he understood, and from them in battle he asked for no mercy. Neither did he show any; but to helpless captives he was always compassionate.

A warrior giant with a giant heart.

CHAPTER 21

Ring out the bells

IN THE WILD scenes that followed the surrender Paddy Mayne found himself in a madly excited, lit-up Brussels, crammed with fighting men of many nationalities, and bursting with anticipation of all the good things in life so long forgotten. And what happened to Paddy? Why, just what would happen to such a man on such a day! He met in the street an RAF officer, whom he had known in his university days, and became involved in the most embarrassing moment of his life. After the pair had downed a goodly measure of whiskey, Paddy suddenly realised that he had nowhere to sleep in the overcrowded capital. They were in an RAF club and his friend spoke to some of his fellow officers who were a little way off.

When he returned he cheerfully announced that all was well and they were now fixed up.

Unsteadily, the two friends picked their way through the cobbled streets to a dingy building sandwiched between two office blocks. It was on the shabby side, thought Paddy, but who could be choosy after what they had been through? Every waking hour had been spent hunting out the enemy, and every ounce of his seemingly boundless energy had been devoted to their pursuit and destruction. Now he was tired, and drunk. Happy, and drunk. Sleep would be a mercy.

If he had known, or cared, where he was going to sleep for the night, Paddy might have had second thoughts. As it was, his good friend let him into a well-patroned brothel run, as often by a hatchet-faced, but a strangely understanding woman of indeterminate years. She took one look at the magnificent fighting Colonel, her beady eyes sweeping along the proud winged dagger and row of medals on his breast, and realised at once – or thought she did – what the huge man wanted. She led him up one flight of stairs, into a cramped bedroom, where he sank gratefully into snoring slumber still dressed.

But, after five minutes, a polite but repetitive knocking noise aroused him. And there, framed in the doorway stood a voluptuous blonde, her cupid's bow slightly parted in a smile of welcome, mingled with expectancy. Of sex, perhaps, and the reward that might come with it from such an impressive, handsome fighting man.

Paddy jerked an eye open, then sat up with a start.

"What in hell's name is going on here?" he growled. "Would you mind getting out? I want to sleep."

Puzzled by this unexpected reception, but seeing the danger if she stayed, the blonde stalked out and slammed the door.

Five minutes later, just as Paddy had settled back once more in restful repose, there came another knock on the door. Madam, fearing that the girl she had sent up had not met exactly with the great Colonel's approval, had selected a shapely brunette for his pleasure. But she might as well have sent up a sack of coal. Paddy, in a near drunken stupor, imagined that he was seeing things. The brunette, very pleasing to the eye, and ostensibly willing to please if she had the chance, sat by his bedside and began to run her fingers through his hair. But she soon jumped up when she saw that the famous Irish Colonel wanted no part of it. Paddy's temper flared.

"Get out!" he roared, pointing to the door. And she fled.

Below the stairs, Madam was almost tearing her hair, wondering what she could do to please this high-ranking and remarkably good-looking officer. Fortunately, or so she thought, her most expensive and exciting girl had arrived in the nick of time. If the Colonel did not like her, she reasoned, then he must be out of his mind. Confidently, she sent the wiggling creature up to where Paddy lay, a slumbering mammoth of a man.

For a moment, she lingered in the doorway, a slinky figure of loveliness. If she had been soiled by usage, it did not show. Where other girls had failed, she never failed to please. Men were men the world over, and when they weren't fighting a war they were fighting over women.

Suddenly, Paddy sat bolt upright and blinked in amazement. The girl thought at first that he was overwhelmed at being confronted by such beauty that he was speechless with admiration. She began to caress him and threw her slender arms around his neck. In alarm, Paddy leapt from his bed, grabbed his bag and stumped out of the room.

"What kind of hotel is this, anyway?" he grunted and staggered drunkenly away into the night.

It was with considerable relief that he returned to England and sanity. Or so it seemed until his transport ship pulled into Gravesend with forty jeep-loads of happy SAS men singing as they waited for the ramps to go down. They gaped in astonishment as a whole team of gold-braided Customs Officers lined up on the dockside, ready to levy duty on, or confiscate, the spoils of war, the silks, wines, watches, cameras and souvenirs that the fighting raiders had brought home with them. Paddy came to the rail and glared down at them. He turned to his men.

"Start up your engines!" he snapped. "Drive your jeeps down the ramps, full speed ahead!" And above the roar of the exhausts he yelled, "Good luck, lads! Enjoy your leave!"

The regiment was not yet ready for the red tapes of Civvy Street, and on the day of their homecoming they felt that the world was theirs. It was to be a short-lived stay for Paddy's men, however, for once back at the unit's headquarters in Chelmsford, Essex, word came through leave was to be postponed. Over in Norway, an occupying enemy army of more than 1,000,000 men under General Falkenhorst was waiting to be disarmed, and the 1st and 2nd SAS Regiments were to be charged with the task. American air transport planes were waiting at stand-by and would take off in four hours.

That night, the SAS veterans landed at Stavenger with a full complement of jeeps and supplies. The Germans were surprisingly polite and friendly and seemed relieved that their deceased Führer had spared them the heroics of a fight to the death. But the following day something like a slight civil war occurred.

It was a clash – nobody ever knew why – between Paddy and his Brigade Commander which set tongues wagging in the Officers' Mess. It was guest night and the drinks flowed freely. Paddy stood with his back to the Brigade Commander, 'Mad Mike' Calvert, the Burma hero, deeply engaged in conversation with a fellow officer. He must have said something provocative about his boss which the boss overheard. For suddenly Mike hurled himself at Paddy in a rugby tackle, and brought him crashing to the floor. What followed is described by 'Mad Mike' himself:

> "We both lay there," he recalls, "until he sprang to his feet and grabbed me with his enormous hands. With apparent ease he lifted me bodily from the floor and threw me over his left shoulder. I landed some distance away and cracked my head on an iron fender. The Medical Officer treated my cuts with ice and lemon taken from the drinks, but both my eyes became blackened and swollen. We still remained good friends. I never bore any ill-will against him, I got what I deserved, and I would rather it came from him than any other man. I've met the top soldiers of a dozen nations, but Paddy was one of the best. He was certainly a better soldier than I was. What made him so distinguished was that even when the job was done, he was ready for more."

The troopers of the Special Air Service were not allowed, however, to sojourn long at Stavenger. Intelligence reports were coming in of a menacing situation at the industrial and tourist town of Odda, ninety miles from Bergen and lying in a cleft below the Folgefonn Glacier at the head of the long, narrow, but stunningly beautiful, fjord of Sör. Here large numbers of tough SS troops were concentrating and it was thought that despite their country's surrender they might blow up the network of hydro-electric plants which were in the area, and generally put on a mad-dog show.

In the event these apprehensions were unfounded and when Colonel Paddy and his men got there they found the Germans docile and correct in every way.

This state of affairs gave the veterans of the desert a much needed holiday and they relaxed in fine style – some courting the comely local girls but most enjoying the strong Norwegian beer. Their billet was a large hotel, part of which, resting on concrete stilts, overhung the fjord.

One night Paddy Mayne and 'Mad Mike' held a private celebration on the hotel roof during which they decided to amuse themselves by walking the parapet and throwing sandbags (put there for air-raid protection) down at vehicles below.

A few moments later Hull appeared and before he knew what was happening he was grabbed by the arms and legs and flung into the icy cold water, 120 feet below.

Fortunately for him, he was wearing light denim trousers and slippers and was able to swim to safety. As he scrambled out he could hear the revellers above roaring with laughter, but he was not angry. The bond of affection between him and his Commanding Officer was too strong to be broken by a piece of drunken horseplay.

From Odda the two regiments were transferred to Bergen, Norway's second City, and here the men were decidedly unhappy. Some of them, and indeed most, felt that they had been away from home long enough and very naturally began letting off steam. Instead of being treated as liberators, or at least as allies, they were looked at askance and frequently subjected to inhospitality, even offensiveness.

Any trooper courting a Norwegian girl – and there were no others – or displaying high spirits in a tavern, would find himself, as likely as not, on the receiving end of a police baton. Even the good-humoured Sergeant Major Bob Bennett and his friend Sergeant Douggie Langston ended up in jail after a harmless spree.

When Colonel Paddy heard about it he was livid and went round to the police station from his hotel billet and brusquely demanded their release. In the mood he was in there was to be no shilly-shallying and the police realised this very quickly when they noticed him fingering his Sten gun in dangerous agitation.

Incidents such as this became even more numerous as time went on and reports of gross brutality being meted out to SAS troopers by the Grey Shadows – the name given to the Bergen police by the Britishers because of the colour of their uniforms – became so persistent that a Major of the SAS Regiment complained to Paddy about it.

The advice he got led to ten jeep-loads of SAS, armed with heavy sticks, driving into the town centre and fighting a pitched battle with the Grey Shadows. It was all quite unofficial but the result was that the Norwegian Government demanded the immediate withdrawal of both SAS regiments to England.

Nobody was sorry to go. And on this Gilbertian note the most daring and quixotic unit in the British Army finished its illustrious record of service in the Second World War.

With them went the memory of the frozen serpent that they had taken to their bosom.

CHAPTER 22

A borderline case

Beating up foreign police is an action unlikely to endear one to the citizens of a foreign city, and Blair Mayne's part in the Bergen fracas could hardly be regarded as a distinguished episode on the credit side of his account. Yet it was perfectly in character, for Mayne was no exception to the immutable Law of Opposites; his immense strength and his infinite gentleness; the cold blooded planning which so often in the past had led to hot blooded action; his ability to inspire friendship – and dislike. All part of the man's make-up.

No man of his stature (in every sense of the word) could go through life without making enemies. He was no exception to the rule, and some of his critics were neither slow nor reluctant to voice their criticisms, usually, of course, behind his back. It was noticeable, however, that this personal prejudice or dislike or jealousy or whatever it was, was almost invariably mixed with at least some degree of admiration and respect. Like that of a famous British general.

At the time he was allowing Mayne a very free hand in his maraudings in the desert and one of his staff officers said to him, regarding Mayne: "I can't understand how you tolerate the man. Why do you?"

The general smiled, that is to say his lips took up the shape of a smile while his steely eyes remained static. "Because," he said, "Mayne is useful to the army. He is useful to me. He is in a class by himself in a really dirty mopping-up operation, and you don't use a tooth brush to clean out sewers. You must use a cruder instrument. I could do with half a dozen more men like him. Ten more or a dozen would, of course, be disastrous. I'd probably have a mutiny on my hands. God knows what he'll do with himself when peace breaks out."

A number of people wondered about that.

War was the man's natural background. Against this background of blood and bullets, mayhem and skulduggery there was nothing incongruous in his behaviour. He was, as it were, a natural part of the pattern. He *enjoyed* war, and it was while he was talking one night, in a club in Cairo, on his favourite topic that he met with one of his very rare defeats.

He was not drunk, but slightly 'unsober', and enjoying the attention of his audience. When Mayne was in full verbal spate it was not always easy to get a word in, but this time somebody did; somebody who was either brave enough or stupid enough to tell him that he was a bloody fool to drink as much as he did. A dangerous remark, but Mayne took it in his stride.

He laughed. "I know I do, I like it and I can't help it. And even if I *could* help it I'd go on doing it. But –", he made a sweeping gesture with his arm – "but then I'll not touch a sup of it when there's killing to be done." He took a gulp of his drink, "A man needs enemies to keep him on the balls of his feet." He looked round as though challenging anyone to contradict him, and his eye met that of a small slim man who had been listening with care to this philosophy on booze and blood. Mayne drew himself up to his vast height and said:

"Don't you agree with me, little man?"

The small man smiled. "I cannot imagine," he said, picking his words with careful deliberation. "I cannot imagine that any man with you for his friend would have any need of enemies."

It took a moment or so for the cruel and undeserved insult to register. When it did, Blair's massive frame became suddenly still. But his hands clenched and there was murder in his eyes. There was the sort of silence you can lean against. Then suddenly he drained his glass, banged it down on the table, turned on his heel and walked away.

"Christ!" said somebody. "Christ! You might have got yourself strangled."

"I might," said the small man. "I might, but I didn't. Anyway, who ever heard of a horse bothering a horse fly?"

What *did* he do when peace came?

Many things. Anything for kicks. Anything from joining in an expedition to the Antarctic to dabbling in hypnotism. And he drank. Heavily on occasions. He also became Secretary of the Incorporated Law Society of Northern Ireland and it was in this capacity – incredible as it seems – that he was to stage and carry out an expedition quite in keeping with his guerrilla exploits in the desert and elsewhere. Equally incredibly the operation began in the benign surroundings of a golf course.

The difference between cracking a man's skull open with the butt of a revolver and striking a golf ball with a golf club is wide, to say the least of it, and Paddy could never be described as an ardent golfer. The eighteen holes of a round were little more than stepping stones to the nineteenth hole where wassail and good-fellowship would prevail but, as Secretary of the Law Society it was one of his unofficial chores to organise from time to time tournaments for jaded and overworked attorneys who, like himself, were ready to grab at any chance to escape from the stultifying atmosphere of an office or a law court.

And so it came about that on a warm and sultry day, beneath the towering majesty of the famed Mountains of Mourne, the legal gentry of Northern Ireland engaged their Southern brethren on the fairways and greens – and even in the club-house bar – of Warrenpoint Golf Club in friendly rivalry.

In the clubhouse group Paddy reigned supreme and, as with the Pied Piper of Hamelin, the sycophants and suckers-up, like the rats, flocked to him in droves. He was, however, pretty discriminating in his choice of friends and gave only a very limited licence to this rag-tag and bobtail. If he could not suffer fools gladly, in his official capacity he had to suffer them.

Alcohol helped. And as the hours ran out and the shadows lengthened so he talked and he drank until the moment came when he discovered that he had outstayed most of his boon companions. Almost worse than the desertion of his friends was the disappearance of the bar steward. Things were becoming serious; their gravity increased by the fact that he was without transport at a time when transport was essential for a foray in search of drink. He felt that having discharged his duty as the Society's Secretary, he was now entitled to look to his own interests, which at this time coincided with the quenching of a very considerable thirst.

Looking, like sister Anne, for help in time of need, his eyes fell on one Desmond, a legal acquaintance and a fanatical admirer of his who, he suspected, would be glad of a closer friendship. So, when they spoke together, it was natural that Desmond should offer him a lift home in his smart new Rover car which had just lately been delivered to him. His friend, Eoin, was delighted too that the illustrious Colonel was coming along with them.

A rising moon was painting streaks of silver on the still waters of Carlingford Lough. At Newry the car turned northward. The large passenger in the back seat leaned forward and a heavy hand fell on Desmond's shoulder.

"Where, Desmond, do you think you're going?" The question was put with the utmost politeness and deceptive casualness. It was almost an academic question, like that of one seeking knowledge for the sake of knowledge and with no ulterior motive in view.

"To Belfast and then to your home at Mount Pleasant," answered Desmond, expecting an immediate accolade of appreciation.

He was well out of his reckoning. "You will do no such thing!" snapped Paddy. "We're going South of the Border for a drink."

It was no use the timid attorney's protesting that it was close to 3.00 am; that he and Eoin were tired, if not actually worn out and verging on insobriety; or that both the Customs posts would be closed and to cross the Border in the circumstances would be a serious breach of the law. As far as Paddy was concerned at the moment there was no Border and there was no law – and the getting of that drink was, in his present mood, just as important as the wrecking of a German airfield had been to him ten years earlier. Furthermore, there was no denying him once his mind was made up.

Desmond and Eoin were both well aware of this and at that moment preferred to face the wrath of the Customs officials than the Hyde half of 'Jekyll and Hyde' now breathing snore-like down their necks from the back seat.

They headed for the Border and to relieve the tension Eoin burst into an old rebel song. Immediately, Colonel Paddy, whose repertoire of all Irish Songs was a treasure house, joined in.

The cool stillness of the summer's night was thrashed by the noisy ballad as they sang:

> "It was down by Brockagh Corner
> One morning I did stray,

I met a fellow rebel there
And this to him did say:
I bear orders from the Captain
To assemble at Drumbar
But how are we to get there
Without a motor car?"

"Now, Barney, dear, be of good cheer,
I'll tell you what we'll do,
The Orangemen have plenty
While we have yet but few,
We'll wire to Stranorlar
Before we walk so far
And we'll give the boys
A jolly ride in Johnston's motor car."

"When Dr Johnston got the wire
He soon pulled on his shoes.
He said, 'This case is urgent.
I haven't time to lose.'
He wore a fancy castor hat
And on his breast a star,
You could hear the din going through Glenfinn
Of Johnston's motor car."

"And when he got to the Reelin Bridge,
There were some rebels there.
He knew the game was up with him
And at them he did stare,
He said, 'I have a permit
For travelling near and far.'
'You can keep your English permit
We want your motor car.'"

"They put the car in motion
And filled her to the brim
With guns and bayonets shining,
And Johnston he did grin.
Then Barney raised the Sinn Fein flag
And they shot off like a star
And they gave three cheers for liberty
And Johnston's motor car."

The Border came, the Border went – and through the night the Rover roared on, with raucous musical accompaniment, like the avant garde of a travelling circus.

By the time they reached Dundalk they had run out of verses and breath. Which was probably as well. The silence – save for the purring of the engine and the whispering rush of the wheels – was broken by a sudden command from Paddy.

"Stop here!"

The market town slumbered. Leaving cats and felons on one side, it is likely that no one was awake at that hour. The car pulled in to the kerb opposite the Imperial Hotel and as it did so the back seat passenger sprang out and practically fastened himself to the door-bell. No answer.

He continued to press on the bell button, but the only sound to be heard from within – apart from the intermittent ringing of the bell – was the ticking and asthmatic whirring of the ancient grandfather clock in the hallway.

Frustrating.

Frustrating that is to the bell ringer, but a considerable relief to Desmond and Eoin. They were pleased, very pleased indeed. Perhaps Hyde might now become Jekyll and they would all get the hell out of it and find the warm comfort of their beds.

Then suddenly the bell ceased and Colonel Paddy was gone.

But where?

His presence had been less than comforting, but now his absence filled them with a greater disquiet. Where on earth had he gone and what was he up to?

Their questions were answered by the rattling of chains and the sliding of bolts. The door of the hotel opened. Dimly silhouetted in the doorway Paddy was beckoning to them.

It was Hobson's choice, but perhaps a few sharp whiskies would liven them up a little.

Inside, Paddy, now behind the bar, dispensed hospitality with a lavish hand and they wondered what charm their host had exercised on the night porter to have been allowed this privilege.

But better things were in store for them, for presently Paddy inquired what they would like for breakfast? Eoin, who had been plied with three large tumblerfuls of neat whiskey, gasped out that anything at all would do. Poor Eoin! at that moment frantically swallowing his saliva to keep the gorge where it belonged; Desmond, not much better but a little relieved by a fingers-down-the-throat experiment a few minutes previously in the toilet.

Anything that would call a halt to this alcoholic nightmare would be a welcome relief and so he suggested rashers and eggs.

Again their host disappeared.

Some time later (one cannot be more precise since time had long since ceased to be of any material importance), Paddy returned, swallowed another shot of neat whiskey, and led them upstairs to the dining room.

"What about a contribution from us?" suggested Desmond meekly and Eoin, despite his plight, nodded agreement.

"Afraid not, gentlemen," replied Mayne, "I have already attended to the bill and, anyway, I consider you to be my guests." (Paddy had left sufficient to cover the bill on top of the locked cash register.)

In addition to his colour and personality and his undoubted eccentricity Colonel Paddy was one of the last of the big spenders. Money seemed to mean nothing to him and he appeared to have an inexhaustible supply of it.

Some contemporaries hinted darkly that he had possessed himself of some of the top Nazis' loot, in Germany. There was no evidence for this. Actually his family was already comfortably off and his income and emoluments as Secretary of the Law Society would have been sufficient to ward off all financial worries. Both his present companions knew well of his big spending reputation, and so they wisely decided to accept his generosity this early morning without further demur.

This Mayne was for sure a charmer, they thought, as they tucked into the meal. But whatever he was, the invisible night porter must be the very salt of the earth.

It was just then that this worthy made his appearance.

There, swaying gently, from sleepiness or drink or a combination of both, he stood at the door. Tousled hair, baggy trousers, greasy waistcoat, rolled-up shirt sleeves and bulging hysterical eyes that looked as if they would tumble down his cheeks any moment. Indeed an apoplectic fit seemed very much in the offing, all the more so because he kept opening and shutting his mouth without uttering a single word.

If his appearance shocked them, the sight of them seemed to threaten his sanity.

"This poor chap is not well," observed Paddy, almost unnecessarily, and rose from the table and passed him at the door. "I think it would be well if we *all left* now," he called over his shoulder to his companions and they noted the warning tone of his voice.

They, too, hurried from the dining room and headed for the hall door at the bottom of the stairs. Suddenly, bedlam broke loose.

"Police! Police! Thieves! Burglars! Blackguards!"

The night porter had obviously found his voice at last. And his legs too, for they heard him rushing down the stairs hot on their heels.

The Rover's self-starter (God be praised and so say all of us!) worked with smooth efficiency and, on a snapped order from Paddy, headed South.

With the Border and safety a mere five miles to the North this seemed a strange manoeuvre until Paddy instructed Desmond to make a detour of the town, and then double back. They might be drunk, but cunning is not the prerogative of the sober, and the direction the car had taken was firmly implanted in the mind of the hysterical night porter. No doubt he would pass on this interesting piece of information at the earliest possible moment.

It was not a matter of "Came the Dawn", because the dawn had already arrived and it was 7.15 am in the morning. The Custom guards would now be at their posts. Desmond, a sober as well as a sombre man by nature and habit, thought about the immediate future with dread in his heart and a sinking feeling in his stomach. Beside him Eoin was not worrying at all. He was not worrying because he had suddenly crumpled into a sound sleep. Desmond envied him. If only this were part of a dream and he could wake to find himself safe and sound in his own bed.

Instead of a dream he was suddenly confronted with the grim reality of two Custom officers standing in the road ahead. They looked unpleasantly cool and efficient in the ruthless morning light. A squadron of butterflies executed an intricate manoeuvre in his stomach. He was in deep trouble. Entering the Republic without having a triptych franked by the Customs (it had seemed *such* fun as they sang their way over the border an hour or so ago) could mean forfeiture of his car and a heavy fine. As to his professional reputation – it simply didn't bear thinking about. From beside him and behind him the only support he was receiving in his hour of peril was double-snoring.

One of the officers approached the now stationary car and asked Desmond what the delay was. Why was he stopping there instead of going into the shed to have his triptych stamped.

Wilting, and scared out of his wits, Desmond tried to explain. He said that he and his companions had gone South on a harmless frolic the night before after the Customs post was closed. He said that he had been a respectable solicitor for nearly twenty-five years and that this was his first peccadillo, and pointed out (without much conviction) that it was, after all, a minor lapse. He finished with the optimistic hope that the officer might see his way to overlook it and allow him and his friends to proceed home. Uriah Heap, washing his hands with invisible soap, could not have been more plaintive or servile.

The cold-eyed official was unmoved. He too had been in his job for some twenty-five years, during which time his heart had been torn out of his rib-cage, or gone of its own accord, and left him with no human feeling.

"Kindly step inside, sir!" he barked. "This is an extremely serious matter and we shall require a full account of your actions."

Dry of tongue, and the butterflies still doing aerobatics in his stomach, Desmond followed the now martial figure into the hut. On parade there were three other gold-braided officers, all sharp-eyed and hostile. They began to crowd him. And all the time he was wondering about that night porter; what he had told the police; what the police were doing; had the alarm gone out yet? At any moment now a telephone call might alert these dreadful customs men to the fact that a certain Rover car and its occupants were 'wanted'. A blacker situation he could not imagine. Now, a sheaf of foolscap paper was dumped in front of him on the desk. It was headed in strange Irish characters, which spelt out the words CUSTAIM A MAL, which he took to mean "Customs and Exercise".

"Holy mackerel!" he swore to himself with unexpected vehemence. "If I survive this, I'll turn my coat and join the Orange Order. The dirty bastard sons of the great whore!"

But unwisely and surprisingly for one so experienced in law Desmond swallowed the official bait, hook line and sinker, and started to scrawl out the evidence against himself.

It is a very true axiom that no lawyer is to be trusted with his own affairs and this distracted wretch was no exception. Now he was in full flight, writing with the ready facility of an author on the wings of inspiration.

But by now, Paddy, after drowning with weariness and drink, was waking up. "What's the hold-up?" he enquired of Eoin.

But he did not wait for the answer. Jumping out of the car he strode into the office to find out for himself. A Customs officer tried to hedge him away from the table where his unhappy friend was madly scratching out his own ruin, but Paddy angrily swept him aside, reached the table and thrust a large hand on the foolscap.

"Now, what's going on here?" he demanded fiercely.

A sour-faced official told him to mind his own business or else he would be charged with aiding or abetting. A glance from Colonel Mayne, and then through his clenched teeth the growl:

"God be with the days when a gentleman could put his whip across the backs of flunkeys like you!"

This was a moment for action not words and taking Desmond by the elbow with one hand while he grabbed the sheet of foolscap with the other, he headed back to the car. One of the Customs officers, bolder than the rest, tried to seize hold of him but Paddy simply lifted him up like a suckling infant and flung him into the nearby hedge.

"Now all aboard!" he ordered. "Get into that car and drive us all home. I've had enough of these jackeens for one night."

Desmond, whose condition now was no better than the hapless night porter's had been half an hour earlier, tottered to the car as finished a picture of horror as one could imagine. Shaking like an aspen leaf, he slumped down behind the wheel and started muttering pious imprecations to high Heaven in a voice that was lost in incoherence and self pity.

The car roared away and swept past the Northern Ireland Customs shed just fifty yards further on. It might have been a carbon copy of one of those desert affairs except that German sentries are always German sentries and Customs authorities are horses of a different colour. Desmond was convinced that he was ruined and, greatly daring, accused Paddy of bringing this about.

"Jesus, Mary and Joseph!" he wailed half turning round to Paddy, in the back seat. "You've ruined me this night and day!"

"Hold your tongue, you blithering idiot!" retorted Paddy. "If it hadn't been for me back there, you would have lost your precious car. You should be thankful, extremely thankful! Buying drink, in fact, to celebrate your narrow escape."

Eoin, still sleepy until the mention of that magic word, cocked up his ears. "Och! by God! Aye, Blair, you're right there," he piped up, lapsing into the country dialect of his native Ballymoney in North Antrim. "We shall need a drop o' something to wash the bad taste of the drink out of our mouths."

In Banbridge town in the County Down, they met a man to supply their want. He was Peter Campbell, and although his bar didn't open officially until 10.00 am he recognised that common humanity was above the law and that these human beings were in a bad way.

Despairing Desmond could not be cheered, even when Paddy slapped him cheerfully on the shoulder and said:

"Buck up, old boy! I will put in a word for you when the Disciplinary Committee has you up for disbarment."

"O, Sacred Heart of Jesus! Blair," moaned Desmond. "Don't be joking at a time like this. I have a wife and four young children, and this is the end. Utter ruination. The absolute end."

Paddy grinned as he beckoned to Peter to recharge their glasses.

"Och, it's not so bad as that, Desmond. Judging by your efforts back there you can always turn your hand to journalism."

Then putting his hand into what he often described as his 'poacher's pocket' he pulled out the sheaf of foolscap paper on which Desmond had written his own condemnation. Bending down to the fire, Paddy placed it on the flaming peat in the grate.

Like the Border trouble the previous night, Desmond's worries came and went and their exit was assisted by more string-pulling than all the harps of Erin's Green Isle had ever got through all the ages. Colonel Paddy, in peace as in war, believed above all in loyalty to his friends.

What strings he was able to pull to hush up the whole affair are not known; it is enough that they were pulled with success.

You could do what the hell you liked with the Germans in wartime and that was that, but the mopping up operation after the Dundalk affair and the Border guards must have been distasteful to Mayne. To fight your way out of trouble is one thing – to talk and buy your way out another. Such are the penalties of peace for a man of war.

But for Colonel Paddy peace was an illusion and the drums were still beating. Somewhere in the temple of his soul there was a bedlam that would not answer the command to peace.

The dramatic and to him unpalatable transition from guerrilla leader to Law Society official induced a mental complex akin to schizophrenia and at times even his best friends became exasperated. Some indeed were actually frightened of him.

Morbid depressions, followed by bouts of heavy drinking, alternated with moods of professional and social responsibility and general bonhomie.

Unfortunately, highly coloured versions of his hell-raising came into general currency and dulled the aura of his wartime heroism. It was a great pity for no more tender-hearted man ever lived.

Remorse attended him perhaps too well and after a heavy spree he was stabbed with guilt. At such times he retired to Mount Pleasant to his beloved flowers and shrubs or to the loneliness of the trout streams to find himself again. And his mother, tender and loving – the very pulse and light of his heart – was always there to comfort and succour him.

Sometimes preoccupation with his work held him together but it was obvious to those close to him that he was hungry and thirsty for something beyond his present vision.

Peace was no more for him than old age.

The way of his death may have been a mockery of the man, but was it tragic? His was not the mind to have been able to cope with the weight of years. Of him and his kind the poet wrote: "They shall not grow old as we that are left grow old."

Paddy Mayne did not grow old. The Black Camel wisely saw to that.

Epilogue

THE FACE OF the world has changed since 1939. The holocaust of the First World War, in which millions died in the mud – at Verdun, at the Marne, at the Somme, in the swamps of Flanders – should have burned deeply into the soul of every European the lesson that War, which is the spawn of pride and arrogance and greed, is a dreadful and desperate mode of arbitration in human affairs, and that the paramount necessity for men on this unhappy planet is the curbing of individual and communal selfishness and the achievement of brotherhood and respect of every human being.

Unhappily, the lesson was not even faintly grasped and the two decades after the 1918 Armistice saw the spread of a poisonous cynicism and the cult of a reckless pursuit of wealth and pleasure emasculate the victorious nations, while in defeated countries there arose an appalling barbarism that was never matched even in the eras of Attila or Genghis Khan.

Inhuman qualities surged upwards in the 1920s and 1930s and made Europe a madhouse. The bedlam of ranting voices – the raucous, shouting voices of brown and black shirted thugs rose to a fearful crescendo from Prussia to Palermo and the fanatical, goose-stepping, jackbooted minions of two monstrous leaders swarmed into the weaker countries and looted, enslaved and massacred the helpless millions.

The democracies, weak and decadent and utterly unprepared looked up with shock and horror and saw that Armageddon was upon them. The old men, who had learnt nothing from the last carnage, stood petrified and the young generation, nurtured on the empty trivial banalities of the post-war era, were lost and bewildered when the lights went out and the kissing had to stop.

Then the call went forth. From factories, offices, great country houses and humble labourers' cottages they had to go. Torn from loving parents, from husbands, wives, sweethearts and children, they had to go. Half trained and utterly uncomprehending the savage demands of the blitzkrieg they had to go – across the stormy Atlantic amid the perils of deadly U-boats; into Norway where the Hun was solidly entrenched; into Flanders to face the steel of Rundstedt's Panzers which drove them into the sea; through the trackless desert sand of Libya where death struck in the blazing sun. It was children against giants. The weak, untutored children of the trifling, jazzing, crooning, democracies helplessly faced the cold-eyed, granite-faced, fanatical, highly trained enemy, nurtured on hate, iron discipline and incredibly advanced techniques of terror and destruction.

There was only one answer. Heroes had to be found and found quickly, from amongst shambling crowds of shopkeepers, schoolmaster, lawyers and artisans who had known only the placid life of village squares and cool sequestered academic backwaters a class of supermen had swiftly to be created. Quiet, tolerant, good-humoured men to be transmogrified into cunning, efficient killers, saboteurs and wreckers. Men who had known only the pleasant atmosphere of idyllic rural surroundings or the harmless kaleidoscope of peace-time city streets had to be transformed almost over-night into intrepid adventurers prepared to roam the night skies over hostile foreign countries; to endure hazardous, sleepless voyages over angry, treacherous oceans, where death came from the clouds or the depths; to strike like Bedouins in the hot sands of Libya and the mountains of the middle East; or to creep like tigers through the fetid jungles of Burma and deal out death more swiftly than the panther or the python. What process could effect this startling metamorphosis and what manner of men could be so transformed?

They were men like Robert Blair Mayne. The athletic, charming young solicitor from Ulster, embarking, as he then was, on a pleasant, placid, foreseeable career in his native province answered, like thousands of others, the terrifying summons to rise up, leave all that made life good – home, friends, career and eventually a happy marriage

– and plunge into a course of training to be a superman.

The fate of Europe, of all civilisation, was suddenly in the balance, and the only salvation lay in the willingness and ability of young men to forsake all they knew and held dear and go forth and submit to an iron discipline, a fierce asceticism, a Spartan life amid snow and ice, in steaming jungles, over trackless deserts, and learn to walk with death and worse than death, to kill or be killed and face tortures as horrible as any devised by the medieval world.

These young men answered the call in thousands and suffered and died in thousands. They died after great heroism and suffering. Many survived, but maimed or bereaved or changed. In the long agony of Europe a terrible beauty was born – the heroism of those young men which was evoked to atone for the blindness, greed and barbarity of their fellow humans. It is not strange that, of those who survived, many never really adjusted to the humdrum tenor of peace-time life.

Whether they did or whether they did not, no one should forget the appalling sacrifice they were called upon to make and which they did make so willingly and with such élan. Only the meanest mind will allow their post-war failings to outweigh their splendid, heroic achievement in the face of the German-Italian barbarism. If these men had not geared themselves to Viking courage and deeds the Europe of today would not exist.

Robert Blair Mayne, one of the greatest of these, is surely now in Valhalla, for ever amongst his own.

Index

11th Scots Commando 24, 26
Afrika Korps 30, 37, 41, 56, 59, 64, 101, 109, 116
Agedabia 41, 42, 55, 102
Agheila 41, 42, 48, 50, 102, 103
Alam Halfa 82
Alexander, General 71, 79, 82, 89, 106
Alexandria 31, 57, 60, 61, 72, 94
Almonds, Sergeant Bill 82, 98, 176
Antwerp 181
Asyut 60, 80
Auchinleck, General Sir Claude 'The Auk' 32, 36, 37, 39, 53, 56, 71, 79, 89
Augusta 120, 125–137
Badoglio, Field Marshal 138, 141, 142
Bagnara 139–141, 144
Bagush 37, 72, 73, 77, 78
Barce 41, 56, 60, 61, 62, 80
Barker, Trooper John 163, 170, 172
Bari 140, 141
Beamish, Cecil 19, 20
Beamish, Air Marshal Sir George 20
Beatrix, HMS 133
Becharre 111
Belfast 17, 19, 21, 24, 27, 39, 76, 114, 154, 206
Belsen 196
Benghazi 41, 50, 53, 56, 59, 60, 62, 63, 67, 68, 71, 80, 81, 82, 86, 89, 93, 126
Benina 41, 63, 65, 67
Bennett, Sergeant-Major Bob 37, 50, 53, 58, 61, 75, 77, 83–91, 98, 121, 123, 130, 132, 153–155, 196, 202

Bergen 196, 201, 202, 203
Berka 56, 60, 63, 65, 67
Bir Facia 102, 103
Bir Guedaffia 103
Bir Zalten 102, 104
Bond, Major 191
Bouerat 50, 53, 54, 55
Bradford, Captain Roy 168
Bradley, General Omar 182
Brindisi 140, 141
Brooke, General Sir Alan 79, 89
Brough, Sergeant 43, 47
Brückner, Sergeant 64, 65
Brussels 183, 184, 198
Buck, Captain Herbert 65
Buckmaster, Colonel Maurice 160
Bunfield, Sergeant 176
Caen 16, 64, 65
Cairo 30, 31, 33, 34, 53, 54, 58, 60, 71, 79, 80, 90, 93, 94, 97, 105, 107, 109, 110, 112, 126, 204
Calvert, Brigadier 'Mad Mike' 188, 200
Cannizzaro 120, 134, 135, 138
Capo Murro di Porco 118, 120, 134
Catania 120, 133, 134, 137, 139, 140
Chambon 176
Chelmsford 177, 184, 200
Choltitz, General 182
Churchill, Captain Randolf 35, 62
Churchill, Sir Winston 11, 37, 84, 128, 157
Citations 18, 22, 106, 134, 165, 179, 190–192

Clandeboye 11
Coates, Lieutenant St John 12, 118
Conlig 11, 12
Corps, Tommy 64, 105, 106, 179
Crete 27, 31, 70, 85, 116, 146
Cumper, Captain Bill 82, 83, 98
Cunningham, General Sir Alan 36, 39, 40, 89
Darvel 149, 151, 154, 160
Dempsey, Lieutenant-General MC 147
Dentz, General 28
Derna 41, 60, 63–65
Dijon 164, 165, 166, 179, 180, 182
Dill, General Sir John 27
Dimane 111
DSO *see* Citations
Duffy, Sergeant Pat 176
Dundalk 208, 213
Dunkirk 157
Dunkley, Sergeant 176
Eisenhower, General Dwight D 101, 103, 116, 117, 141, 181, 186
El Alamein 60, 71, 72, 79, 82, 88, 93, 98, 101, 149
El Daba 77, 98
El Kharga 60, 81
Fairford 160, 161
Falkenhorst, General 200
Fenwick, Major Ian 174–177, 179, 180
Finnegan, Major Jack 111
Foggia 140, 144
Fontainebleau 169, 174–178
Fraser, Lieutenant Bill 30, 32, 42, 48, 49, 51, 53, 56, 61, 98, 105, 164–166, 168, 177, 178
Fuka 60, 72, 101
Garstin, Captain Pat 163, 169, 170, 171, 172, 174
Gaulle, General Charles de 156, 157
Gazala 40, 41, 56, 63
Geneifa 27, 30, 32, 111
Gerows, General 182

Gneisenau (German battleship) 20
Great Sand Sea 40, 41, 55, 57, 60, 70, 80, 93, 96, 97, 99
Grese, Irma 196
Gunning, Lieutenant 196
Harrison, Captain DH 125, 145, 190
Haselden, Colonel John 80
Hasselet 51
Hatiet Etla 96
Heidrich, General 145, 146
Heliopolis 34, 35
Heraklion 70
Hitler, Adolf 11, 13, 102, 126, 129, 138, 143, 149, 167, 169, 171, 172, 182, 183, 186, 189
Holliman, Captain Gus 44, 51
Howard's Cairn 100
Hull, Corporal William (Bill) 12, 153, 154, 191, 193, 194, 201
Jalo 40, 41, 48, 50, 51, 55, 60, 80, 81, 86, 88, 102
Jebel 41, 56, 59, 60, 61, 81
Jellico, Captain Lord 35, 70, 75
Jones, Corporal 'Ginger' 171, 172, 173
Jordan, Lieutenant Augustin 63
Kabrit 33, 35, 38, 53, 54, 55, 57, 60, 62, 71, 77, 79, 80, 85, 87, 97, 102–105, 112, 153
Keevil 170
Kesselring, Field Marshal 117
Keyes, Lieutenant Colonel Geoffrey 25, 26, 27, 29, 30
Kramer, Commandant Josef 196
Kufra 60, 70, 71, 80, 81, 85, 89, 90, 93, 97, 102
Langston, Sergeant Douggie 202
Laycock, Colonel Robert 'Lucky' 27, 36, 117
Leclerc, General 182
Lewis, Lieutenant Jock 32, 34, 36, 39, 42, 48, 49, 51, 53, 97
Lilley, Corporal 66, 67
Limoges 164, 180

INDEX

Litani River 28
Long Range Desert Group, *see* LRDG
LRDG 32, 37, 38, 40-44, 46-48, 51, 55, 61, 62, 67, 68, 70, 72, 80, 93, 96, 102
Luntz, Karl 20
Lutton, Lance Corporal 173
McCready, Captain Michael 165
McGonigal, Lieutenant Eoin 28, 30, 32, 39
McLeod, Brigadier 185, 186
McLuskey, Rev Fraser 10, 12, 150, 151, 152, 165, 178
Maclean, Brigadier Sir Fitzroy 54, 62, 63, 81, 83, 108-110
Malta 63, 70
Maquis (*see also* Resistance) 23, 158-162, 164, 165, 169, 172, 176, 178, 187
Marble Arch, Libya 49, 50, 51
March, Major Tony 184
Marriott, Brigadier John 40, 42
Marsh, Major Tony 98, 99, 165, 178
Martuba 60, 63, 64
Mazignen 166, 167, 178
Melot, Captain Bob 58, 61, 62, 81, 82, 85, 110-112, 183
Mersa Berga 48
Mersa Matruh 31, 60, 71, 72, 79, 93, 99
Misurata 50, 102
Montgomery, General Sir Bernard 71, 79, 82, 89, 93, 98, 101, 117, 133, 136, 142, 144, 186 Mont Sauche 166, 177
Mount Pleasant 17, 18, 206, 214
Muirhead, Captain Alec 166, 177
Mussolini, Benito 44, 122, 128, 129, 136, 138, 141-143, 162
Naples 140, 141, 146, 148
Narvik 25, 116
Nevers 164, 165
Newtownards 11, 17, 18, 44, 133, 135, 153, 154, 191
Nofilia 49, 50, 51
O'Connor, General Richard 37, 89
Odda 201, 202

Oldenburg 189, 190, 192, 193, 195
Overlord, Operation 158, 162
Paris 156, 162, 164, 166, 169, 170, 174, 175, 179-182, 188
Pedder, Colonel 26, 29
Pétain, Marshal 28, 156
Pithiviers 174, 175
Pleydell, Captain (Dr) Malcolm 35, 72, 73, 75, 97, 104
Poat, Captain Harry 125, 134
Poitiers 164, 180
Poligny 156
Primasole Bridge 134
Qattara 79, 98
Rathara 68,
Reid, Brigadier Denys 40, 42
Resistance (*see also* Maquis) 160, 161, 175, 176, 181, 182, 186
Riding, Lieutenant 176, 177, 178
Ridler, Sergeant 197
Ritchie, General Neil 39, 40, 71
Rommel, General Erwin 27, 30, 32, 37, 39, 55, 56, 63, 70, 71, 80, 82, 101, 103, 109, 126, 162, 167, 169
Rose, Corporal 61, 83, 98
Royal Scots Greys 25, 26
Royal Ulster Rifles 4, 13, 24, 153
Sadler, Sergeant Mike 43, 91, 179
Salerno 140, 141
Sand Sea *see* Great Sand Sea
Scharnhorst (German battleship) 20
Seekings, Corporal Reg 58, 68, 98, 165
Sidi-Enich 77
Sillito, David 'Jack' 95, 114
Sirte 41-44, 47, 49, 50
Siwa 38, 41, 55, 57-62, 64, 68, 70, 71
Skorzeny, Colonel Otto 142, 143, 162
Slonta 56, 60
Stavenger 200, 201
Stirling, Colonel David 12, 13, 31, 32, 33, 35, 36, 39-44, 47-51, 53-56, 62, 63, 65, 67, 70-74, 77-83, 86, 90, 93, 102, 103, 106, 107, 117, 126, 186

221

Storey, Corporal 66
Straits of Messina 120, 136, 137, 139, 140
Street, Captain 103
Suez 27, 33, 114
Syracuse 120, 123, 125, 132, 134, 136
Tamit 43, 44, 47, 49, 50, 53, 55, 65, 102
Taranto 140, 141
Termoli 140, 141, 144–148
Thimory 175
Tobruk 32, 37, 39, 40, 41, 60, 70, 71, 80, 81, 82, 95
Tonkin, Major John 145, 146, 164, 196, 197
Tours 156, 180
Tripoli 46, 50, 102, 103, 111
Ulster Monarch 114, 117, 119, 121, 123, 125, 127, 131, 132, 134, 141, 143
Vaculik, Corporal Serge 170–173
Vichy 28, 156
von Paulus, Colonel-General 110
Walker, Trooper Joe 172
Warburton, Corporal 66
Wavell, General Sir Archibald 27, 32, 37
Willmott, Lieutenant Commander Nigel 118
Wiseman, Captain 134, 166
Young, Trooper Billy 172
Zahedi, General 108